LONDON
OFF-SEASON AND ON

Also by Doris Lehman

The Riviera Off-Season and On

Also by Robert Haru Fisher

Crown Insider's Guide to Japan
Fisher's Annotated Guide to Japan
Klee
Picasso

LONDON
OFF-SEASON AND ON

A Guide to Special Pleasures, Better Rates,
and Shorter Lines

Doris Lehman
and
Robert Haru Fisher

Illustrated by Amy Lehman

ST. MARTIN'S GRIFFIN ⚐ NEW YORK

For Carly and Lindsay Lehman
and
Harukuni Nishizawa

LONDON OFF-SEASON AND ON. Copyright © 1999 by Doris Lehman and Robert Haru Fisher. All rights reserved. Printed in the United States of America. No part of this book may be used or reproduced in any manner whatsoever without written permission except in the case of brief quotations embodied in critical articles or reviews. For information, address St. Martin's Press, 175 Fifth Avenue, New York, N.Y. 10010.

Design by Nancy Resnick
Illustrations by Amy Lehman

Library of Congress Cataloging-in-Publication Data

Lehman, Doris.
    London off-season and on / Doris Lehman and Robert Haru Fisher.—
1st St. Martin's Griffin ed.
        p.   cm.
    Includes index.
    ISBN 0-312-20447-7
    1. London (England) Guidebooks.   I. Fisher, Robert Haru.
II. Title
DA679.L45   1999
914.2104'859—dc21   99-36165
                                                          CIP

First Edition: October 1999

10 9 8 7 6 5 4 3 2 1

Contents

Introduction   xiii

1. Practical Information for Visiting London   1

2. London Off-Season and On (Mostly Off)—
   the Calendar   21

3. Theater, Music, and Nightlife   39

4. Sightseeing London, Off-Season Sites
   (and On-Season, Too)   44

5. Museums and Churches   61

6. Inauthentic Alternatives   70

7. Mysterious London   73

8. Where to Stay in London   80

9. Where to Eat in London   95

10. Shopping in London   114

11. Leisure Activities   129

12. London Sports   133

13. London for Children   139

14. Day Trips from London   150
    *Aldeburgh • Bath • Blenheim Palace • Brighton •
    Cambridge • Canterbury • Coventry • Dublin • North of
    Dublin • South of Dublin • Edinburgh • Greenwich •
    Hampton Court Palace • Ipswich • Oxford • Paris •
    Stratford-Upon-Avon • Warwick • Windsor*

Index   229

Acknowledgments

We would like to thank all of our friends (old and newly-found) who helped us in many ways to make this book possible:

Zorka in London, who helped scout out new restaurants; John and Tom in Dublin, who took us sightseeing to many of the places we recommend there; Christine and Edgar, who guided us through Aldeburgh (and who were also kind enough to read the manuscript of the book, offering helpful suggestions); Hazel, who guided us to Wisley Gardens and Hampton Court. Thank you for your help and friendship.

And special thanks to Amy, who drew the beautiful illustrations; Michael Lehman, who advised on legal matters; Heidi Lehman, who encouraged us with her enthusiasm; and, of course, Mike, who always is there to help with kindness and support. Also to Carly and Lindsay, who assisted us in discovering London for children.

Of course, deepest gratitude to our editor, Greg Cohn, for believing in the "off-season" concept.

Finally, to Harukuni Nishizawa, as always, the inspiration.

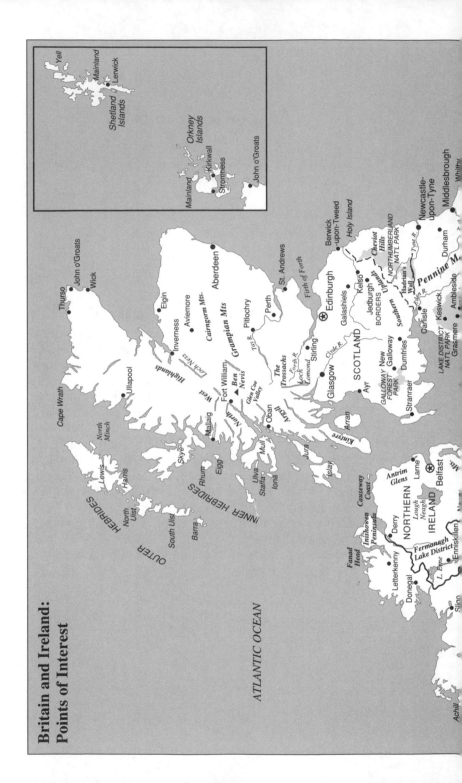

Britain and Ireland: Points of Interest

Introduction

Everyone agrees that London is one of the great cities of the world, any time of the year. But London off-season is the luckiest of treats. On-season is summertime, June through August, when the majority of people plan their trips thinking the always-changeable English weather will be best.

But we plan our trips off-season, before or after the rush, when the sights, shops, restaurants, theaters, and most activities are in full swing. Perhaps the weather is not as warm, but dressed properly you can have a wonderful time. As far as we're concerned, the summer is far too crowded. Most places except deluxe hotels and restaurants are not air-conditioned, and the hot indoors can be miserable.

Furthermore, we love visiting small towns nearby (all described in this book) off-season, because you can really enjoy them. Just try going to Bath or Stratford-Upon-Avon in July. You might as well park your car on the outskirts of town and never pick it up again until you are ready to leave. In January, when the weather may still be delightful, you can stroll the streets, stop in any restaurant, and see all the sights without waiting in line. Brighton, too, is a nightmare in the summer. Off-season, it is glorious. We could mention other towns and sights that are best off-season, but you get the idea.

1. Practical Information for Visiting London

Try to do as much preparing at home for your trip as possible, so when you arrive you will not be disappointed. If you know your departure date far in advance, it's a good idea to reserve and pay for your trip as early as you can. Low fares sell out early, so take advantage of them as soon as you hear about them. We also advise booking a hotel room for the first night of your trip so that when you arrive, you have a place to go. It is possible to get a reservation at the last minute, but it can be disconcerting to do so from a London airport phone booth or hotel-booking desk. After that, just have your maps and this guidebook, and you are set to go.

TOURIST OFFICES

For additional information, or to provide answers we haven't given in this book, contact the British Tourist Authority, which maintains the following offices in North America:

> New York. 551 Fifth Avenue, 7th floor, New York, NY 10176. Phone 212-981-2200, fax 212-986-1188; Web site www. visitbritain.com and www.bta.org.uk.
> Chicago. 625 N. Michigan Avenue, Suite 1510, Chicago, IL 60611. Phone 312-787-0464.
> Los Angeles. P.O. Box 71087, Los Angeles, CA 90071. Phone 213-628-5731.
> Miami. 5201 Blue Lagoon Drive, Miami, FL 33126. Phone 375-9444.

Toll free information: 1-800-462-2748. Web site www.visitbritain.com.

ENTRY REQUIREMENTS

There are no visa requirements for Canadian or American citizens. A valid passport is required for all visitors, however. Check visa requirements for all other nationalities prior to travel. If you plan to stay longer than six months, check the special requirements for extended visas.

HOW TO GET TO LONDON FROM THE UNITED STATES

Boat

The *QE2* sails from New York to Southampton, England, regularly during the months of April through December. Cunard offers many packages such as fly/sail, Concorde one way, and hotel packages (and once in England to return on a *QE2* sailing). When the *QE2* docks in Southampton, passengers must take a train, bus, taxi, or car to continue on to London. The Southampton airport is a taxi ride away if you plan to fly to Dublin or other destinations.

For more information, call the Cunard Line at 1-800-7-CUNARD or write to: Cunard, 6100 Blue Lagoon Drive, Suite 400, Miami, Florida 33126. Web site http://www.cunardline.com

The *QE2* is wheelchair accessible, but be sure to ask all the appropriate questions when booking.

Air

If you plan to travel from North America by air, there are many options. The flying time from Newark and New York is six and a half hours, from Chicago seven and a half hours, and from Los Angeles ten hours. The two major British arrival airports from the United States are Gatwick and Heathrow, which are both within easy train reach of London.

Be sure to check in at least two hours prior to the flight. All airlines overbook and then can deny boarding to those who check in later than the required time. Off-season travel usually eliminates this problem, however!

The major airlines include:

> American Airlines. 1-800-433-7300 or 817-267-1151; in London 181 572 5555.
> British Airways. 1-800-274-9297; in the UK 0345 222 111.
> Continental Airlines. 1-800-525-0280; in London 0800 776 464.
> Delta Airlines. 1-800-241-4141; in London 0800 414 767.
> Northwest Airlines. 1-800-447-4747; in London 0990 561 000.
> TWA. 1-800-892-4141; in London 0181 814 0707.
> United Airlines. 1-800-241-6522; in London 0845 844 4777.
> US Airways. 1-800-428-4322; in London 0800-783-5556.

EUROPE FLIGHT PASS (FORMERLY KNOWN AS EURAIR PASS): Phone 888-387-2479, fax 310-665-0954; Web site www.europeflight pass.com.

You must buy a minimum of three $90 coupons, each of which is good for a nonstop flight between any two available cities. In this program, there are sixty cities in several countries including England, Ireland, France, Spain, Germany, Greece, and Denmark. Airlines participating in this program are: Aer Lingus, Icelandair, Air Bristol, Estonian Airlines, PGA Portugalia, Spanair, VLM Flemish, Virgin Express, Air Greece, Air One, and Augsburg Airlines. Perhaps more airlines will join this plan; at press time, CityJet (out of Dublin), Alpi Eagles (Italian), and Croatia Airlines were planning to join. For six coupons ($540), you could travel from London to Madrid, then to Rome, then to Venice, then to Barcelona, then to Brussels, and back to London.

This pass is available only to North American residents. You must buy the coupons before leaving North America, but you can make your reservations in Europe. Unused tickets are nonrefundable and nontransferable. The tickets expire 120 days after purchase. Airport taxes are not included. There are no cancellation fees or change fees. The only requirement is a 24-hour notice to the airline if you plan to change or cancel.

BRITISH AIR CARRY-ON RESTRICTIONS: BA has started something new as of this writing. Carry-on baggage will be weighed at check-in and will be tagged with a green tag indicating that it can be carried on board. Economy class carry-on must be thirteen pounds or less; business and first-class carry-on has to be less than twenty pounds. If you arrive at the boarding gate without the green tag, BA has the right to put your baggage in the hold. Don't put valuables into your carry-on bag if you think it is over the weight limit.

Consolidators

Discount consolidators or bulk-fare operators—"bucket shops"—many of them using regularly scheduled flights on the airlines listed above, can offer cheaper seats because they buy in bulk and often at the last minute. In many cases you'll be on the same plane with people paying higher fares, and will get the same good service.

Here are a few reputable consolidators and clubs:

> 800-FLY-4-LESS
> Moment's Notice Discount Travel Club. Phone 718-234-6295;
> there's a modest fee for joining this travel club.
> Worldwide Discount Travel Club. Phone 305-534-2082; you
> pay a fee for joining club.

Charter Flights

Charter flights are usually available at a lower fare than the scheduled airlines charge, but they are also less reliable. We have found that they often do not depart when they say they will and sometimes can be as late as a full day behind schedule. They have been known to overfly the scheduled arrival airport and stop at another one without notice. If you decide on a charter, we strongly advise paying by credit card (so that you can stop payment or otherwise get your money back if there is trouble).

TRAIN SERVICE FROM GATWICK AND HEATHROW AIRPORTS TO LONDON: Gatwick Airport has had train service to Victoria Station since 1984. It is less expensive than a taxi and takes only half an hour.

Heathrow Airport has just started its train service, called Heathrow Express. (Phone 0845 600-1515.) The trip from the airport to London's Paddington Station takes fifteen minutes and connects with four different Underground lines. If you have carry-on luggage, you can even check in for your flight at Paddington Station. Full check-in facilities should be open for most airlines by the end of 1999. Cost: $16 each way ($32 first-class!).

Though both train services charge a fee, they are much more economical than a taxi. Less expensive options include the Underground from Heathrow and a bus ("coach") from Gatwick.

Animals

Sorry, Fido or Fluffy will probably have to stay home. Animals cannot enter the UK without being quarantined for many months. There is considerable debate in England today about scrapping this requirement, but don't hold your breath. Some people try to smuggle their pets in and out but we strongly advise against it, as the penalties are severe and expensive. If you're lucky, you'll just be deported, along with your pet, with instructions never to come back. Sometimes, you can choose to put the pet in quarantine and pay a huge fine (or maybe go to jail).

CHILDREN

Britain is a wonderful country to travel in with children. London is full of excellent sights, as are the towns you can visit on day trips. Zoos, castles, barge trips, museums, and wonderfully big cabs make travel easy. The London Tourist Board publishes "Where to Take Children," a pamphlet that can be picked up at newsstands and travel offices. There is also a "Kidsline" which operates daily except weekends, reached by calling 171-222-8070 in London. This number will provide information on what's doing in London for kids.

Children are usually entitled to discounts on the airplane and in hotels. Also ask about special children's meals if you have a fussy eater with you. They are available on most airlines if reserved in advance. Always tell the booking agent if you are traveling with a child. When renting a car, pre-reserve a child seat. They're required by law.

CLIMATE

The wonderful thing about going to London off-season, and to all the places we describe as side trips in this book, is that the weather is usually mild—even in the winter. The summers can be hot, and the lack of air-conditioning does not help, but the winters—with the correct clothing—can be great. (Just don't forget the umbrella.) And spring and autumn are heaven. But in winter, it is true . . . it does rain in England (though the total rainfall is less than in New York).

CURRENCY

Britain hasn't yet figured out what to do with the new European currency called the euro. Though financial and commercial organizations are already dealing in Euros, you don't have to worry about them, as the pound sterling is still king (or queen, or whatever).

Be sure to take along a pocket calculator to convert English pounds into U.S. dollars. Pound notes come in denominations of 5, 10, 20, and 50 pounds. Coins come in 1, 2, 5, 10, 20 and 50 pence, a one-pound coin, and the new two-pound coin. There are 100 pence to the pound. Credit cards are also accepted, as are travelers' checks. Most international credit cards are widely accepted.

Banking hours are Monday to Friday from 9:30am to 3:30pm. Some centrally located banks stay open until 5pm.

The main London banks are Barclays, National Westminster, Midland, and Lloyds. If you have an ATM card, bring that too, as you will usually get the best possible rate of exchange when you use it, and most bank machines will accept them. Be sure you have your pin code with you, and note that it should be no longer than four digits or letters.

At press time, the exchange rate was approximately $1.60 to the pound sterling (£), but the rate fluctuates daily. The best rate is obtained when you obtain cash directly from an ATM, the second best when you use credit cards, third best at banks or *bureau de change* shops, which charge a commission, and the worst when you exchange at hotels, restaurants, or shops which charge a commission for the exchange.

Can You Spare a Euro, Madame?

The euro will be replacing most of Europe's currencies in the near future. On January 1, 1999 the foreign exchange rates of the currencies of eleven European countries were fixed against one another and against the euro. The dollar exchanges in the future will also be set against the euro, not the franc, peseta, lira or mark. It will take another three years until the different currencies are phased out, so don't panic. We'll have plenty of time to adjust to the euro. Euro bills and coins will not go into circulation until January 1, 2002. You will still be able to use each country's currency until June 2002. On January 1, 1999 merchants of the eleven countries already agreeing to use the euro were asked to price goods in their own currencies and in the euro. This will begin to make people comfortable with the new currency and help us learn what it is worth. One thing for sure, the euro will make it easier to compare prices from country to country.

American Express started issuing euro travelers' checks on January 1, 1999, but when they are cashed you will receive the currency of the country you are in until 2002, when the euro goes into general circulation.

The countries that will use the euro are: Austria, Belgium, Finland, France, Germany, Ireland, Italy, Luxembourg, the Netherlands, Portugal, and Spain. Other countries, including Britain, may eventually join. The exchange rate between the dollar and the euro was set on January 1, 1999 and at time of writing was 0.95 to the U.S. dollar, but if you're sticking to Britain on this trip, don't let it bother you!

It is a good idea to buy a hundred dollars worth of pounds sterling at your home bank or at the U.S. airport of departure so that you have bus, taxi, tip, and postcard money handy the moment you arrive. If you forget, you can always convert your money at the airport on arrival, but you may have to stand in line and delay the beginning of your vacation.

MEDICATION

If you take any medication that requires a prescription, be sure to have the prescription with you, and not in your luggage. Also have a letter from your doctor stating what you need and why. If you need to take insulin and require a syringe while on board a flight, be sure to have a doctor's note stating why you are carrying syringes.

DRIVING IN THE U.K.

Important when renting a car if traveling with a small child: Reserve a car seat at the time you rent the car.

A current driver's license or international driving license is required. You must be twenty-one years of age and no older than seventy to rent from most major companies.

Here are some helpful hints for driving in England:

Remember that the British drive on the left side of the road and pass on the right. To avoid knocking off sideview mirrors on parked cars when you try to park, be sure you leave enough room between you and the parked car next to you.

It is best (though much more costly) to rent a car with automatic transmission instead of a manual. Shifting gears with the left hand makes driving more difficult.

Look both ways before making a turn. Turning is more difficult when driving on the "wrong" side of the street.

At roundabouts (traffic circles), stay on the inside lane, be sure you know where you want to exit, and go around a few times if necessary to get your bearings before exiting. Off-season, of course, the traffic will be lighter.

If you are staying only in London, you do not need a car. But if you are taking day trips and prefer to drive instead of taking the train or bus, go ahead, be brave, and rent a vehicle. Driving always adds to the fun since you can stop whenever you wish to see a sight, have lunch, or just not have to watch the clock to get back to the station.

Always check about insurance, which we feel you *must* have.

Britain uses miles, not kilometers (thank heavens!). Note that imperial pints and gallons are 20 percent larger than pints and gallons in the U.S. Gasoline (called petrol here) is also more expensive than in the U.S. One U.S. gallon equals 3.8 liters if you get a liter-marked pump; one UK gallon equals 1.2 U.S. gallons. (Also, one mile equals 1.6 kilometers, if you get a kilometer-marked car or signpost along the way.)

Drivers

If you feel you do not want to drive yourself, there is an option: Take-A-Guide Ltd. From the U.S. Phone 1-800-825-4946, fax 1-800-635-7177. From London, 181-960-0459, fax 181-964-0990.

ELECTRICITY

The electric current in Britain is 240 Volts AC. Bring a converter for your own hair blower or other electric device. Britain uses three-prong square-pin plugs, unlike any other plug to be found in Europe, so a plug adapter is a good idea, too.

EMBASSIES

Canadian. Macdonald House, 1 Grosvenor Square, London WIX OAB. Phone 171 258 6600.

United States. 24 Grosvenor Square, London WIA IAE. Phone 171 499 9000.

EMERGENCY NUMBER

Dial 999, and you will be connected by an operator to the police, fire department, or ambulance. Remember, it's *not* 911 as in the U.S.

GETTING AROUND IN LONDON

Bus and Underground Travel

LONDON TRANSPORT: (Phone 171 222 1234.) If you plan to use the Underground (subway) or bus, it is best to buy a pass. They are available at newspaper stands, rail stations, and underground stations.

Types of passes available:

One-Day Travelcard. For use weekdays after 9:30am, and on weekends and national holidays. This pass is good for Underground and bus. Adults from £3.50 (Zones 1 and 2) to £4.30 (all Zones), children £1.80 (all zones).

Weekly Travelcards. For Underground and bus travel. You'll need a passport-sized photo to give them. Adults from £13 (Zone 1) to £34 (all Zones), children £5.20 (Zone 1) to £12.40 (all Zones).

Unrestricted One Day Pass. Costs more than the One-Day pass, but can be used at any time during the day.

Visitor's Travelcard. Must be purchased outside the UK (in the U.S. or Canada, for instance) for three-, four-, or seven-day travel. This card can be purchased from BritRail 888-422-2748. They also sell tickets for the new Heathrow Express train to the airport.

(Note that "subway" in Britain means a pedestrian underpass beneath a street, so you should refer to those trains running underground as, well, the Underground, or the tube, another British term for the same thing.)

FERRY SIGHTSEEING: Tel. 171 488 0344. Tickets are sold on the ferry. A new service that began during the summer of 1997 and has been very successful is the Hop-On Hop-Off Thames Ferry. It operates on the Thames River between London Bridge and St. Katherine's Dock, and stops at five piers: Tower Pier, London Bridge Pier, *H.M.S. Belfast,* Butlers Wharf, and St. Katherine's Dock. The fare as of this writing is £2 and is good for the entire day with as many stops as you wish. Along with the ticket, you receive vouchers for discounts at some of the museums and shops along the way. The ferry operates daily every 30 minutes between 11am and 5pm, from April 1 to October 26. From October 26 to March 31 it operates on weekends only.

HOME EXCHANGE

This is an excellent idea for anyone planning to spend any length of time in London. You exchange homes or apartments for the cost of buying an annual publication with the home-exchange listings. Or, a wonderful new way to find home exchanges is through the Web.

Intervac International. Box 590504, San Francisco, CA 94159. Phone 415-435-3497, fax 415-435-7440. The fee is $65.00 per year.

International Home Exchange Network. can be found at http://www.homexchange.com with a yearly fee, which entitles you to change your listing, browse as often as you wish, and include a color photo.

Computex. http://www.computex.co.uk has an annual fee, but the first year is free. You can include a color photo in this listing, too.

HOME AND APARTMENT RENTALS

Another way to save money might be to rent your own flat for one week or as long as you desire. Rates can start as low as £300 per week off-season, including weekly linen change and maid service. During off-season, your choices will be greater and the prices usually lower than in-season. A very good book about rentals in Europe which includes a section on the U.K. is: *Guide to Vacation Rentals in Europe,* by Michael and Laura Murphy, published by The Globe Pequot Press of Old Saybrook, CT.

Other reliable sources:

> At Home Abroad, 405 East 56th Street, New York City, N. Y. 10022. Phone 212-421-9165, fax 212-752-1591.
> Blandings Country Homes in England, Scotland and Wales. Blanding The Barn, Musgrave Farm, Horningsea Road, Fen Ditton, Cambridge, England CB5 8SZ. Phone 011 44 1223-293444, fax 011 44 1223 292888.
> Rental Directories International, 2044 Rittenhouse Square, Philadelphia, PA 19103. Phone 215-985-4001, fax 215-985-0323.
> Villas and Apartments Abroad, 420 Madison Avenue, Suite 1003, New York City, N.Y. 10017. Phone 212-759-1025, fax 212-755-8316.
> Villas International, 605 Market Street, Suite 510, San Francisco, CA 94105. Phone 415-281-0910, fax 415-281-0919.
> Kay & Co., 45 Chiltern Street, London W1M 1HN, England. Phone 011 44 171 486 6338, fax 011 44 171 487 3953; e-mail: kayco@globalnet.co.uk.

LOST CREDIT CARDS

Access	01702 362988
American Express	01273 696933
Diners Club	01252 516261
Mastercard	01702 352211
Visa	01604 230230

MAPS

We recommend the Michelin map of England and *London Off-Season and On* as the only map and guidebook you will need for a successful trip.

MEDICAL ASSISTANCE

Consider purchasing insurance before departing on a trip. It can be bought from a travel agent or your own insurance company. Insurance should cover lost airline tickets, baggage, money, and, most important, health. There are comprehensive policies sold to cover emergencies, including some that will transport you back home in an extreme case.

Worldwide Assistance Services. 1133 15th Street NW, Suite 400, Washington, DC 20005. Phone 202-331-1609, 1-800-821-2828; fax 202-828-5896. Includes emergency evacuation.

Information by Phone

The London Tourist Office has a telephone guide to London, which can be dialed easily from London.
    Dial 0839 123 PLUS the three-number code below for the topic that interests you:

400	"What's on" this week
401	What's on during the next three months
403	Current exhibitions
404	What's on for children
407	Sunday in London
411	Changing of the Guard
416	West End Shows
418	Christmas and Easter events
422	Rock and Pop Concerts
428	Street Markets
429	Museums
430	Getting Around London
431	Guided Tours and Walks
432	River Trips
433	Getting to the Airports
480	Popular Attractions
481	Palaces
482	Greenwich
483	Famous Houses and Gardens
484	Day Trips from London
485	London Dining

IAMAT

IAMAT (International Association for Medical Assistance to Travellers) is a non-profit organization that has a list of English-speaking doctors who provide medical help for a small fixed fee. Although the list is provided free of charge, a small donation is appreciated. (If you donate at least $25, you receive a large package of IAMAT publications, including charts on where it is safe (or not) to drink the water and milk, eat the food, as well as what inoculations you need, and much more.) Membership in IAMAT is free. They can be reached at 417 Center Street, Lewiston, NY 14090.

HIV and AIDS Services

Body Positive Helpline, London. Phone 171 373 9124. Daily 7:00am to 10:00pm.
National AIDS Helpline, USA. Phone 1-800-567-123.

Dental Emergency Care

Phone twenty-four hours a day for referral to a local dentist or clinic. Phone 171 937 3951.

Eye Care

For a referral to an eye doctor. Phone 171 928 9435.

Rape Crisis Center

Phone in London twenty-four hours a day, 171 837 1600.

Travelers with Disabilities

The most important thing to do when booking air, ship, or hotel is to ask all of the questions ahead of time. Don't arrive and be disappointed. We have noted "wheelchair access" in many of our descriptions of hotels, restaurants, and sights, but please ask anyway. Some access might have been added, or what is provided may not be adequate.

> Access to the Underground. Phone 171 918 3312 for information on each tube station and what is provided.
>
> *London Made Easy* is published by the British Tourist Authority, and supplies information on wheelchair access.
>
> *Travelin' Talk Directory* is a 500-page directory listing organizations that help travelers with disabilities. Write to: Box 3534, Clarksville, TN 37043. Phone 615-552-6670, fax 615 552-1182. Cost $35.
>
> RADAR is the Royal Association for Disabilities and Rehabilitation, which provides advice and information. They can be reached at: 12 City Forum, 250 City Road, London EC1V 8AF; Phone 171 250 3222. A *Guide to British Rail for the Physically Handicapped* can be ordered through RADAR at 25 Mortimer Street, London W1N 8AB, England.
>
> A *World of Options for the 90's: A Guide to International Educational Exchange, Community Service and Travel for Persons with Disabilities* can be ordered through: Mobility International USA, P.O. Box 10767, Eugene OR 97440. Phone 503-343-1284.

SAFETY

Like every other city, London has its share of crime. When sight-seeing, wear a fanny pack, turned in front, with your valuables. At night, when walking try to stay in well-lit areas. Have a copy of the front page of your passport, plus credit cards and traveler check numbers back at your room. Do not have the copies and originals in the same place.

SENIOR CITIZENS

Senior citizens in the UK are persons over 60. Discounts are available on trains, and admission fees to museums, castles, and other sights, as well as to some movie theaters, but not to legitimate theaters (stage shows). Anyway, there's no harm in asking!

AARP (the American Association of Retired Persons) 601 E Street NW, Washington, DC 20049; Phone 202-434-2277. Dues $8.00 per person or couple per year. Membership includes discounts on many hotels and car rentals, and and other perks.

SHOPPING

Each person is allowed $400 worth of goods duty free upon entering the U.S. from Europe, if you have been out of the country for forty-eight hours or more. *Remember:* No Cuban cigars are allowed in the U.S. They will be confiscated, regardless of where you purchase them.

For additional information on tax-free shopping contact: Fexco Tax Free Shopping Limited, Fexco House, 15 Galena Road, London W6 OLT, England. Phone 011 44 181 748 0774; fax 011 44 181 741 5520.

STUDENT TRAVEL

If you are a student (or traveling with a child), be sure to ask for a discount, of which there are many. You should have an identification card with your date of birth, or your passport. A photo ID is also a good idea. Some discounts offered are on BritRail, buses, car rentals, and sights. Students should purchase a ISIC Student ID card in the United States. It can also be purchased in Canada and the UK.

If you are not a student, but are under age twenty-six, you can obtain a GO 25 International Youth Travel Card, which also entitles you to many discounts. The cards are $18 each and can be purchased through the Council on International Educational Exchange, 205 East 42nd Street, 16th floor, New York, N.Y. 10017; phone 212-661-1450. If you call or write to this number or address they will furnish you with a number or address for an office in the part of the country you live in, or mail you the application from the New York office.

SWEATER REPAIR

If you have a cashmere sweater you love, and you discover a hole in it, don't panic. Call 011 44 171 584 9806, the number for the Cashmere Clinic in London. They will tell you to whom to mail the sweater, how long it will take to repair, and how much it will cost. They will wash, defuzz, and repair a sweater to make it look like new. An old-style sweater can also be reshaped if you want to update it.

TELEPHONE

The British country code is 44. Calling from the U.S to Britain, dial 011-44, then the city code, and then the phone number. London has two area codes: 171 for inner London and 181 for outer London. Do not dial any zero (0) appearing just before the city code.

Calling the U.S from Britain: Check with AT&T, MCI or Sprint for your direct-dialing code from Europe to the U.S. if you plan to use a calling card. Calling from an outside phone can be done either using a coin phone or a BT phone card. The least expensive times to make calls are from 6pm to 8am Monday through Friday, and all weekend. The BT phone card can be purchased in various denominations in shops showing the BT logo. Instructions for using the card are on the phone box. Just be sure to have enough money on your card for your call, or an extra card if you plan a long conversation. When the card runs out, you will hear a beep and will have to insert a new card. If you do not have one, you will be disconnected. Pay or coin phones require you to put your coins in first, listen for the tone, and dial. The display on the phone tells you how much money is left. Keep inserting coins until you finish the conversation. If you have overpaid, you will get change. We find it best to use small change toward the end of the conversation just in case you are at a phone that does not refund change.

Calling the U.S. from a phone in the UK, dial 00, the country code (which is 1 for the U.S.), and then the area code and number.

Operator Assistance dial 100
International Operator dial 155
Emergency dial 999

Meet Me At 1945?

Most of the world now uses the 24-hour system. Americans who know about it often refer to it as military time, though it is used by much of U.S. industry, especially by airlines.

Here's a 24-hour time converter for the UK and Europe:

Midnight = 2400 (rarely, 0000) hours
11pm = 2300
10pm = 2200
9pm = 2100
8pm = 2000
7pm = 1900
6pm = 1800
5pm = 1700
4pm = 1600
3pm = 1500
2pm = 1400
1pm = 1300

A.M. hours are the same as on the U.S. 12-hour scale: 1, 2, 3, 4, 5, 6, 7, 8, 9, 10, 11 and 12 noon. But 1 A.M. is often written as 0100, 2 A.M. as 0200, and so on.

TIPPING

In England, a ten to fifteen percent tip is adequate for restaurants, pubs, taxis, hair dressers, and all services. If you feel that the service you received was excellent, feel free to give more. In a pub, you can tip by telling the bartender to "put one for yourself" on the tab, meaning a drink similar to the one you ordered. He or she will then add that amount to your bill.

TRAIN TRAVEL

BritRail passes provide excellent discounts on regular fares, so if you plan to travel outside London, buy them before you leave home. (They must be bought outside of Britain.) There are many possibilities, so be sure to ask before you buy. There are passes for travel on consecutive days, a certain number of days a month, as well as student passes, senior passes, AARP and so on. You can also buy a BritRail + Ireland Pass for travel by ferry to Ireland or travel in Ireland. And remember, off-season, the trains aren't crowded.

Call BritRail in the U.S. (1-800-677-8585) or use their Web site (www.railpass.com) for the latest information.

Remember: All BritRail passes must be bought in North America. They *CANNOT* be purchased in the UK.

Types of Passes

1. BritRail Classic Pass
2. BritRail Classic Senior Pass (over 60)
3. BritRail Youth Classic Pass(16–25 years old, standard fare only)
4. BritRail Flexipass (allows use on nonconsecutive days)
5. BritRail Family Pass (for more than one person)
6. BritRail Pass + Car (combined rail and rental car)
7. BritRail Pass +Ireland (United Kingdom and Republic of Ireland)
8. BritRail Southeast Pass (a regional pass)
9. Freedom of Scotland Travelpass (unlimited rail travel in Scotland on BritRail)

Tickets To. 10 East 21st Street, New York, NY 10010. Phone 212-529-9069, fax. 212-529-4838; Web site http://www.ticketsto.com.

This is a company specializing in tickets to and within London, Paris, and Europe. You can obtain tickets and passes for Eurostar, European trains, tours, museums, BritRail (all of the passes listed above), airport shuttle buses, and day-trip excursions. Fax or phone in your order, and your request will be mailed within forty-eight hours. It is worth sending for their very complete brochure and using this company, especially if you are buying more than one pass. Along with the ease of using Tickets To, you can buy any Michelin guide or map at a 20 percent discount along with your order.

Underground or Tube

There are over 250 stations in London, each with the London Underground logo. The Underground is generally safe, clean, and cheap. And off-season, it's apt to be less crowded. Trains run daily from 5:30am until midnight except on Christmas Day. After midnight, you are on your own finding a way home. Be prepared if you plan to stay out late. Smoking is not permitted in stations or on trains. See Getting around in London, starting on page 9.

WALKING IN ENGLAND, IRELAND, AND SCOTLAND

Be sure to look both ways until you feel secure about crossing streets. Remember, the traffic comes from the other direction than in the U.S., so look right, left, then right again. Cross at the "zebra" white-striped crossings, where cars must stop for you, or at corners where the push-button operated light will change for you to cross. More and more one-way streets now have white painted signs on the pavements that say look left, to remind the British themselves that traffic is coming from the left, and not, as usual, from the right. Remember that when crossing.

Walking Tours of London

Wear good walking shoes, take your folding umbrella, and off you go. Walking is the best way to see a city, and London is a wonderful city to walk in.

Listed here are a few of the very good walking tour companies:

The Original London Walks. Phone 171 624 2978 or 171 794 1764

Historical Walks of London. Phone 181 668 4019

The Londoner Pub Walks. Phone 181 883 2656

Footsteps. Phone 162 275 4451. Tours in different languages

Madeline Quinn. Phone 181 650 7640. Tours of Greenwich

WEATHER

Do not come to Britain without an umbrella. The weather can be beautiful, but it is best to be prepared, off-season. Average daytime temperature during the summer is 70°F. During the winter the average daytime temperature is 40°F. To get a weather report day or night for anyplace in the world, call 1-900-WEATHER.

Average Temperatures

Average London temperature (and remember this is "average"):

January	36–43°F
February	36–44°F
March	38–50°F
April	42–56°F
May	47–62°F
June	53–69°F
July	56–71°F
August	56–71°F
September	52–65°F
October	46–58°F
November	42–50°F
December	38–45°F

P.S. Britain, as most of the world, uses Centigrade, not Fahrenheit, so get used to 22° (Celsius or Centigrade), meaning about 70°F.

---

2. London Off-Season and On (Mostly Off)—the Calendar

Note that many holidays, particularly those with religious or formerly religious significance, are based on the church calendar, and thus do not fall on a fixed date. We have tried to anticipate in which months these holidays (e.g. Ascension Day, Easter, and the like) will fall. Some secular dates are also very movable, including Chinese New Year and even some trade shows. So check our index if you can't find something in the "right" month of our listings.

Navigating By The Stars

Stars in front of the listings in this chapter indicate how we judge the event, with five stars being the maximum, zero stars the minimum. If you're in a hurry, just check out how many stars we give something, then set off to enjoy those spots. We hope you agree with our assessments—if not, let us know!

★★★★★ You should come to London just to see this!
★★★★ Once in London, plan your stay to include this.
★★★ Plan your day around this.
★★ Plan half your day around this.
★ Include this if you have the time.

DAILY EVENTS (YEAR-ROUND)

★★★★★ The Changing of the Queen's Guard at Buckingham Palace.

This takes place at 11:30 daily in summer, and every other day from October through March. You can join the throngs (the earlier the better if you want to be up front), or you can follow our suggestion and walk down the route the guards take. They depart from either Hyde Park Barracks at 10:45, or from Wellington Barracks at 11:00. (Phone the London Tourist Board, 0839 123 456, on the morning you plan to go, to find out which route the guards will take.) The easiest place to watch from is at the entrance of the Wellington Barracks, on Birdcage Walk just due east of the palace, where the guard forms for its march. There are three units, namely the band, the St. James's Palace detachment, and the Buckingham Palace detachment. They march into the forecourt to change the guard there. You can tell the different guards' groups by the colors of their plumes: red for Coldstream, white for Grenadiers, blue for the Irish, and green and white for the Welsh. The Scots have no plume.

★★★★ Changing of the Queen's Life Guard, at Horse Guards Parade.

Ceremony takes place daily at 11:00, except for Sundays, when it is at 10:00. We suggest you take up your position inside the courtyard instead of outside on the street for more maneuverability. The cavalry units leave Hyde Park Barracks at 10:25 every day but Sunday (when they leave one hour earlier) and proceed along the South Carriage Drive adjoining Hyde Park, through Hyde Park Corner, and down Constitution Hill and The Mall, arriving at Whitehall for the ceremony.

★★★ Changing of the Guard at St. James's Palace.

A small unit changes the guard here at 11:15 on the same days as at Buckingham Palace (see schedule above). You can no longer get up close to the guards at Clarence House, where the Queen Mother lives, but you can watch this through the fence. Better yet, watch them on the St. James's Street side of St. James's Palace, where there is no fence to obstruct your view.

★★ The Ceremony of the Keys of the Tower of London.

Every night of the year at 9:40, the fortress is shut down in a little ceremony (no band music), which is carried out by the Chief Yeoman Warder. You have to write ahead for permission to see this. Write to: Resident Governor, HM Tower of London, London EC3, and enclose a self-addressed and stamped envelope (you can use an International Postal Reply Coupon, obtainable at your local U.S. post office, if you write from outside Britain).

OFF-SEASON

January

AFTER-CHRISTMAS SALES IN LONDON (ONLY OFF-SEASON) These fabulous sales are held for a month starting the day after Christmas and ending around January 31. The most famous sale is at Harrods, but almost all stores participate in this annual event. Department stores and small shops are packed with locals and overseas tourists who come to take advantage of the sales.

★ January 1. The Lord Mayor of Westminster sponsors a New Year's Day Parade, starting at about 2:30, from Westminster Abbey to Berkeley Square, followed by a concert at the Royal Albert Hall.

Early January. An unusual array of craft at the International Boat Show in Earl's Court.

January 25. Burns Night. Scots celebrate the birthday of Robert "Robbie" Burns, usually with a poetry reading and a meal of haggis, at private parties, or at selected hotels (ask your concierge).

★ January 30. Commemorative Service for Charles I, beheaded by act of Parliament in 1649. A wreath is laid at his statue in Trafalgar Square.

Mid-January. Rugby fans will love the Triple Crown and International Championships at Twickenham.

January or February

Chinese New Year celebrations on Gerrard Street, Soho. Firecrackers, dragons, the works. Lunar calendar determines the exact date.

February

Mid-February. International Motor Show, Earl's Court.

February 22. Boy Scouts and Girl Guides Memorial Service in Westminster Abbey.

★★ Around March 11 to 14. Crufts Dog Show, the world's most fascinating, once at Earl's Court, now in the National Exhibition Centre, Birmingham, worth the short rail trip directly to the Centre.

February or March

February 6 (or if it falls on a Sunday, February 7). Forty-one-gun cannon salute for Accession Day, in Hyde Park, near the southeast corner above Hyde Park Corner. Marks the Queen's accession to the throne on the death of her father, George VI.

February, March, or April

★ Shrove Tuesday. Pancake races along the Thames, at the Embankment, and down Carnaby Street in central London. Contestants toss pancakes in a frying pan as they run (and musn't drop the batter).

★★★ Maundy Thursday (even years only). The Queen or another member of the royal family distributes special coins (Maundy Money) to representatives of the elderly. Often at Westminster Abbey, check ahead if you wish to attend.

On the same day, Maundy Purses are distributed at St. Bartholomew-the-Great in Smithfield.

★ Good Friday. Hot cross buns are distributed to children before the 10:30am service at St. Bartholomew-the-Great in Smithfield.

★ Holy Saturday, Easter Sunday and Monday. Kite Festival on Blackheath Common.

Easter Sunday. Easter Parade in Battersea Park; a carnival atmosphere with stalls, rides, the works.

★★ Easter Sunday. Tower of London Church Parade. The Beefeaters and others in splendid ceremonial garb are inspected and parade before and after the 11:00 service.

★ Easter Monday morning (about 9:30 to noon). London Harness Horse Parade, Battersea Park.

March

★ March 1. On St. David's Day, the Duke of Edinburgh (or alternate) hands a bunch of leeks to the commandant of the Welsh Guards at Windsor Castle.

★ Mid-March. Spring Antiques Fair at Chelsea Old Town Hall.

★ March 17. On St. Patrick's Day, the Queen Mother (or alternate) hands a batch of shamrocks to the Irish Guard, out at Pirbright, in Surrey.

Second week. Ideal Home Exhibition at Earl's Court—if you really want to see British kitchens and bathrooms on display.

Third week. International Book Fair, Olympia Exhibition Centre.

March or April

March or April through January. Royal Shakespeare Theatre season in Stratford-upon-Avon.

★ Late March. At St. Clement Danes church, handbell ring for the distribution of oranges and lemons to Cockney children.

★★ Head of the River Race. Hundreds of crews row their boats on the Thames from Mortlake to Putney.

Late March. Classic Car Show, Alexandra Palace.

★ Usually early April, on a Saturday afternoon. Oxford-Cambridge four-mile boat race on the Thames, from Putney to Mortlake.

Late March or early April. John Stow Memorial Service, Church of St. Andrew Undershaft, City. At 11:30 on the appointed Sunday, the Lord Mayor puts a new quill pen in the hand of the statue of Stow, an early author.

April

★ Second and fourth Tuesday and Wednesday of April. Royal Horticultural Society Spring Flower Show, at the Royal Horticultural Society in Westminster.

Mid- or Late April. London Marathon from Greenwich (starts at 9:30) to Westminster Bridge and Buckingham Palace.

April 21. On the Queen's real birthday, forty-one-gun salute from cannon in Hyde Park (also on Tower Hill).

★★ April 23. St. George's Day Service in St. Paul's Cathedral, with knights of the Order of St. George in their splendid robes.

Last week. Shakespeare's birthday celebrated at Southwark Cathedral, on the south side of the Thames.

April or May

★★ Whitsunday (Pentecost). Tower of London Church Parade. The Beefeaters and others, in their marvelous ceremonial garb, are inspected and parade before and after the 11:00 church service. (Also on Easter Sunday and Sunday before Christmas.)

Late April or early May. Football Association Cup Final, Wembley Stadium.

Late April or early May. Rugby League Challenge Cup Final, Wembley Stadium.

May

First Monday. May Bank Holiday. Everything closes.

Mid-May. Royal Windsor Horse Show at Home Park, Windsor.

May 1. Horse racing at Newmarket, near London, begins. Includes the Guinness Stakes.

★★ Late May. Chelsea Flower Show at Royal Hospital Grounds. Closed to the public on certain days, so check ahead before going.

Early May. Rugby Union Cup Final at Twickenham Rugby Football Ground.

★★ May 29. Oak-Apple Day Parade, Royal Hospital, Chelsea. Old soldier pensioners put on their seventeenth-century costumes and pay tribute to Charles II, founder of the hospital. (To avoid capture at the Battle of Worcester in 1651, the king hid in an oak tree.)

★★★★★ Mid-May through end of August. Glyndebourne Festival Opera Season, about an hour by train out of town near the village of Lewes, East Sussex. Take the train (sometime they add a special

"The Season" Then and Now

Traditionally, back in the good old days, "The Season" in London began in May and went through September. It was de rigueur to attend as many social events as possible, especially if you were planning to have your daughter presented at Buckingham Palace. Most of the old activities are still on the social calendars of savvy (and affluent) Londoners, but a few have died natural deaths. Moreover, for most people in modern times, "The Season" has shrunk to mean the summer months.

Highlights included:

May

Season officially begins with Royal Academy's Private Viewing in May, the day before it opens to the public.

Opera season opens.

Debutantes were presented at court (a practice long since ended).

Chelsea Flower Show.

Polo matches at Hurlingham and elsewhere.

June

Trooping the Colours.

Running of the Derby at Epsom.

Speech Day at Eton.

Ascot Week, especially Gold Cup Day.

The Aldershot Tattoo.

International Horse Show.

Royal Air Force Tournament.

Wimbledon Lawn Tennis, into July.

July

Polo matches continue.

Henley Regatta.

Oxford-Cambridge cricket matches.

Eton-Harrow cricket matches.

Goodwood Races, which end the London-centered portion of "The Season" on July 30.

August

Regatta Week at Cowes, Isle of Wight.

Highland Season, with grouse and partridge shoot-
ing, in the Scottish Highlands.

September

The Highland Games in Scotland (second week).

Highland Gatherings throughout the month, Scotland.

Royal Garden Party, back at Buckingham Palace,
marking the official end of "The Season."

train) or hire a car, put on your best suit or frock (black tie pre-
ferred), and go to this wonderful display of ostentatious culture at
its best. Tailgate picnic hampers and folding tables out of your
rental car in the parking lot, picnic on the grass, or dine at intermission in the nifty restaurant here. Cocktails before, digestifs afterward, and relatively little-known operatic works performed in a
newly expanded bijou opera house. Expensive, but fun and edify-
ing, too!

Late May. Mind-Body-Spirit Festival at the Royal Horticultural Society,
Westminster.

Last three weeks. Brighton Festival in Brighton, Sussex. Music, theater, displays.

May or June

Late May or early June. Royal Academy opening of Summer Exhibition. Until mid-August.

Late May or early June. Samuel Pepys Commemoration. The Lord
Mayor places a wreath on Pepys' monument in St. Olave's Church.

★ On Ascension Day, students march around the Tower of London,
beating the bounds of the tower by hitting the markers with sticks. At
5pm there is a service at All Hallows Barking-by-the-Tower church
attended by the Lord Mayor; and every third year, it is said, warders
from the tower come to critique the students' work.

Late May to early September. Open Air Theatre Season, Regent's Park.

Late May. Salisbury Festival in Salisbury. Presentations of fine arts, music, and theater.

IN-SEASON

June

★★★★★ Saturday nearest June 11. Queen's Official Birthday, with the Trooping of the Colour at Horse Guards Parade. The Queen rides in an open carriage from Buckingham Palace down The Mall (from 10:30 to 11:00), and returns the same way (about 12:30) after reviewing the troops. Tickets only by advance reservation. Write well in advance to: Brigade Major, Trooping the Colour, Household Division, Horse Guards, Whitehall, SW1A 2AX, enclosing a stamped, self-addressed envelope. Then, at 1pm, the Queen appears on the balcony of Buckingham Palace and the Royal Air Force does a fly-past overhead. Finally, another forty-one-gun salute is fired at the Tower of London.

★★★★★ Early June. Beating Retreat, Horse Guards Parade. Massed bands, a thrilling spectacle. Might be held outside Buckingham Palace as alternate venue, so check ahead.

★★★ Early June. The Derby is run at Epsom Downs racecourse in Surrey.

June through August. Royal Academy Summer Exhibition. The show that used to open the traditional London Season (see box, pages 27–28). New works by lots of artists, mostly unknown. Some years opens in late May.

★★★★★ Mid-June. Royal Ascot (in Berkshire). The Queen attends Royal Ascot (after parading in an open carriage before the crowd). Formal attire is required in the Royal Enclosure. The bigger the hat, the better. Races every afternoon.

★★★★★ Monday afternoon of Ascot Week, usually second or third week of June. Garter Ceremony, Windsor Castle. Procession of yeoman and cavalry to the chapel inside castle precincts.

Mid-June. Greenwich Festival, Greenwich. Dance, concerts, theater, events for the kids.

Mid-June to mid-August. Outdoor Theatre Season at Holland Park. Mostly opera and ballet.

Second and third weeks. Aldeburgh Festival, in Aldeburgh, Suffolk. (See chapter 14, Day Trips from London.)

★★★ Late June to early July. Royal Henley Regatta, Henley-on-Thames, Oxfordshire.

★★★★★ Late June to early July for two weeks. All England Lawn Tennis Championships, Wimbledon. Centre Court tickets by ballot after you apply (see page 135).

Annual Music Festival, Spitalfields. Mostly classical music at Christ Church.

Late June. Antiquarian Book Fair. Venue varies, usually a large hotel.

June through September, Saturday evenings only. Kenwood Lakeside Concerts, Kenwood House. Famous orchestras.

June or July

Cricket Test Matches at Lord's Cricket Ground and at the Oval. Often start mid-May, end late June at Lord's, where World Cup is held.

July

City of London Festival for three weeks, in all sorts of venues, including St. Paul's Cathedral, the Tower of London, you name it. Theater, music, dance, the works.

Early July. Hampton Court Flower Show, Hampton Court Palace, Surrey.

★★ Mid-July to mid-September. Prom concerts at Royal Albert Hall. On the last night, September 15 or nearest Saturday (tickets hard to get), audience indulges itself in a gigantic sing-along, including "Land of Hope and Glory" and "Rule, Britannia!" You haven't really seen flag-waving unless you've seen this (and you don't have to be British to enjoy it).

★★★ Late July (usually third and fourth weeks). The Royal Tournament (military displays, massed bands, contests by the troops, and the like), Earl's Court. Members of royal family attend. On the Sunday before the tournament, everyone participating joins in a gigantic march-past on the Horse Guards Parade, very exciting to watch if you like spectacle.

Late July. Doggett's Coat & Badge Race. Oldest race in England, rowed by boatmen of the Watermen Company in single sculls.

★ Third week. Swan Upping on the Thames in Surrey (between Whitchurch and Sunbury). Traditionally costumed swan counters row upstream, marking birds that belong to the City of London, only counting (not marking) those that belong to the Queen. (They can tell those belonging to the City by notches on the beak.)

July. Warwick Arts Festival, in Warwick, Warwickshire. Theater, music, fine arts displays.

Last weekend. Cambridge Folk Festival, in Cambridge. Music from international artists.

August

Early August through September. Buckingham Palace open to the public. Get tickets same day at Green Park office near palace.

August Bank Holiday weekend. Last Monday. Everything closed. Hampstead Heath Fair. Also Notting Hill Carnival, Ladbroke Grove. The Caribbean comes to London. West Indian community stages a street fair, with bands, food stalls and a parade.

Westminster Horse Show, Hyde Park.

Mid-August. Summer Flower Show at Royal Horticultural Society in Westminster.

OFF-SEASON

September

First week (even years only). Farnborough Air Show, in Hampshire.

Mid-September. Antiques Fair, Chelsea Old Town Hall.

September 15. Battle of Britain Week begins with a Royal Air Force fly-over above Westminster Abbey about noon and a thanksgiving service at the abbey on the Saturday nearest the 15th.

Second and third weeks. Canterbury Festival, in Canterbury, Kent, with drama, music, and fine arts presentations.

★ On or near September 21. Christ's Hospital March, when children from the school, wearing their traditional long, blue coats, march through the city on St. Mathew's Day.

★★ Third Sunday (usually). Horseman's Sunday, when worshipers mount their horses and assemble outside Church of St. John & St. Michael in Hyde Park Crescent between 11:30 and 1:00. The vicar is on horseback, too. After the open-air service, they all go for a ride in Hyde Park along Rotten Row.

★★ Third weekend. Aldeburgh Britten Festival, celebrating the works of Benjamin Britten, and also works by other composers.

★ Last weekend. Horse of the Year Show at Wembley Arena, with fine displays of jumping and the like.

★ September 29, Michaelmas Day. For the election of the Lord Mayor, there is a procession of electors, from St. Lawrence Jewry church to the Guildhall, in ceremonial robes and wigs.

September or October

Windsor Festival, in Windsor. Fine-arts presentations, music, theater, and the like.

October

★★   First Monday. After a service at Westminster Abbey, Her Majesty's judges and counsels proceed in full regalia to the House of Lords, where they have a bang-up breakfast, and the Law Term is opened. America's Supreme Court also opens on the first Monday

---

London Open House

Every fall, almost always in September, on a weekend that varies from year to year, there is an opportunity to see the capital's most fascinating buildings, intriguing not only for their importance, architectural flair, or history, but because they are not usually open to the public. (In 1999, the dates were September 18 and 19. The event has now been held for six years.)

For the first time in 1999, Bush House, home to the BBC World Service and an Aldwych landmark, was open, as was its neighbor, Australia House. For the first time ever, the Horseguards Parade was open to the public.

Repeat openings were held by the Foreign Office, the Treasury, the ITN (Independent Television Network) building, and a number of private homes, many of the latter designed by famous contemporary architects.

In 1999 there were nearly 500 buildings open across the capital and the number of visitors was estimated at over 500,000.

For more details, look at the London Open House Web site www.londonopenhouse.demon.co.uk. From about mid-June of every year, you can get recorded phone information at 0891 600 061 (costs 60p per minute).

---

in October but there is nothing as colorful as this. The judges in London carry little posies—the better to ward off the plague, it is said.

★★ First Sunday, at 3pm. Pearly Kings and Queens gather at St. Martin-in-the-Fields for Costermonger's Harvest Festival.

Sunday nearest October 21. Trafalgar Day Parade at the square, sponsored by the Navy League.

Royals Watching

If your hotel concierge can't clue you in on royal events when you ask (and don't be bashful—he or she would love to see royalty, too), check out the two serious newspapers among London's several daily rags: *The Times* and *The Daily Telegraph*. Inside, nearly every day, will be a Court Calendar. This will detail the public activities of the royal family. After you note the location, you can phone that place for the exact time of arrival or departure, also finding out whether the public is allowed inside. You may see only the royal getting out of a car, but if you're lucky, there might be a royal walkabout, with the Queen (or other royal) stopping to chat with the public. (You can be sure a bodyguard or two will be close by.)

If a royal will attend a theatrical or musical performance, you can try to get a ticket (usually difficult at the last minute) or again enlist the aid of your concierge in doing so.

Finally, if you're planning to be in London during the summer, you can write ahead (far, far ahead) to the American Embassy in London and ask to be given tickets to one of the Queen's annual garden parties (of which there are several). (Foreign embassies are allocated only a few tickets, so a smaller nation's embassy might be a better bet if you have any connections there.) You may just end up on the waiting list, but then you can make a second trip the next summer, can't you?

Late October. (Odd years only). British International Motor Show, formerly Earl's Court, now is held in the National Exhibition Centre, a short train ride from London to the door of the Centre, near Birmingham.

Late October. International Ballroom Dancing championships. Venue changes from year to year.

★★★ Date depending on the tide. The annual Full Tidal Closure of the Thames. A sight you can't see elsewhere; a hidden barrier "dam" is lifted completely out of the water above the waves to close off the river entirely, in a test to ensure that it is in working condition against future floods.

November

★★★★★ Early November. State Opening of Parliament. The Queen, wearing her imperial state crown, rides in state from Buckingham Palace (leaving at 10:30), down The Mall and Horse Guards Parade to Parliament, then returns the same way after she opens Parliament with a speech written for her by the current government. Royal salute of cannon from St. James's Park.

★★★ Sunday closest to November 11, Remembrance Sunday. Remembrance Day ceremonies at the Cenotaph, always attended by the Queen. Salute of cannon in Hyde Park as well.

★★★ Saturday closest to November 11. Remembrance Day ceremonies at Royal Albert Hall, almost always attended by the Queen and other members of the royal family.

First Sunday. Veteran Car Run to Brighton. Starts at Hyde Park Corner.

November 5. Guy Fawkes' Day. Fireworks in the evening, everywhere.

★★★★★ Saturday nearest to November 9. The Lord Mayor's Procession & Show through the streets of the City, in which the newly elected mayor rides in a great coach from Guildhall to the Law Courts along the Strand to take his oath of office. Floats and bands, too.

London Film Festival (for three weeks), mostly at National Film Theatre.

Un-royal Protocol

You probably won't have a chance to meet a member of the royal family while in London. If you do, do *not* follow the example of American comedian Alan King, who was coached in advance on how to behave. King was part of a Command Performance—an annual charity event for which you might want to obtain tickets, if you can afford the price. After the performance, usually a variety show, the Queen or some other royal comes backstage to meet the cast, which lines up to shake her hand. Strict instructions are given to the performers: "Her Majesty will come to your position in the line, extend her hand, and say your name (after being prompted by an aide whispering it into her ear). Take her hand and bow (little more than a nod of the head), or (for women) curtsey (if you wish; optional for non-subjects of Her Majesty), respond to her greeting, and call her 'Your Majesty.'"

So, when the Queen reached Alan King, she extended her hand and said, "Good evening, Mr. King." To which Alan replied, almost automatically, "Good evening, Mrs. Queen."

Close, but no cigar.

In fact, should you get lucky and have a chance to be presented to a royal person, women should remember that the curtsey went out of style with Americans on July 4, 1776, and is very difficult to learn properly, anyhow. Should you try it on meeting a royal, you risk not only a wrenched lower back but the ridicule of your fellow countrymen, and not a few British subjects, too. The proper greeting for non-British subjects to give a royal (of any variety or country) is a friendly handshake (if the royal proffers a hand to shake) and a small nod of the head. And don't try to crush the royal hand, guys—they don't care how "sincere" your grip is, and besides, a tight squeeze can hurt a hand that gets shaken hundreds of times a day.

Last Sunday in November. Christmas Parade in the West End, with floats and the like. Very modern and very commercial. You could miss this, you know.

December

First Thursday. London's "official" Christmas tree is lighted up in Trafalgar Square for the first time this year, with carol singing afterward.

Mid-December. International Show Jumping Championships, where horses display their strength. At Olympia Arena.

★★ Sunday before Christmas. Tower of London Church Parade. The Beefeaters and others assemble for parade and inspection in their marvelous ceremonial garb before and after the 11:00 church service.

Pre-Christmas. Carol services everywhere, including Westminster Abbey.

December 25, Christmas Day. Almost everything closes.

December 26, Boxing Day. Many places closed. Named for the boxes of things (often unwanted Christmas presents, hand-me-downs or leftovers) that the well-to-do handed out to servants, tradesmen, employees, and the other less socially esteemed on the day after Christmas. The recipients from outside the household would usually come calling to get their boxes on this day.

December 31. Exiled Scots spend Watch Night on steps of St. Paul's Cathedral.

New Year's Eve. celebrations in Trafalgar Square, something like those in New York's Time Square. Can get rowdy.

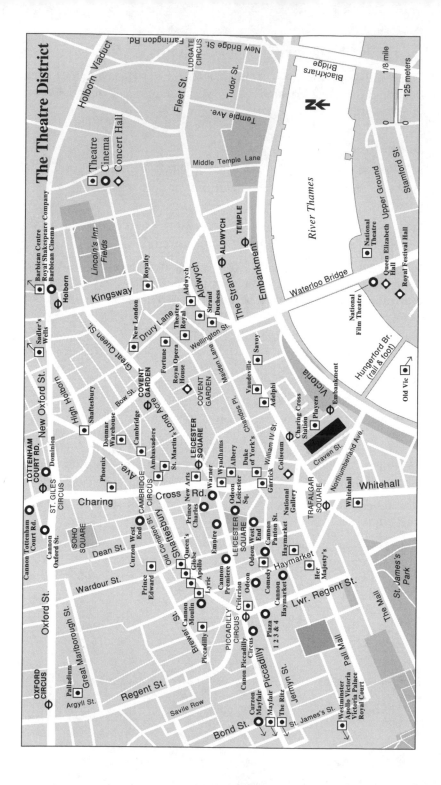

The Theatre District

Holborn Viaduct

Farringdon Rd.
New Bridge St.
LUDGATE CIRCUS

Fleet St.
Tudor St.

Middle Temple Lane
Temple Ave.

Blackfriars Bridge

River Thames

0   1/8 mile
0   125 meters

■ Theatre
○ Cinema
◇ Concert Hall

■ Barbican Centre
  Royal Shakespeare Company
● Barbican Cinema

◯ Holborn

Lincoln's Inn Fields

Kingsway

■ Sadler's Wells

New Oxford St.
TOTTENHAM COURT RD.

■ Dominion

ST. GILES CIRCUS

◯ Cannon Tottenham Court Rd.
◯ Cannon Oxford St.

High Holborn
Great Queen St.

■ New London
■ Drury Lane
■ Theatre Royal

◇ Royalty

Bow St.

Shaftesbury
■ Donmar Warehouse
■ Cambridge
■ Ambassadors
■ St. Martin's

■ Fortune
◇ Royal Opera House
COVENT GARDEN

◯ COVENT GARDEN

Long Acre

Wellington St.

◇ Aldwych
■ Aldwych
■ Strand
■ Duchess

◯ ALDWYCH

◇ TEMPLE

The Strand

◯ Embankment

Maiden Lane
■ Vaudeville
■ Savoy
■ Adelphi

Chandos Pl.
William IV St.

■ Charing Cross Station
■ Players
◯ Embankment

Craven St.
Northumberland Ave.

■ National Theatre

■ National Film Theatre

■ Queen Elizabeth Hall
◇ Royal Festival Hall

Waterloo Bridge

Upper Ground
Stamford St.

Hungerford Br. (rail & foot)

● Old Vic

Phoenix

Charing Cross Rd.
CAMBRIDGE CIRCUS

■ Phoenix
■ Palace

◯ Prince Charles
■ New Arts
■ Warner
■ Wyndhams
■ Albery
■ Duke of York's
■ Garrick
■ Coliseum

LEICESTER SQUARE
◯ LEICESTER SQUARE

◯ Odeon Leicester Sq.
◯ Warner

National Gallery

TRAFALGAR SQUARE
◯ Charing Cross

Dean St.
SOHO SQUARE
Old Compton St.

◯ Curzon West End

■ Queen's
■ Globe
■ Apollo
■ Lyric
■ Empire
◯ Empire

◯ Odeon West End
◯ Odeon

■ Comedy
■ Her Majesty's
■ Haymarket

Haymarket
Panton St.

■ Whitehall
Whitehall

Wardour St.

■ Prince Edward
◯ Cannon Moulin
■ Lyric

◯ Curzon Premiere
◯ Criterion
◯ Cannon Haymarket

PICCADILLY CIRCUS
◯ Cannon Piccadilly Circus
◯ Plaza 1 2 3 & 4

Brewer St.

Oxford St.
OXFORD CIRCUS
◯

■ Palladium
Argyll St.

Great Marlborough St.

Regent St.
Savile Row

Piccadilly

Lwr. Regent St.

Jermyn St.

St. James's St.
◯ Curzon Mayfair
■ Mayfair
■ The Ritz

Bond St.

Pall Mall

■ Westminster
  Apollo Victoria
  Victoria Palace
  Royal Court

The Mall
St. James's Park

3. Theater, Music, and Nightlife

Since London is equal to New York in its wildly diverse opportunities to see theater and hear good music, we won't even attempt to list what's going on. There is, in fact, an excellent weekly publication that does just that, called *Time Out*, which has been so successful over the past few decades in London that the owners have started similar publications in New York and even Paris.

In the pages of *Time Out* and the daily newspapers (by which we mean mostly *The Times* and *The Daily Telegraph*, *The Guardian*, and *The Independent*), you'll find plenty of information on the spectacular theater offerings available, as well as the very broad musical menu from which you can choose on a daily basis throughout the year.

Off-season, theater productions and concerts are far more plentiful than they are in summer, when, in fact, some musical groups are off, usually touring elsewhere.

You should be aware of certain changes on the London theater and musical scenes, however, if you have never been here in the past or have just been keeping up with events in a desultory fashion and from a distance.

Most important, the Royal Opera House in Covent Garden has been closed down for repairs, and is now expected to reopen at the end of 1999. The Royal Opera and the Royal Ballet are performing at different venues, wherever and whenever they can find an empty stage.

Don't overlook out-of-the-way venues for concerts and plays. It's fun to walk across the Thames on Hungerford Bridge (pedestrians only), from the center of tourist London to the South Bank, where, in honor of the Queen, new concert halls (including the Royal Festival Hall) and other performing-arts buildings were erected back in the 1950s. Here you'll also find the National Film Theatre, which specializes in showing rare and often unique films that nobody else screens. There's also the Barbican Centre, unpopular because of its location "way out East" in the City of London, not far from St. Paul's Cathedral. Ticket prices are lower, the presentations often most unusual, new things always happening.

TICKETS

As to buying tickets for any kind of performance, you can do so in advance from North America by calling Keith Prowse, England's major theater, concert, and sports ticket broker:

In New York: 234 West 44th Street, Suite 1000, NY 10036. Phone 1-800-669-8687 or 212-398-1430; fax. 212-302-4251; e-mail tickets@ keithprowse.com

In England: 153 487 0709
In Dublin: 353 (01) 679 5333
In Paris: 33 (1) 42 81 31 13

Other sources of theater tickets

Edwards and Edwards: In U.S., phone 1-800-328-2150
London Showline: In U.S., phone 1-800-962-9246

In London, if you have time to visit the box offices, do so by all means. If not, ask your friendly hotel hall porter (English-speak for concierge), and don't forget to tip him or her for procuring the tickets.

OPERA

Grand-opera fans should not forget for an instant that the Royal Opera is not the only game in town, the English National Opera (phone 171 632 8300) being as distinguished, if not as old. The ENO's permanent home is the wonderfully old Coliseum, on St. Martin's Lane. And don't forget the Welsh or Scottish national operas, which come to London on a regular basis, sometimes performing lesser-known vehicles.

The most fun venues of all are the Glyndebourne Opera, south of London, and the Wexford Opera Festival, over in Ireland. Glyndebourne is in summer; see p. 28. Wexford is in autumn, and although, like Glyndebourne, it is a black-tie affair, it is really rather jolly, and definitely more friendly. Black tie is never required, of course. Oddly enough, black tie at the Royal Opera is not so common, except on very grand occasions, such as a gala or a rare attendance by a member of the royal family (most of whom don't like opera, in any case).

THEATER

Most extraordinary on the new London theater scene is Shakespeare's Globe Theatre, a splendid replica of the original down on the south shore of the Thames in Bankside. The original burned down not long after it opened back in the seventeenth century, but an American actor, Sam Jaffe, made it his life's work (after leaving Hollywood) to rebuild the place. The work, after many tribulations, was finally finished shortly after his recent death. The Globe is open on-season and off, June through September only (mainly because it has no roof). Phone 171 620 0202.

First among many firsts in British theater is the Royal Shakespeare Company, now based at Barbican Centre, off-season from November through April. Phone 171 638 8891.

High on a theater-lover's list, too, is the Royal National Theatre, on the South Bank. Off-season and on, year-round. Phone 171 928 2252.

For half-price West End theatre tickets on the day of the show, queue up at the Leicester Square Half Price Ticket Booth. Cash only. Open Monday through Saturday 2:30 to 6:30, on the south side of Leicester Square.

Though we aren't giving a comprehensive listing of theaters here, we can't resist adding a couple of favorites:

The Royal Court Theatre, St. Martin's Lane—a temporary spot until its permanent home in Sloane Square is refurbished. Phone 171 565 5000.

Her Majesty's Theatre, Haymarket, as much for its appearance as for its plays. Phone 171 930 8800.

DANCE

Without Covent Garden, the Royal Ballet is homeless, but the company displays its usual brilliance wherever it performs these days. Sites include the Coliseum, the Royal Festival Hall on the South Bank, and a place out in Hammersmith! Phone 171 304 4000.

And don't forget Sadler's Wells, which is now based at the Peacock Theatre, 23 Portugal Street, off the Kingsway near the Strand. Phone 171 314 9002.

MUSIC

Some of the best classical music in the world, from piano performances to chamber music programs, can be found at Wigmore Hall, 36 Wigmore Street, in the West End. Phone 171 935 2141.

London has five major symphony orchestras, which play in many venues, including the South Bank—everyone's favorite. The five are the Royal Philharmonic, BBC Symphony, London Symphony, BBC Philharmonic and Philharmonia orchestras. Famous smaller groups, such as the Academy of St. Martin-in-the-Fields and the English Chamber Orchestra, also perform regularly.

The Royal Albert Hall presents many programs, including the infamous Pops (about which we write in our chapter 2, Daily Events (Year-Round), see p. 22; see index); you should try to attend a concert here just to see this magnificent and unusually designed place, now over one hundred years old. Phone 171 589 8212.

JAZZ

If you think of London and jazz in the same sentence, you must be an addict of the latter, so here's where to go: Ronnie Scott's, London's best and oldest jazz club (Ronnie died in 1996, by the way). It's in Soho, of course, at 47 Frith Street. Phone 171 439 0747.

Royal Albert Hall

NIGHTCLUBS

The best in London, if not the world, is the Ministry of Sound, 103 Gaunt Street, way down near the Elephant & Castle tube station. It opens at about 10:30 at night (Saturdays at midnight) and goes, goes, goes all night, until dawn or later. Phone 171 378 6528.

4. Sightseeing London, Off-Season Sites (and On-Season, Too)

Our Sightseeing Star Rating System

If you are pressed for time, you will probably want to see the most impressive sights London has to offer. To help you with this, we've assigned stars to the sights as we judge them, as follows:

★★★★★   Come to London just to see this.
★★★★   Plan your trip around this.
★★★   Plan your day around this.
★★   Go out of your way to see this.
★   Detour a little to see this.

IF YOU HAVE ONLY ONE DAY

If you have only a day, it makes sense to see the best of London, so aim for as many of the five-star sights as possible.

★★★★★   Her Majesty's Tower of London. Weekdays and Saturdays 9:30 to 5:00, Sundays 2:00 to 5:00. Closes at 4pm November through February.

Undoubtedly the world's most famous castle, the Tower of London was built by William the Conqueror in 1097 to assure his recently conquered Anglo-Saxon subjects that he meant to stay. The name for a collection of towers (there are nineteen of them in "the Tower") is

often used to refer to just one of them—the Bloody Tower, where Richard III is said to have ordered his nephews to be strangled. Most visitors here come to see the Crown Jewels (replicas now are on display, the real things tucked away and used on state occasions only), and secondly, perhaps, to breathe in the atmosphere created by so much history and tragedy.

Here, you'll see the spot on Tower Green where hundreds of famous people were executed, including Anne Boleyn, Thomas More, Sir Walter Raleigh, and Saint John Fisher. Take note also of the dungeons. The last person to be imprisoned here, by the way, was Rudolph Hess, Hitler's loony deputy, after he fled Germany during World War II.

Among the much-publicized sights, there are some unusual ones, which you have to look out for:

The Whispering Gallery in the Beauchamp (pronounced "Beecham") Tower, where royal spies lurked, hoping to overhear condemned prisoners' conversations implicating other persons as yet unknown in plots against the current monarch.

The Middle Chamber of Beauchamp Tower, where Lady Jane Gray's husband, Lord Dudley, carved her name twice in the wall before they were both executed.

See also our section on Ghosts in chapter 6 for other Tower memories.

★★★★★ Westminster Abbey. Daily from 8:00 to 7:00. Though admission to the Abbey itself is free, there is an admission charge to see the abbey's own museum, the Chapter House, the Chamber of Pyx in the Cloisters, and the royal chapels. Wheelchair accessible.

Doubly famous as a site for coronations and other royal ceremonies and for its Poets' Corner and memorials to other famous persons, this church is first or second on most visitors' itineraries. Built at the same time as the Tower, Westminster Abbey has seen the coronation of every monarch since William the Conqueror's on Christmas

Day, 1066. You should look here for the Coronation Chair (the Stone of Scone that once rested here was finally returned to Scotland in 1996) and, of course, Poets' Corner, where Charles Dickens, Rudyard Kipling, Samuel Johnson, Geoffrey Chaucer, and others lie buried. The tombs of Queen Elizabeth I and her sister, Mary, are in the nearby Henry VII Chapel.

Queen Elizabeth II was crowned here in 1953, as were all her predecessors. Many of Britain's great writers and scientists, as well as statesmen, are buried here, including William Shakespeare and Sir Isaac Newton. Don't miss the cloisters, the museum or, for that matter, the guided tour.

★★★★★ The British Museum; Great Russell Street. Weekdays and Saturdays 10:00 to 5:00, Sundays 2:30 to 6:00.

Since the Reading Room has been moved from this building, the museum is now devoted almost entirely to being a museum, which most visitors assumed it was, anyhow. Not the largest museum in the world, it is still one of the three or four most important. (Its sisters are the Louvre in Paris, the Metropolitan in New York, and any other of your choice.) There is room here to list only a few of the must-sees: the Magna Carta, the Elgin (pronounced with a hard "g") Marbles from the Parthenon in Athens, the Portland Vase, and the Rosetta Stone are but four of the best-known treasures.

Westminster Abbey

That Damned British Museum!

An archconservative American friend of ours who lives in London used to curse the British Museum every time he drove by. "That damned Karl Marx wrote *Das Kapital* in there, and started the whole Communist mess. And the British taxpayer let him get away with it!"

Since the collapse of Soviet communism, our friend has turned his wrath elsewhere. With the books removed from the old museum and placed in the new British Library up by St. Pancras Station, our friend now snorts, "It's no longer a place where you can go to have a quiet read. There were always too many tourists in the museum rooms, but once you were inside the Reading Room, it was heaven. And I won't be using the new British Library—Prince Charles was right when he said it looks like a KGB training school."

If *you* want to visit the new British Library, you'll find it near St. Pancras Station, at 96 Euston Road (phone 0171 412 7000). It's open from 10:00 to 5:00 Monday through Saturday, 2:30 to 6:00 on Sundays. It's quite a striking building, despite what Prince Charles said about it.

IF YOU HAVE TWO DAYS

In addition to the five-star listings, see as many of the four-star sights as possible:

★★★★ The Houses of Parliament, including Big Ben and the view from across Westminster Bridge. Saturday year-round, also Monday, Tuesday, and Thursday in August and September. A few tickets are available for watching debates from the Strangers' Gallery. If you have British connections, ask them to get tickets through their Member of Parliament.

You use the Victoria Tower entrance (that's the biggest tower, in the center) for your tour. Only some of its rooms are open to the public. If you join a guided tour, you're likely to see more, and to hear about one of Britain's most marvelous customs: Prior to the opening of Parliament annually, while the Queen sits waiting on her throne in the House of Lords, an usher (Gentleman Black Rod) walks toward the door of the House of Commons to summon them into her presence. Just before the usher reaches the Commons' door, it is slammed in his face, a not-so-gentle reminder that the Commons can do what it wishes to do. (Back in 1649, it sentenced Charles I to death for defying its wishes.) A moment later, the door opens and the members of the House of Commons humbly follow the usher back to hear the Queen's speech.

The current Labour government has introduced legislation to abolish the right of hereditary peers to sit (and vote) in the House of Lords, leaving only life peers (political appointees, mostly) with that privilege. As this would be a major constitutional change, passage of the bill (the House of Lords must approve it, as well as the Commons) may take a long time and most certainly will provoke a continuing debate. Our advice: If you want to see a hereditary lord in full cry in the House of Lords, do it soon, as that species may be a vanishing breed, at least in this venue.

★★★★ The Changing of the Queen's Guard at Buckingham Palace. See Daily Events, page 22, for details.

IF YOU HAVE THREE DAYS

To the five- and four-star sights, add these three-star places:

★★★ St. Paul's Cathedral. Tours daily 8:00 to 6:00.

London's largest house of worship, St. Paul's (built 1675–1710) is the masterwork of Sir Christopher Wren, whose famous epitaph graces his tomb inside ("Here lies Christopher Wren. If you would see his monument, look around you."). There has been a church on this site since the seventh century. Both Wellington and Nelson are buried here. Of special interest is the so-called American Chapel, actually the Jesus Chapel, dedicated to the men and women of the American armed forces who died in World War II. The stout of limb can go up to the Whispering Gallery around the base of the dome; even hardier souls can climb the 530 steps up to the Golden Gallery, at the base of the lantern atop the dome.

★★★ Buckingham Palace. Early August through September, daily 9:30 to 5:30. Get tickets at Green Park office from 9:00 on the same day you wish to visit.

Sophia Loren Was Being Rude

Insensitive tourists from every continent, it would seem, are fascinated by the idea of disturbing a sentry on duty, causing him to abandon his ramrod-straight posture, his eye-front look and no-nonsense demeanor. Ignorant of courtesy, people of both sexes, all ages and all cultures wave their hands in front of the sentry's eyes, dance around him, try to make him laugh, and otherwise behave like louts. Some even proposition the sentries, tucking notes into their pockets or boots. That some might be successful in making assignations this way was attested to by a *London Evening Standard* front-page article a few years back, headlining the news that the Changing of the Guard ceremony had been canceled a few times in the past because of nonattendance by some of the troopers, who weren't back in their barracks by roll call in the morning! It was Sophia Loren, in a 1970s movie about Arab spies, who tried to make a sentry move so she could retrieve some secret paper that he had inadvertently stepped on. In the film, the sentry, inexplicably, fainted dead away after putting up with her antics for a while. Our advice: Why act like an idiot?

Not open to tourists at all until recently, Buck House, as the British irreverently call it, is the unofficial seat of the British Royal Family. Officially, the seat is still at the Palace of Saint James. When ambassadors are sent to London from abroad, they are accredited to "the Court of St. James," and the most serious official announcements (births, weddings and deaths) are still announced from a balcony there. But Buck House is where the Queen and Prince Philip live when in London, and it is from one of its balconies that the Royal Family still waves on state occasions such as the Queen's Official Birthday (in June), after the opening of Parliament, and so forth. You're only allowed in eighteen of the palace's 660 rooms—including the Throne Room. In addition to the palace proper, visitors can see the Royal Mews behind the palace and the Queen's Art Gallery, attached to it on the Buckingham Gate before it becomes Buckingham Palace Road.

★★★ Hampton Court Palace. Daily 9:30 to 6:00 (4:30 in winter). Go out by boat, back the same, or travel by bus or train.

Built by Cardinal Wolsey, Henry VIII's chief minister, and appropriated from him by the king, Hampton Court is a marvelous palace, far superior to Buck House in architecture, scope, and purpose, and surrounded by lovely lawns and gardens. All of that, and a river, to boot! Instead of living here and turning Buck House into a pied-a-terre, which any right-thinking sybarite would do, the present royal family has followed the lead of many of its antecedents and turned Hampton Court over to grace-and-favor flats—and, of course, tourists. Nearly a thousand small apartments exist here, occupied ("by grace and favor of Her Majesty") by as many faithful retainers, past and present, of the royal establishment. Many are in "reduced circumstances," as the genteel British often term diminished income.

In addition to the State Apartments and the Picture Gallery, be sure to look out for the mammoth kitchens and the Maze, the latter outside in the gardens which run down to the Thames itself.

There'll Always Be An England!

Reduced circumstances, which many of the grace-and-favor inhabitants of apartments in Hampton Court Palace suffer from, reminds us of another great British institution, the charitable trust. Most of these organizations issue Christmas cards to raise money for their causes. One of our personal favorites has always been the Society for the Relief of Distressed Gentlefolk.

Critics of the alleged British love for animals over, say, ordinary people, note that the Queen has lent her patronage to the *Royal* Society for the Prevention of Cruelty to Animals, but not to the *National* Society for the Prevention of Cruelty to Children. Her support means the difference in names, if nothing else.

But, at least, England has a society for insufficiently financed gentlemen and gentlewomen, who presumably wouldn't want to resort to living on the dole!

IF YOU HAVE FOUR DAYS

Add on the following two-star sights (and see our Museum listings in chapter 4).

★★ St. James's Park

This is London's prettiest park, and one of the smallest, easily seen in an hour or so. There are splendid views of Westminster through the trees and above the lake, where plenty of waterfowl live, breed, and mooch from visitors. There is no better way to navigate your way from Buck House to Westminster Abbey or Parliament than to wander slowly through this gorgeous bit of greenery.

I'm Always the Last to Know!

One of our oldest friends is the granddaughter of a woman named Penelope, who was a regular reader to Queen Victoria in that grand lady's last years (Her Majesty's eyesight had seriously diminished). On one occasion, Penelope entered the royal presence a bit flustered, apologizing profusely. "I'm sorry, Your Majesty, for being late today. But the most wonderful thing occurred while I was passing through St. James's Park. There was an Italian organ grinder there, and he had the most attractive little monkey, doing all manner of clever tricks! I simply had to stay and watch for a few minutes!"

"An Italian organ-grinder?" queried the old queen. "With a monkey? In St. James's Park?" She sighed. "Why doesn't anyone ever tell me these things?"

★★ St. James's Palace. Interior not open to the public, except Queen's Chapel, which is open only for services (see Churches, page 68).

Ambassadors from foreign countries are appointed to the Court of St. James, not to the Court of Buckingham Palace, or, for that matter, to the Government of the United Kingdom. They must be received by the Queen to start their terms as ambassadors, and when they leave, they say a royal good-bye to her. Nonetheless, they meet her in Buckingham Palace, down The Mall, as the royal family doesn't like St. James's small and dark apartments. (Some retainers do live here, however.) This is the place where you can walk right up to the sentries at their guard posts, if you are insensitive enough to do that kind of thing, or at least photograph them quite close up, which they are used to. A sensitive Londoner's recommendation (he himself was once a guard): Stay at least ten feet away, and the farther away you are, the happier the sentry will be. "Just put yourself in his place," our friend says. At about the same time as the Changing of the Guard is staged at Buck House (see page 22), you can see a small-scale version of the same thing up-close, here at St. James's, where Pall Mall (pronounced "*pell mell*") meets St. James's Street.

★★ Whitehall, especially the Banqueting House. Weekdays 10:00 to 5:00, Sundays 3:00 to 5:00.

The site of Charles I's execution, the Banqueting House is famous also for its splendid ceiling paintings by Rubens (1635). The king, who commissioned the paintings, stepped to the execution scaffolding from a window in the same hall fourteen years later (January 30, 1649). A bust on the exterior marks the probable site of the since-altered window.

★★ Royal Courts of Justice. Temple Bar, at the junction of Fleet Street and the Strand.

You can tour the buildings anytime they are open; the galleries are always open during actual trials.

★★ The Guildhall. Weekdays 10:00 to 5:00. Closed on days when official functions take place, and sometimes for several days after.

This is a lavishly decorated building, both inside and out. You'll appreciate this place if you like London and its history, especially the lore of the City itself. Most interesting of all is the crypt. Look especially for the world's oldest clock museum here, and for the Guildhall Library.

★★ Harrods Department Store. Weekdays 10:00 to 6:00 (Wednesday, Thursday, Friday to 7:00), Sunday closed.

Come here not necessarily to shop, but to look over the goods and to people-watch. Don't miss the food halls, especially the great hall for meat and fish. Our suggestion: See these two halls first, then go upstairs to the floors of your choice and work your way down. Everything is an anticlimax after these highlights, in any case.

★★ Greenwich. Cutty Sark, National Maritime Museum. Greenwich Observatory. Go round-trip by boat.

The museum was once a royal palace; in fact, it was from here that Anne Boleyn departed for the Tower to have her head removed. The Cutty Sark is an interesting old vessel. At the observatory, you can stand on a line indicating zero degrees longitude, with one foot east of Greenwich Mean Time and one foot west (or vice-versa!).

Near here the giant Millennium Dome has been constructed to house whatever wonders the current government will have dreamed up by the time the dome is finished.

The Millenium Dome & Other Extravagances

Opening officially at midnight of December 31, 1999, London's giant Millennium Dome will be a permanent celebration that Prime Minister Tony Blair says will make it "embody the spirit of the future of the world." But, then, the inventor of Cool Britannia, as Blair is known, was never one for understatement, once the defining mark of any British gentleman. The building, though, is the world's largest fiberglass domed structure, embracing an area about the size of three football fields.

The Dome, which will house all sorts of theme attractions (including a giant reproduction of the human body through which you can walk), cost over £750 million (about $1.215 billion), and is expected to attract about 12 million visitors during the year 2000. It sits in Greenwich, near the Prime Meridian line, the exact point from which the world's time is measured ("Greenwich Mean Time").

There will be 12 attractions arranged around the dome's interior, and in the center will be a live performance area. The idea of the exhibits is to take visitors through time, from the Big Bang origins of the universe through the evolution of mankind, and on through human history to the present day. It will be a combination of live performances, virtual reality, and other special effects.

Some of the attractions include the Body Zone (a huge sitting figure), a Spirit Level (a place for reflection in a garden), The Learning Curve (virtual reality rides and interactive exhibits), Serious Play (including wearing suits that let you stick to the walls), and Living Island (a typical British seaside resort), among others. (Meanwhile, British authors are upset about no books being represented in the Dome, "not even the Bible," as one spokesperson said.)

You have to prebook, as there are just two "operating sessions" a day during peak times, with a capacity of "only" 35,000 people at a time. Your concierge in London can arrange tickets for you, as can the Keith Prowse ticket agency or your travel agent back home.

If you don't plan to be in the Dome on January 1, 2000 or anytime later, you will also find other Millennial projects all over the counrty, many of them funded by the relatively new National Lottery. Among them are a high-tech Millennium Bridge, the first pedestrian bridge to be built across the Thames in London for one hundred years (linking St. Paul's Cathedral on the north bank to the new Tate Gallery of Modern Art on the south bank); the new Millennium Stadium in Cardiff, which in fact was ready to host the Rugby World Cup in late 1999; and more. There will even be a giant British Airways Millennium Ferris Wheel (500 feet in diameter) near County Hall on the Thames to give you a new perspective of London.

New hotels are being built, the Millennium organizers tell us, and grants have been made to villages to fix up their village greens, halls, churches, and church bells. More walking and cycling trails are being created and inland waterways are being opened up.

The Tate Gallery of Modern Art (mentioned above), a new sister to the existing Tate Gallery of British Art, will be opened in London, and major improvements are being made to such old warhorses as the British Museum and the Science Museum, too.

To get to the Millennium Dome, you can take a new extension of the Jubilee subway (Underground) line, 24 trains an hour running in each direction between central London and the Greenwich site of the dome, the station there being named the New North Greenwich Station. It will be the largest underground rail station in Europe when finished. There will also be boat service to the site, plans to be announced nearer to opening day.

For more information on the Millennium Dome and other plans, look at the London Tourist Board's website, www.LondonTown.com.

★★ Royal Botanical Gardens, Kew, in Richmond, a London suburb. Daily 10:00 to sunset. Greenhouses (called "glasshouses" here) open from 1:00.

Perhaps the world's best collection of botanical specimens grows here, nearly every kind of plant there is. The garden dates back to 1759, and has established the pattern from which nearly all other botanical gardens have been modeled. Also known as Kew Gardens.

IF YOU HAVE FIVE DAYS

Now, add on the one-star sights—as many as you can:

★ Cabinet War Rooms, Clive Steps, King Charles Street. Daily from 9:30 to 6:00.

In this rabbit warren below ground, Winston Churchill and his commanders engineered Britain's amazing battle for survival, first alone, and then, after more than two years, with the decisive help of the United States.

★ Shepherd Market, off Piccadilly.

Tucked away off Piccadilly (look for White Horse Street) is this little bit of Olde Englande right in the posh West End, behind one of London's finest hotels (the Athenaeum) and just two short streets from another (the Hilton). There are food, fish and fruit markets, small restaurants, cozy pubs, local dentists and doctors—and yes, people live here, including in recent years, newly-started couturiers and more than one call girl and male "escort service."

★ Hyde Park & Kensington Gardens. Daily, sunrise to sunset.

The two adjoin one another, park to the east, gardens to the west. Highlights include the statuary, Rotten Row (for horseback riding), the Serpentine (for sunbathing in summer, strolling the rest of the year), the Serpentine Gallery (for frequently changing exhibitions and a good place to have tea), the Round Pond (for sailboats, nannies and their charges, the occasional romantic meeting), and at the west end, Kensington Palace, rear view. Famous statues here include one of Peter Pan.

★ Hyde Park Corner, northeast corner of the park, where plebeian Oxford street meets posh Park Lane. Also known as Speaker's Corner.

Here is the spot where everyone can have his or her say, usually on Sundays. There are usually more foreign speakers—many from what's left of the British Commonwealth—than there are British. The Irish Republican Army, however, evidently doesn't believe its freedom to speak would last long here. If you're lucky, you might find a flat-earth exponent; you might hear even a more mysterious speaker demanding that "the bishops open Joanna Southcut's box"!

Joanna Southcut's Box

Late in the nineteenth century, one Joanna Southcut bequeathed a box containing her prophecies about such minor things as the date of the end of the world, the return of Christ (the "second coming") and more. She left her box to the bishops of the Church of England, and enough money to administer a fund to ensure that they opened the box and took heed of the warnings. Apparently, they refused to do so, and for over a hundred years, the executors of her estate (who said lawyers don't know a good thing when they see it?) have been taking out ads in British publications (and at least one American guidebook to England) asking: "When Will the Bishops Open Joanna Southcut's Box?" An English friend swears he has heard the same question thundered from a stepladder (the favored form of support, not a mere soapbox) at Hyde Park Corner.

★ Lincoln's Inn, Chancery Lane. Monday to Friday 8:00 to 7:00.

You can wander freely through the courtyards and inner lawns of the Inn (as you can at Grey's Inn, also a lawyer's haven), but you need appointments to enter the buildings themselves. Here many of London's highest-paid lawyers, the barristers who actually argue cases before the courts (as opposed to the solicitors who merely do the paperwork), have their offices. You might see one or two, male and female, dashing out to court in their robes and white powdered wigs.

★ The Temple, just off Fleet Street. Daily, sunrise to sunset.

This is about as medieval a London as you are likely to find. The old buildings here, some dating back to the twelfth century, are occupied mostly by members of the legal profession. Look especially for the old Knights Templar church, also twelfth century, based on the floor plan of the Church of the Holy Sepulcher in Jerusalem.

★ Church of St. Bartholomew-the-Great, West Smithfield. Daily, sunrise to sunset.

Although the oldest of London's churches, little remains of the original; but the thirteenth- and fourteenth-century remnants are impressive enough.

★ New and Old Bond streets (and Burlington Arcade) for the window shopping. Most shops open weekdays 10:00 to 6:00.

New Bond Street lies south of Oxford Street, near the tube station of the same name, stretching toward Piccadilly but turning into Old Bond Street at the bottom, two blocks before reaching Piccadilly. Here you'll find Asprey (jewelers to Her Majesty) and a host of other very fancy stores.

★ One of London's street markets (see chapter 10, Shopping in London). Take your pick.

★ Trafalgar Square.

This place vied with Piccadilly Circus as center of the known universe when Britain controlled a quarter of the world's area and population at the zenith of the Empire, back in the 1930s. The snobs opted for the square, with its statuary, National Art Gallery, and High Commission (embassy) offices of Commonwealth countries. The toffs thought Piccadilly Circus much more exciting and to the point, with its department stores and amusement arcades, not to mention the porno palaces and pubs on the side streets. In the square, look for

The Temple, Inns of Court

Nelson's Column (in the center) and the big lamppost with the police box built into it (southeast corner). The pigeons will come to you unless you actively shoo them away.

Nelson's Column dominates Trafalgar Square, commemorating the admiral's victory over Napoleon's navy off the coast of Spain, during which Nelson was killed. Every Christmas since 1947, the city of Oslo sends a tree to London in thanks for Britain's help to Norway during World War II; this is where the tree stands throughout the holiday season.

★ Covent Garden.

Though the Royal Opera House is closed for complete renovations and expansion (its reopening is scheduled for the year 2000), the area around it is of great interest, especially to shoppers. To keep developers out, local residents willingly turned the area into a tourist haven, though the trendy restaurants and shops here attract large numbers of young Londoners as well. As at Les Halles in Paris, most of the produce and market functions of the old garden have been moved to a distant location.

★ Old Bailey. Public galleries open weekdays 10:30 to 1:00 and 2:00 to 4:00. No tours.

If you want to watch a criminal court in action, this is the place; it is probably the world's most famous such court. As Forrest Gump would say, it's like a box of chocolates—you never know what you're going to get. Maybe you'll be lucky, most likely not.

★ Kensington Palace, Broad Walk, Kensington Gardens. Daily 9:00 to 5:00 (Sundays from 11:00). There is some talk of closing the place down for renovations, so check ahead. At any time, of course, you can admire the exterior of this residence of, among others, Princess Margaret.

★ Westminster Cathedral. Daily 7:00am to 8:00pm.

The leading Roman Catholic place of worship in London, it dates only from 1903. From the top of the tower, you can get a quite good view of all of London.

★ Southwark Cathedral, London Bridge. Daily sunrise to sunset.

The William Shakespeare Memorial here, plus the Harvard Chapel and the fine Gothic architecture, make this worth the journey south of the river.

IF YOU HAVE SIX DAYS

Here are a few more of the other interesting sights in London to add to the previous days' listings. (It would take an encyclopedia to list them all.) We also list two you might want to see but can't.

★ London Aquarium, Regent's Park.

Daily 10:00 to 5:00 in summer, 10:00 to 4:00 in winter. (Closed on Christmas Day). Inside the London Zoo, very nicely done.

★ London Zoo, Regent's Park.
See London Aquarium, above.

Kensington Palace

**The Spencer House

Little known and not often visited, the Spencer House is a marvelous place to get an idea of how the really rich (and famous) live. At 27 St. James's Place, SW1, right off St. James's Street and a stone's throw from the palace of the same name, this is the London residence of the famous Spencer family (as in Princess Diana, born into this family, and Winston Spencer Churchill). You can go tour it with a guide, which takes about fifteen minutes. It is open only on Sunday from 11:30 to 4:45; closed in January and August, and to children under ten. Phone 171 499 8620.

Lloyd's of London is no longer open to the public, and why would you want to see this awful, modern structure anyhow? The old one had at least a sense of history.

The Monument, Monument Street.

Climb to the top if the renovation work is finished (310 steps). Commemorates the Great Fire of 1666, which destroyed much of the City.

The Stock Exchange, Old Broad Street, London EC2, is also closed to the public. About as exciting as Wall Street, or less so, even when it was opened.

5. Museums and Churches

Not everyone is a museum fan, so we didn't include museums in our "Must See" category, with the sole exception of the British Museum, which is as much an historic relic as a museum in many ways, and has to be seen if you want to say you were in London.

For those who wish to spend time in these (sometimes) hallowed halls, here is our private listing of museums, with their star ratings,

FIVE-STAR

★★★★★ British Museum, Great Russell Street. (See If You Have Only One Day, in chapter 4.)

★★★★★ National Gallery, Trafalgar Square. Daily 10:00 to 6:00, (Sunday, from 2:00).

Perhaps the best collection of European paintings in the world, with masterpieces by Botticelli, Leonardo, Tintoretto, Hogarth, Gainsborough, Turner, El Greco, Rembrandt, Manet, Monet, and more.

★★★★★ Victoria & Albert Museum, Cromwell Road. Daily 10:00 to 5:00 (Mondays from noon).

This is the world's best museum for the decorative arts, in the opinion of many experts. Outstanding for Indian art, but with plenty of recognizable treasures by Raphael, Holbein and Bernini, to name only a few.

FOUR-STAR

★★★★ National Portrait Gallery, St. Martin's Place. Daily 10:00 to 6:00 (Sunday from noon).

One of the world's best collections of portraits, with artists ranging from Whistler to Warhol.

★★★★ Natural History Museum, Cromwell Road. Open Monday to Saturday 10:00 to 5:50, Sunday from 11:00 to 5:50. Closed December 24–26.

Comprises the Natural History Museum and the Geological Museum. Rocks and plants, dinosaur exhibits, and diamonds.

★★★★ The Tate Gallery of Modern Art. Open now daily 10:00 to 5:50.

Combines the old (like the National Gallery) and the new (like, well, the Tate), with a magnificent collection of paintings by artists ranging from Turner, Reynolds, and Constable through Picasso and Francis Bacon. Henry Moore's most famous sculptures are here also. Will soon divide into two buildings, the Tate Gallery of British Art on Mill Bank, and a new Tate Gallery of Modern Art, across the Thames.

THREE-STAR

★★★ Percival David Foundation of Chinese Art, 53 Gordon Square. Monday to Friday, 10:30 to 5:00.

Has, perhaps, the best display of Chinese art outside China or Taiwan. Don't miss the porcelain collections.

★★★ The Science Museum, Exhibition Road, SW7. Daily 10:00 to 5:00 (closed December 24–26).

From the first train engine to the first jet, it's all here, with hands-on displays.

TWO-STAR

★★ Institute of Contemporary Arts, Nash House, Duke of York Steps. Galleries open daily noon to 7:30.

Just off The Mall, the ICA is London's brightest exhibition space for every kind of avant-garde art. Also films and lectures.

★★ The Courtauld Institute Picture Gallery, Somerset House, the Strand. Monday to Saturday 10:00 to 6:00, Sunday from 2:00.
French impressionist paintings by the dozens, as well as old Italian masters.

★★ The Wallace Collection, Manchester Square, W1. Open Monday to Saturday 10:00 to 5:50, Sunday from 11:00 to 5:50. Closed Christmas and New Year's.
Mostly French paintings here, by artists including Boucher, Fragonard, and also Rembrandt. A lot of armor from around the world, as well.

ONE-STAR

★ Imperial War Museum, Lambeth Road. Daily 10:00 to 6:00 (closed December 24–26).
Appropriately, perhaps, occupying the former mental hospital known as Bedlam (short for Bethlehem Royal Hospital), the displays attest to the efficacy (or lack thereof) of war.

★ Museum of London, 150 London Wall, EC2. Open Tuesday to Saturday, 10:00 to 5:00, Sunday 10:00 to 5:50.
Relics of old London, some still used, such as the marvelous Lord Mayor's Coach.

★ National Maritime Museum, Romney Road. Open daily 10:00 to 5:00 (closed December 24–26).
You have to go down to Greenwich for this, but it's worth the trip, especially if you can make it in fine weather by boat (catch Thames launch at Westminster Bridge Charing Cross, or the Tower Piers). In the royal park that houses the Old Royal Observatory (Greenwich Mean Time, remember?), the museum is a tribute to the Britain that ruled the waves. Paintings and models, among other things.

The Royal Borough
of Kensington

QUEEN'S GATE
S.W. 7.

★ The Queen's Gallery, Buckingham Palace. Tuesday to Saturday 11:00 to 5:00, Sundays from 2:00.
Adjoining the palace itself. Contains pictures from Her Majesty's collection.

★ Wellington Museum, Apsley House, 149 Piccadilly, W1. Tuesday to Sunday 11:00 to 5:00.
Right at Hyde Park Corner, this is the former mansion of the Duke of Wellington, victor of the Battle of Waterloo, who sent Napoleon to St. Helena. Strangely, there is a giant statue of Napoleon in the lobby, but otherwise, the house is filled with Wellington's battle trophies and the like.

Special Exhibitions

Major exhibitions are often held at the Royal Academy of Arts, Burlington House, Piccadilly, W.1. Check with the local newspapers to see what exhibition, if any, is open while you are in town. The Annual Summer Exhibition, June through August, is a favorite with many.

SPECIAL-INTEREST MUSEUMS

No stars are assigned, as only fans of the special interest will be interested in most cases.

Bank of England Museum, Threadneedle Street. Monday to Friday, 10:00 to 5:00. History of the bank, with interactive video display.

Carlyle's House, 24 Cheyne Row. April through October, Wednesday to Monday 11:00 to 5:00.
Thomas Carlyle, the historian, lived here. Come to see everything left just as it was at the time of his death in 1881. Note also the Victorian-style garden.

Clink Prison Museum, 1 Clink Street, SE1. Daily 10:00 to 6:00, closed Christmas and New Year's Day.
This is where the slang word for prison came from—London's oldest jail, torture devices and all.

Clock Museum, in the Guildhall. (See If You Have Four Days, in chapter 4).

Dickens's House, 48 Doughty Street. Monday to Saturday 10:00 to 5:00.
Dickens wrote *Oliver Twist* here, among other works.

Doctor Johnson's House, 17 Gough Square. Monday to Saturday,
11:00 to 5:00.
If only to see a nicely restored seventeenth-century residence, you
should visit the lexicographer's house.

Fan Museum, 12 Crooms Hill. Daily 11:00 to 4:30.
You have to come to Greenwich for this, but fans of fans won't mind.

Florence Nightingale Museum, St. Thomas's Hospital, 2 Lambeth
Palace Road. Tuesday to Sunday 10:00 to 4:00, and on British holidays.
Florence Nightingale's possessions and other items from the Crimean
War are displayed in the Nightingale School, which is in the hospital.

Freud Museum, 20 Maresfield Gardens. Wednesday to Sunday noon
to 5:00.
This is where the father of shrinks lived and worked after his
escape from the Nazis.

Guards Museum, Wellington Barracks, Birdcage Walk. Daily 10:00 to
6:00 (closed Christmas season and all of January).
History of the foot guard regiments (Grenadiers, Coldstream,
Irish, Scots, and Welsh).

Hogarth's House, Hogarth Lane. Open April to September on Monday, Wednesday to Saturday from 11:00 to 6:00, on Sunday from 2:00
to 6:00. Rest of year, same days and hours, but closes at 4:00. Also
closed September 1 to 15 and December 11 to 31.
Out in Chiswick Park (you pass it en route to Heathrow Airport), is
this little house, with several of Hogarth's engravings.

Jewish Museum, 129 Albert Street. Open Sunday to Thursday 10:00 to
4:00.
You'll find this exhibit, with many significant items of interest, in
Camden Town.

Keats's House, Wentworth Place. Summer weekdays 10:00 to 1:00 and
2:00 to 5:00, weekends and winter, afternoons only.
The poet wrote "Ode on a Grecian Urn" here.

London Canal Museum, New Wharf Road, Kings Cross. Open Tuesday
to Sunday, 10:00 to 4:30, also on British holiday Mondays.
This exhibit covers life on the canal, and more, including all you
ever wanted to know about the ice business.

London Toy & Model Museum, 21 Craven Hill. Daily 9:00 to 5:00.
    Up in the Bayswater area is this charming collection of toys and
models, including dolls, of course. The kids should love it.

London Canal Trips

If you have time, a pleasant way to see parts of London is to take a trip on one of the two canals left—
Regent's Canal and Grand Union Canal. Go to Little
Venice, just north of Paddington Rail Station, to
catch these craft:

Jason's Trip. Regent's Canal, which passes Regent's
Park. Opposite 60 Blomfield Road. Phone 171 286
3428.

Jenny Wren Cruises. 250 Camden High Street.
Phone 171 485 4433.

London Waterbus Company. Camden Lock Market,
Camden Lock Place, Chalk Farm Road. Phone 171
482 2660.

London Transport Museum, Covent Garden, WC2. Daily 10:00 to
6:00 (closed December 24–26).
    Buses, locomotives and tube trains, among other items.

MCC Cricket Museum, St. John's Wood. Book in advance for tours
daily at 12:00 and 2:00, 10:00 on match days. No tours on Cup and
Test match days.
    At the Mecca of cricket, you can see all you want to know about the
game, and the "Ashes" over which England and Australia compete
every few years.

Museum of Garden History, Lambeth Palace Road in the Tradescant
Trust complex. Open Monday to Friday, 10:30 to 4:00, Sunday 10:30
to 5:00.
    Outside is a seventeenth-century garden, with the tomb of the
HMS Bounty's Admiral Bligh; inside, tools and a permanent exhibit.

Museum of Mankind, 6 Burlington Gardens. Monday to Saturday
10:00 to 5:00, Sunday 3:00 to 6:00.

Next door to the Royal Academy, this is a great ethnographic museum, one of the world's best.

Museum of the Moving Image, South Bank, under Waterloo Bridge. Daily 10:00 to 6:00. Movie and TV history and technology.

Musical Museum, 368 High Street, Brentford, Middlesex. Call ahead for demonstration days and hours 181 560 8108. Out west of London, in the suburbs near Kew. Lots of automatic musical machines, from boxes to mighty Wurlitzers.

National Army Museum, Royal Hospital road, in heart of Chelsea; next to Royal Hospital, a pensioners' home. Open daily 10:00 to 5:30.
Here you get the story of Britain's earlier wars.

National Postal Museum, King Edward Street. Open Monday to Friday 9:30 to 4:30.
Stamps and more stamps, including the world-famous Penny Black, the world's most expensive.

Pollock's Toy Museum, 1 Scala Street. Open Monday to Saturday 10:00 to 4:30.
Adults will like this as much as children. Many toy theaters, dolls and teddy bears.

Royal Air Force Museum, Grahame Park Way, Hendon. Daily 10:00 to 6:00.
The national aviation museum, with Sopwith Camels and Spitfires as well as more recent craft.

Royal Mews, Buckingham Palace Road. Open Wednesday and sometimes other days in summer. Phone ahead 171 799 2331.
The royal carriages, their horses and equipment.

Sir John Soane Museum, 13 Lincoln's Inn Fields. Open Thursday to Saturday 10:00 to 5:00.
Not like a museum, this is just the house Sir John died in—his will demands that nothing be changed. Wonderful, as it tells us how a rich man lived in 1837. His art collection includes Canalettos and Turners, not to mention Hogarths.

Syon House, Brentford, Middlesex, just to the west of London (en route to Heathrow). Open April to September, Wednesday to Sunday 11:00 to 5:00.
You'll see the work of Robert Adam here, as well as gardener Capability Brown, and the amazing London Butterfly House.

Theatre Museum, Russell Street. Open Tuesday to Sunday 11:00 to 7:00. Part of the Victoria & Albert Museum, with exhibits on stage design, costuming and more.

William Morris Gallery, Forest Road, Walthamstow. Open Tuesday to Saturday and first Sunday of each month 10:00 to 1:00 and 2:00 to 5:00.
If you're interested in the Pre-Raphaelite writer and designer's work, from wallpaper to furniture, glass to textiles, it's all here.

The Dulwich Picture Gallery

Located in south London, at College Road, West Dulwich, this is a little-known, but outstanding museum, the oldest public art gallery in England. There is an amazing collection of Old Masters here, including works by Rembrandt, Rubens, Van Dyck, Canaletto and Gainsborough. Closed Mondays. Phone 181 693 5254. (Tube: West Dulwich or North Dulwich.)

FAMOUS CHURCHES

In addition to the small number of churches mentioned in our list of starred sightseeing attractions (such as Westminster Abbey, St. Paul's Cathedral, and the like), here are a few more which we think are outstanding in their own ways, though only for real lovers of church architecture or history:

All Hallows, by the Tower of London, Byward Street.
Dates from the year 675; you can still see a Saxon arch here.

Brompton Oratory, Brompton Road.
Only 110 years old, but with a splendid organ and a very wide nave (the third widest in England). British Roman Catholicism's most social church.

St. Clement Danes, The Strand.
Official church of the Royal Air Force, made famous by a nursery rhyme that likened the sound of its bells to the phrase "oranges and lemons." Interior destroyed in the blitz of 1941 but restored in 1955.

Services in the Palace

You can attend morning church services at the Queen's Chapel in St. James's Palace on Sundays at 8:30 and 11:15, from Easter through the end of July. It's the only way to see one of Inigo Jones's masterpieces, especially its fine woodwork. It's also the only way you're ever likely to be allowed inside St. James's Palace.

St. Giles Cripplegate, corner of Fore and Wood streets.
John Milton is buried here.

St. Helen Bishopsgate, Great St. Helen's Street.
An ancestor of George Washington's mother, Mary Ball, was vicar here before moving (in 1650) to America during England's Civil War. Many imposing sculptured monuments and brasses.

★ St. James's, Piccadilly.
One of Wren's masterpieces (1684). Damaged during World War II, its steeple (made of Styrofoam) was lowered into place by helicopter in the late 1960s. Outstanding for its extensive social work. Heavy concert and musical program.

St. Martin-in-the-Fields, Trafalgar Square.
The most musical church in London. Concerts Thursday, Friday and Saturday evenings; lunch-time concerts weekdays except Thursday.

St. Mary-le-Bow Church, Cheapside. Wren designed the present church over a 900-year-old crypt. If you're born within hearing range of "Bow's bells," you are a true Cockney.

Wesley's Chapel, House & Museum of Methodism, City Road. Three for the price of one here: this is the mother church of worldwide Methodism since it was built in 1778, and it also contains a museum. Next door is where John Wesley lived.

6. Inauthentic Alternatives

One visitor's delight is another's despair, we know, but there are some things we think nobody should waste time or money on while in London. Some of the places we dislike the most are, in fact, marvelous places to take the kids, especially those old enough to go unsupervised. But, fun for the kids or not, they are still not really London experiences. Here are just a few, and our suggested alternatives to their supposed charms.

Guinness World of Records, Coventry Street, Piccadilly.

Okay, maybe it is fun for the kids, but after all, Guinness is selling a kind of beer, and this is little better than the Believe-It-or-Not museums scattered around the United States.

Taking a tour of the real London, to almost any part of its wide range of historic sights, is bound to provide you and any children you might have in tow with more authentic impressions that should last longer than the temporary thrill of some of these oddball first, longest, biggest, strongest, whatever "records."

London Dungeon, 28 Tooley Street.

They don't allow children under ten to enter on their own, but no one over ten could appreciate this kind of place, seven being about the right age in the opinion of many. Fake-creepy and icky, it depicts the Plague, a guillotine "theatre," and plenty of torture and strange noises. Yuk!

More authentic would be a trip to the Tower of London (see page 44), where there is still a dungeon, and where there was plenty of misery, torture included, to go around.

Madame Tussaud's, Marylebone Road.

Wildly popular, mostly with visitors from the European continent, and again, pitched at a low intelligence and age level (perhaps an average eleven-year-old). The place contains wax models of famous people, contemporary and historical, including the entire royal family, pop stars, and film royalty. Worst: the Chamber of Horrors. Only saving grace: Your ticket allows you to see the London Planetarium, next door, with shows of the universe every forty-five minutes. For planetarium show times, call 171 486 1121.

A suggested alternative to Madame Tussaud's might be any British pub, where you can meet all sorts of characters, every one authentic, and all willing to reply to you should you choose to initiate a conversation. The British have a reputation for being diffident (perhaps "shy"?), but if you start up a conversation, you'll find most of them dying to talk, about almost anything.

Quasar, Trocadero Centre, Piccadilly Circus.

Live-action laser games, they say, but they mean virtual reality. You have to be seven to get in one of the games, and that's about the right age, too, to enjoy them. There are plenty of other, better, things to do than shoot paint balls, real or imagined, at each other.

Instead of make-believe types of games and virtual reality, you might want to indulge in real reality, by taking in a game of tennis, by hiking or jogging around London's parks, or just watching a real sport played by real people. We have a sports chapter (page 133) on all these activities, and more.

Sherlock Holmes Museum, 221b Baker Street.

Isn't it better to just read the books and use your imagination? But if you insist, you'll find nearly every item mentioned in the books displayed here, in a cunningly contrived commercial venture that we found quite disappointing. Still, it's better than a similar reconstruction we saw in Switzerland, in the town of Meiringen, near Reichenbach Falls, where Professor Moriarty supposedly killed off the nosy detective. The shop here is the main reason for the operation, we suspect. And, by the way, 221b didn't exist as an address until the present owners made it up out of neighboring addresses for this commercial venture.

Instead of relying on a museum, a better alternative would be to visit the sights mentioned in the Sherlock Holmes books and see what they look like today. Such places might include a rail station, a police headquarters, a dark lane in the City, or a West End thoroughfare, just for starters.

Tower Hill Pageant, Tower Hill.

You get into a small car and ride through dioramas depicting London's history, with computerized commentary.

Better you walk around the streets outside and see the present for yourself, and imagine the past from what you've learned from the time you were in school.

7. Mysterious London

What would London be without fog-filled nights, unknown footsteps in the dark behind you, dimly lit cobblestoned streets, a werewolf or two? Off-season especially, when days are short and shadows long, is the time for these kinds of fancies to occupy your time and mind. Not all are connected to crime and hauntings—some of this city's mysteries are just, well, puzzling.

GHOSTS

Adelphi Theatre.
The ghost of a Victorian actor, William Terriss, has been seen here on the deserted stage as recently as the 1950s. (See also Covent Garden Tube Station, below.)

The British Museum.
There is a mummy here of a minor princess, which is said to be cursed and to have brought evil to everyone touching it. Hence, "the curse of the mummy's tomb." So don't go around handling the mummies in this place!

Covent Garden Tube Station.
The ghost of William Terriss has been seen several times in this station near the scene of his murder in 1897, usually when the last train is leaving around midnight.

Drury Lane Theatre.
The Man in Grey, one of London's most famous ghosts, was killed in a fight on the stage here in the eighteenth century. His ghost has been seen many times, as recently as the 1930s. He is said to appear

only when a show is having a successful run, and he usually haunts the
Upper Circle (fourth row).

The Gargoyle Club.

This antique strip club in Soho was once the home of Nell Gwynne
(c. 1632), whose ghost has repeatedly been seen by the girls working
here. The ghost wears a large hat and emits the odor of gardenias, it
is said.

Green Park.

This rather plain park adjoining Buckingham Palace and Piccadilly
is the site of the Dead Man's Tree, which is said to be haunted, mostly
by a young man in gray. Directly in front of the Park Lane Hotel and
about 150 feet from Piccadilly, it was the scene of many suicides (vic-
tims hanged themselves from the branches) in the nineteenth century, and duels in the century before that.

The Grenadier Pub, Wilton Row.

A young guardsman is said to have cheated while gambling in this
former officer's mess, and for that, he was tried by a kangaroo court of
his peers, then flogged to death. Ghostly hauntings, including the
guardsman's mounting the staircase, come to a peak in September,
witnesses say.

Hampton Court Palace, Surrey.

There are three ghosts here: Jane Seymour, Henry VIII's third
wife, is said to haunt the Queen's Staircase, traversing the Silverstick
Gallery on her way from the Queen's Room to the stairs, and then
descending them. People who have seen her ghost say she is dressed
in white and holds a lighted candle in her right hand. Henry VIII's
fifth wife, Catherine Howard, is said to beat her fists on the palace's
chapel door, where the King was deep in prayer after deciding to have
her beheaded for failing to produce a son. She also has been seen
running along the Haunted Gallery (named for her activities there).
A former nurse to Edward VI, Sybel Penn, is said to appear, making
her way through the apartments, dressed in a long, dark robe.

Haymarket Theatre.

The ghost of a former manager, John Buckstone (d. 1878), has
appeared on stage before a full audience as recently as the 1960s. He
is said to appear only for productions that will be a hit.

Kensington Palace.

The ghost of George II is said to be seen often here, looking out
of the window toward the weathervane above the main entrance, to

see whether the winds are favorable for ships from his homeland, Germany.

Lincoln's Inn Fields.

This impressive old quadrangle is haunted by the ghost of Anthony Babbington, who plotted to overthrow Elizabeth I in favor of Mary, Queen of Scots. For this act of treason, he was executed here in 1586 (hanged, drawn and quartered). The ghost of Lord Brampton, a leading barrister in the eighteenth century, is often seen here, too, complete with wig and robes.

Old Queen's Head Pub, Islington.

The Earl of Essex, beheaded in the Tower of London, once lived here, and Elizabeth I often stopped over en route to or from London. The resident ghost here, a woman more often heard than seen, is thought by many to be Bess herself.

Red Lion Square.

This lovely old square was the burial site of many illustrious figures, the most prominent being Oliver Cromwell, leader of the parliamentarians in Britain's Civil War. Two years after he died in 1658, when the Restoration once again put royalty on England's throne, Charles II's followers dug up Cromwell's body in Westminster Abbey, hanged it at Tyburn, then cut it up and buried it in Red Lion Fields, at the time a totally undeveloped area. The ghosts of Cromwell and two of his accomplices whose bodies met the same fate are often seen here, walking together through brick walls and the like.

St. James's Church, Garlick Hill.

In a glass case here there's a mummy, found in the early nineteenth century but probably much older. Its ghost sometimes roams around the place, occasionally settling down to pray in the balcony.

St. James's Park.

This elegant park, the nicest in all of London, lies directly between Buckingham Palace and Whitehall. Near Birdcage Walk, on its southern flank, the ghost of a woman is said to haunt the lawn. She was killed by her jealous husband after an alleged affair, beheaded and thrown into the lake in the park. Most often, she is seen trying to get from the lake to her home in the nearby Wellington Barracks.

Spaniards Inn, Hampstead Heath.

The ghost of highwayman Dick Turpin, riding a ghost horse named Black Bess, is often seen (and heard) on the heath, galloping to and from the inn, which was his headquarters. The inn got its name from the fact that it was a former Spanish embassy.

Tower of London.

Among the ghosts seen here are those of Lady Jane Gray, Anne Boleyn, and Catherine Howard (the latter two wives of Henry VIII), and the Earl of Essex, all beheaded here. Lady Jane, niece of Henry VIII and the daughter of the Duke of Suffolk, actually ascended the throne on the death of Henry VIII's son, Edward VI. She reigned for only nine days before being beheaded at the age of seventeen in 1554. Anne was Henry's second wife, and gave birth to the girl who later became Elizabeth I. Her headless ghost is seen most often coming from the Queen's House, where her cell was, toward Tower Green, where she was beheaded. Catherine was Henry's fifth wife.

Guy Fawkes (who planned to blow up Parliament) was tortured on the rack in the White Tower's dungeon here and killed in 1605; his ghost is said to haunt the dungeon. Under the chapel stairs in the same tower were buried, allegedly, the two young nephews of Richard III—Edward V and his brother, the Duke of York—killed by Richard's orders in the Bloody Tower. Their ghosts are said to roam together, holding hands. Sir Walter Raleigh's ghost, carrying his head beneath his arm, is often seen on Raleigh's Walk, which runs from the Queen's House to the Bloody Tower, a stretch he favored for exercise before he was executed in 1618.

University of London, University College, Gower St.

Since his body is embalmed in a glass display case in the entrance hall of this college, the famed philosopher Jeremy Bentham's ghost hasn't far to go, though it is said to wander the halls of the place frequently.

Westminster Abbey.

A well-known ghost in the abbey is Father Benedictus's, a monk killed here in the fourteenth century; his specter is said to walk in the Cloisters every afternoon between 5:00 and 6:00. The Ghost of the Unknown Warrior, a World War I soldier is also resident here. A third ghost said to haunt the abbey is that of John Bradshaw, head of the court that sentenced Charles I to death; Bradshaw signed the king's death warrant in the abbey's deanery.

MURDERS

Jack the Ripper.

There are several sights connected with this legendary (but real) killer, all in the East End, where tourists are still unlikely to go. There are tours of the area, but going on your own is easy enough. "Jack" killed five prostitutes in the fall of 1888 near Spitalsfield Market and the surrounding area. The scene of one murder in Mitre Square, Aldgate, is called "Rippers Corner."

The Kensington Vampire.

At 79 Gloucester Road, just a few steps across the street from the Gloucester Road tube station, John Haigh murdered four people in the late 1940s, drank their blood, then dissolved their bodies in acid. The site is now occupied by an English-as-a-Second-Language School.

LEGENDS

Boadicea's Tomb.

This marvelous tribal queen, who led her troops against the Roman conquerors back in the first century A.D., and who committed suicide rather than be captured when her cause was lost, is said to be buried under Platform 8 of the King's Cross Railway Station in London. But it's just a legend, and probably not a fact at all.

Curse of St. Giles Circus.

Centre Point, where Oxford Street meets Tottenham Court Road, is the spot where Sir John Oldcastle, the original upon whom Shakespeare based his Falstaff character, was roasted to death in 1417 for heresy against the Roman Catholic church. As he was dying, he cursed the nearby hospital, where authorities were celebrating his demise. The curse has said to have made real-estate speculation in the area a distinctly unfavorable exercise for the more than 550 years since.

HIDDEN TREASURE

French crown jewels under Trafalgar Square? Madame duBarry, Louis XV's mistress, brought the crown jewels of France when she came to London in 1793, trying to raise funds for a counterrevolution and restoration of the monarchy in her native land. Since she didn't take the jewels with her when she returned to France, it is believed she buried them near Pall Mall, where she was staying in London. The spot she chose is said to be the Royal Mews, which then lay where Trafalgar Square is now located.

ODDITIES

Westminster Abbey.

The Stone of Scone is no longer here, havng finally been returned to the Scottish people on St. Andrews Day in 1996, 699 years after Edward I stole it from them and brought it to the abbey. During the time it was here, it rested beneath the Coronation Chair. The stone is said to be Jacob's Pillow, upon which the Old Testament character rested his head as he dreamed of angels, and which was the foundation stone for his ladder to heaven. It was said to have come to Scotland from the Holy Land, via Ireland.

Some of the skin of a thief who stole the wealth of Edward I and who was flayed alive for his crime is still stuck to a door in the Chamber of the Pyx, under the door's iron hinges. But you'd need a microscope to spot it.

Trafalgar Square.

The police station in the lamppost. At the southeastern corner of

---

Where the Downstairs Staff Hang Out

Just around the corner from Pickering Place, leading from Pall Mall to King Street, is Crown Passage, a little bit of Olde London that hasn't changed too much in hundreds of years. Here you'll find a small market selling newspapers, cigarettes, and candy, not to mention lottery tickets, and a simple diner specializing in cold sandwiches and soft drinks, which looks as if it hasn't been decorated in at least the past fifty years. It is much used by staff of nearby posh establishments, from St. James's Palace to Christie's, and some of the exclusive clubs in the district. In other words, in an Upstairs/Downstairs world, this is where downstairs hangs out in its limited free time.

the square, inside one of the large stone lantern bases, is a tiny police station, with room for one Bobby and a phone, linked, it is said, directly to Scotland Yard. Good for demonstrations, no doubt.

Republic of Texas Embassy in Pickering Place.

Friends of Texas and just plain oddity-seekers will want to take a peek at the site of that state's former embassy to the Court of St. James. Just a few hundred feet from St. James's Palace itself, right next door to Berry Brothers (the elite wine shop), is a narrow pedestrian alley leading to Pickering Place. On the wall in the passageway is a plaque indicating that 3, Pickering Place was the site of the Republic of Texas Embassy in the early 1840s.

8. Where to Stay in London

Here we list some carefully selected hotels in all price ranges, some not on anyone else's lists at all.

We've assigned star ratings to the hotels we list in order to help you choose. In nearly every case, the number of stars matches a price range, as the days when marvelous establishments charged only moderate prices are long since gone. There may be an occasional bargain somewhere in the world, but not in London. You pay for what you get, London having some of the world's highest-priced hotels. In many cases, we think the prices demanded are far more than the rooms are really worth, but, with supply and demand the keyword everywhere, the hoteliers have the customer by the nose and usually get what they want. (What visitors to London want is more reasonably priced hotels in or near the center!)

If the rates frighten you (as they do us), consider asking for a corporate rate, which can be lower, or for any packages the hotel might be promoting (unless you want to throw your money around for some reason).

Many hotels, especially those belonging to chains, have packages for discounted rates, particularly off-season. See our listings for the Berkeley, Grosvenor House, and Le Meridien Piccadilly for offerings by three chains (the Savoy Group, Forte, and Le Meridien, respectively). Other chain hotels also have packages, such as the Inter-Continental, Hilton, and Sheraton. Ask at all hotels when making reservations. There is usually some discount available.

Unless we note otherwise, in addition to the rates noted below, which are for two persons in a room, you'll probably have to pay a service charge (in lieu of tipping) of 10 percent to 15 percent, and will definitely have to pay a VAT (Value Added Tax) of 17.5 percent. On the other hand, many hotel rates include breakfast, either Continental (skimpy) or full English style.

Hotels are open year-round, unless otherwise noted.

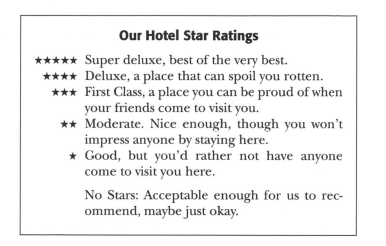

Our Hotel Star Ratings

★★★★★ Super deluxe, best of the very best.

★★★★ Deluxe, a place that can spoil you rotten.

★★★ First Class, a place you can be proud of when your friends come to visit you.

★★ Moderate. Nice enough, though you won't impress anyone by staying here.

★ Good, but you'd rather not have anyone come to visit you here.

No Stars: Acceptable enough for us to recommend, maybe just okay.

★★★★ The Athenaeum Hotel, 116 Piccadilly, London W1V 0BJ. Phone 1-800-335-3300 or 171 499 3464, fax 171 493 0644. Rates $370 and up. (Apartment rates upon request.)

Recently refurbished and with a new health club (with small pool), the Athenaeum is one of London's nicest finds—if nothing else, at least the location, across the street from Green Park, makes it just about the best address in town. The staff is noted for being friendly, something you can't say for many high-priced hotels in London these days, and the concierges are considered the most proficient in all of England. There are 133 rooms, and some self-catering apartments, the latter quite costly. Largish rooms, all deluxe amenities; outstanding (and elegant) restaurant.

★★ Basil Street Hotel, 8 Basil Street, London SW3 1AH. Phone 171 581 3311, fax 171 581 3693. Rates $192 to $288.

Stay here for one of two reasons: You like Edwardian decor and a quiet, genteel ambiance; or you want to be near Harrods and Harvey Nichols, two of London's most important department stores. The ninety rooms (most with bath) are large but unimaginatively furnished. But you won't spend much time in them, anyhow. Hotel facilities include a restaurant, and a lounge for women only (a nice place to have a quiet tea).

★★★ Beaufort Hotel, 33 Beaufort Gardens, London SW3 1PP. Phone 1-800-888-1199 or 171 584 5252, fax 171 589 2834. Rates $240 to $344.

One of London's finest and earliest boutique hotels, this is run by a lady who is also a television producer. It feels like someone's home, and there is even an honor bar to add to that ambiance, along with beautifully furnished rooms and all sorts of little comfy amenities, like books in the room, flowers, and more. You're just around the corner from Harrods.

Built in 1890 as a townhouse, it was renovated in 1995.

★★★★★ Berkeley Hotel, Wilton Place, London SW1X 7RL. Phone 1-800 53-SAVOY or 171 235 6000, fax 171 235 4330. Rates start at $400.

Just refurbished with all the electronic paraphernalia you'll need for a decade or so, this is a place much favored by English nobility (and this is one place they don't laugh at that word), including the Queen herself, who has dined here quite often. Modern (1972), yet traditionally elegant, the Berkeley has one of London's best locations, too. The 160 large rooms are divinely decorated. Indoor/outdoor pool, two restaurants, every amenity you can think of.

★★★ Brown's Hotel, 29-34 Albemarle Street, London W1X 4BP. Phone 1-800-225-5843 or 171 493 6020, fax 171 493 9381. Rates $376 to $440 for double rooms.

One of the most traditional places to stay in London, and the opposite of flashy; staying here is like being in a friend's town house. The decor is subdued traditional, the service ditto. Having afternoon tea here will remind you of visiting your well-off aunt and uncle and being on your best behavior. Facilities include a restaurant and bar. There are 110 rooms and several suites.

★★★ Capital Hotel, 22 Basil Street, London SW3 1AT. Phone 1-800-926-3199 or 171 589 5171, fax 171 225 0011. Rates $300 and up.

Right behind Harrods, this hotel boasts one of London's best restaurants. The forty-eight rooms are largish and comfortably furnished, some in Ralph-Lauren style. A modern building, it nevertheless seems to fit in with its Victorian neighbors.

★ Caswell Hotel, 25 Gloucester Street, London SW1V 2DB. Phone 171 834 6345, no fax. Rates $112 and up.

There aren't many rooms here, only 18 in fact, and less than half these have a bath. You don't get any frills, though the rooms are well-furnished and clean. You are near Victoria Station, where there are many similar hotels, but few as nicely maintained.

Central Club, 16-22 Great Russell Street, London WC1B 3LR. Phone 171 636 7512, fax 171 636 5378. Rates $96 and up.

An imposing building, this was a YWCA from the early '30s until quite recently. You have a gym as well as a coffee shop, but none of the 100 rooms has a private bath attached. (There are opulent showers, baths and toilets in the hallway bathrooms.) Prices in London being among the world's highest, the charge for a room here is quite low, but you get what you pay for—just a place to sleep.

★★★★★ Claridge's, Brook Street, London W1A 2JQ. Phone 1-800-63-SAVOY or 171 629 8860, fax 171 499 2210. Rates $400 and up. Wheelchair access.

A British institution, Claridge's has put up many kings, queens, and heads of state, including the late Emperor of Japan. The red-brick exterior may seem plain, but the interiors are fabulously done, touches of art deco blending with Edwardian throughout. There are 190 large rooms; and a new (1995) health club, too. The two restaurants are justly famous for their cuisine.

★★★★★ Connaught Hotel, Carlos Place, London W1Y 6AL. Phone 1-800-63-SAVOY or 171 499 7070, fax 171 495-3262. Rates $400 and up. Wheelchair access.

The Connaught is like a huge country home transported to London, its oak-clad lobby and corridors murmuring "baronial" to you as you enter. The 90 rooms are huge, many with fireplaces, the staff like well-trained butlers in a titled person's house. The Grill Room here is one of London's best restaurants. The location is marvelous, midway between Berkeley Square and Grosvenor Square.

★★ Diplomat Hotel, 2 Chesham Street, London SW1X 8DT. Phone 171 235 1544, fax 171 259 6153. Rates $184 to $232.

Halfway between expensive Knightsbridge and fashionable Sloane Square, the Diplomat is a real find, and recently renovated at that. There are only 27 rooms, but each is comfortable and pleasant.

★★★★★ The Dorchester, 53 Park Lane, London W1A 2HJ. Phone 1-800-727-9820 or 171 629 8888, fax 171 409 0114. Rates $424 to $472 for a double. Wheelchair access.

One of London's best hotels, the Dorchester has been a favorite of the English, and is used for some of the very best social events, in season or out. There are 190 rooms and 50 suites. The hotel, a marvelous example of understated English elegance, also has one of London's best restaurants, the Grill, plus a business center and health club.

★★★ Dorset Square Hotel, 39-40 Dorset Square, London NW1 6QN. Phone 800-553-6674 or 171 723 7874, fax 171 724 3328. Rates $192 to $280 for a double.

Near Regent's Park, this hotel consists of two town houses joined together, to make room for thirty-five rooms and two small suites. Decorated by the owners, the place looks and feels like a country home in many ways, and it's nearly as quiet as one. Lovely ambiance, with just the right tone of friendliness.

★★★ Duke's Hotel, 35 St. James's Place, London SW1A 1NY. Phone 1-800-381-4702 or 171 491 4840, fax 171 493 1264. Rates $280 to $344 for a double. Limited wheelchair access.

Duke's is exactly the right size for a hotel, with only 64 rooms and about a dozen suites. The pleasant rooms are decorated in several styles, all elegant, and you have the comforting feeling that you're as close as any hotel can get to Buckingham Palace, Clarence House, and Spencer House—and you're on the "right" side (the St. James's side) of those three noble buildings. The restaurant is popular with local business tycoons at lunchtime, but quieter at dinnertime.

★★ Durrants Hotel, George Street, London W1H 6BJ. Phone 171 935 8131, fax 171 487 3510. Rates $184 to $200 for a double. Wheelchair access.

A pleasant place, run by the same family for over one hundred years, Durrants is made up of several adjoining houses. The nearly 100 rooms (a few suites) are nicely decorated and quite comfortable. There's also a pub on the premises, as well as a restaurant.

★ Edward Lear Hotel, 28-30 Seymour Street, London W1H 5WD. Phone 171 402 5401, fax 171 706 3766. Rates $128 for a double, includes breakfast.

When the limerist of the same name lived here, it was just a town house, but now it has been joined to another to form this small hotel with 31 rooms (only a few with bath), and four suites. Nicely located in the Marble Arch area, a busy part of town.

★ Eleven Cadogan Gardens, 11 Cadogan Gardens, London, SW3 2RJ. Phone 171 730 3426, fax 171 730 5217. Rates $190 and up, tax included.

Lovely Victorian hotel at Sloane Square, moderate first class. All rooms have private bath or shower. Health club.

★ Fielding Hotel, 4 Broad Court, Bow Street, London WC2B 5QZ. Phone 171 836 8305, fax 171 497 0064. Rates $136 to $152 for double room.

You stay here for the location, not the ambiance, though the place is pleasant enough. The twenty-six rooms (most with bath) are tiny, and there are no perks or frills to mention, but you can't beat the Covent Garden atmosphere and ambiance.

★★★ 47 Park Street (Westin Demeure Hotel), 47 Park Street, London, W1Y 4EB. Phone 171 491 7282, fax 171 491 7281. Rates $500 and up for a one-bedroom suite.

Deluxe hotel, fifty-two suites all beautifully decorated with sitting room and kitchen. Maid service available. Cocktail lounge.

★★★★ Four Seasons Hotel, Hamilton Place, Park Lane, London W1A 1AZ. Phone 1-800-223-6800 or 171 499 0888, fax 171 493 6629. Rates $400 and up. Wheelchair access.

Formerly known as the Inn on the Park, this is one of London's first modern luxury hotels (1970), and is superbly located on the eastern edge of Hyde Park. There are 228 large rooms, a health club, two

good restaurants, and the outstanding service the Four Seasons chain is known for, not to mention amenities such as three phones in each room.

★★ Gore Hotel, 189 Queen's Gate, London SW7 5EX. Phone 1-800-637-7200 or 171 584 6601, fax 171 589 8127. Rates $248 to $351 for a double.

A lovely old hotel with only 55 rooms, all Victorian and dark, the Gore has one of London's better hotel restaurants. You're in one of the nicer residential parts of Kensington (which is actually in the Royal Borough of Kensington & Chelsea), and near museums, parks, and most transportation.

★★ Goring Hotel, 15 Bestow Place, Grosvenor Gardens, London SW1W 0JW. Phone 171 396 9000, fax 171 834 4393. Rates $280 to $344 for a double.

Just near Buckingham Palace (on the "wrong," or non-St. James's side), the Goring is a pleasant old pile, with seventy rooms and a few suites. Standard furnishings make the rooms drab, but the location is perfect, especially if you plan to use Victoria Station more than once. Facilities include restaurant and bar.

★★★★ Grosvenor House Hotel, Park Lane, London W1A 3AA. Phone 1-800-225-5843 or 171 499 6363, fax 171 493 3341. Rates $400 and up. Wheelchair access.

In the two huge buildings that make up this Lightens-designed hotel, the northern one is mostly apartments, 140 of them. There are 454 very large rooms inside the hotel itself as well as the Crown Club floor with special amenities, and a business center, health club with pool, shops, and more, all overlooking Hyde Park. Enjoy the hotel's two restaurants, especially Nico's, better than which it is hard to find in London.

★★ Great Eastern Hotel, Liverpool Street, London EC2M 7QN. Phone 171 283 4363, fax 171 283 4897. Rates $139 to $163.

The location isn't fashionable, but the price is right and the rooms are big. You're also well placed for the City and for quick getaways from Liverpool Street Station (adjacent) to the Continent or up to Cambridge, for example. Most of the 160 rooms have baths—big tubs and all from the good old days—and you'll love the stained-glass dome hanging over one of the hotel's two restaurants.

★★★ Halcyon Hotel, 81 Holland Park, London W11 3RZ. Phone 171 727 7288, fax 171 229 8516. Rates $400 and up.

Holland Park is one of London's nicest residential areas, and this luxury hotel fits right in. The pub is as classy as the neighborhood, the guests equally so. Many of the 44 rooms have four-poster beds, and all the rooms are decorated in an elegant upper-class manner.

★★★ The Hemp, 31-35 Craven Hill Gardens, London W2 3EA. Phone 171 298 9000, fax. 171 402 4666., Rates $400 and up, suites from $700. Limited wheelchair access.

New, interesting, superior first-class hotel opened in 1996 near Hyde Park and the West End. Beautiful guest rooms have every amenity including fax machine; some have a small kitchen and balcony. Restaurant, bar, library, and gym.

★★★★★ Hilton Park Lane, 22 Park Lane, London W1Y 4BE. Phone 1-800-HILTONS or 171 493 8000. Rates $400 and up. Wheelchair access.

Only recently totally refurbished at a cost of $25 million , this is the Hilton flagship in Europe. Towering some twenty-five stories, it overlooks Buckingham Palace's gardens, as well as Hyde Park and almost everything else for a couple of miles around. It has 447 rooms and suites, with executive floors and a Club Room. Close to all the sights in Mayfair. In addition to the great views, you have large rooms, excellent service, and two fine restaurants.

★★★ Howard Hotel, Temple Place, Strand London WC2R 2PR. Phone 171 836 3555 or 1-800-221-1074, fax 171 379 4547. Rates $300 and up.

This is a fairly small, 136-room deluxe hotel overlooking the Thames River, and near the theater district. All rooms are nicely furnished, many with Louis XV furnishings. Some rooms overlook the river. Amenities include a French restaurant, bar, and best of all, free indoor parking.

★★★★★ Hyde Park Mandarin Oriental, 66 Knightsbridge, London SW1Y 7LA. Phone 1-800 (MANDARIN) or 171 235 2000, fax 171 235 4552. Rates $400 and up. Wheelchair access.

Only the name has changed—otherwise, this is still the wonderful old Hyde Park Hotel, favorite of the royal family and diplomats. Located right on Hyde Park at Knightsbridge, it has one of London's nicest locations. The fine old Edwardian atmosphere hasn't been changed, though the 185 large rooms (especially the bathrooms) have recently been refurbished and updated for the latest amenities. Splendid restaurant overlooking the park. Also new: a great health club, with a small pool.

★★★★★ Inter-Continental Hotel, One Hamilton Place, London W1V 0QY. Phone 800-327-0200 or 171 409 3131, fax 171 409 7460. Rates $400 and up. Wheelchair access.

Stay here if you want all the modern conveniences this chain is famous for, plus a nice health club (with small pool) and a first-rate business center. There are 450 fair-sized rooms decorated in many different styles, plus two fine restaurants, a bar, and great views of Hyde Park itself.

★★★ Kensington Close Hotel, Wrights Lane, London W8 5SP. Phone 171 937 8170, fax 171 937 8289. Rates $250 and up.

This is a huge place, with 525 average-sized rooms, but the price is right. It has been recently renovated, and there are nonsmoking rooms as well as executive rooms with special amenities. Close to Kensington High Street, it's a good place for shoppers, too. There's a very nice health club here, and jogging in Kensington Gardens is just a short, well, jog away.

★★★★★ The Lanesborough, Hyde Park Corner, London SW1X 7TA. Phone 171 259 5599, or 1-800-999-1828, fax 171 259 5606. Rates $500 and up. Wheelchair access.

Superior Deluxe. This is a gorgeous grand hotel built on the site of an old hospital in Belgravia, just opposite Hyde Park and across the street from Buckingham Palace's gardens. The rooms are beautifully decorated with two-line phone, fax, safe, and more. Hotel facilities include rooms for non-smokers, bar, and meals served all day. Excellent business center.

★★★★ London Marriott, Grosvenor Square, London W1A 4AW. Phone 1-800-228-9290 or 171 493 1232, fax 171 491 3201. Rates $352 and up. Wheelchair access.

Formerly known as the Europa, this hotel enjoys a privileged place on Grosvenor Square, along with the U.S. Embassy and the Canadian High Commission, among other tony neighbors. The red-brick facade, masking a very modern but traditional interior, blends well with neighbors, which is more than you can say for the U.S. Embassy. There are twenty-two rooms and fifteen suites, all done in elegant fashion, with many antiques scattered about both public and private rooms. Facilities include nonsmoking rooms, an excellent restaurant, and fitness and business centers.

Mandarin Oriental Hyde Park London. See Hyde Park Mandarin Oriental.

★★★ May Fair Hotel, Stratton Street, London W1A 2AN. Phone 1-800-327-0800 or 171 629 7777, fax 171 629 1459. Rate $350 and up. Wheelchair access.

One of London's older hotels (1927), the May Fair is in an enviable location, in the fashionable commercial and residential area that bears the hotel's name, yet near Piccadilly and the two parks closest to Buckingham Palace—St. James's and Green Park. There are 285 smallish rooms decorated in the best English middle-class taste of the 1960s. Nice health club with small pool, plus two restaurants and other amenities.

★★★★ Le Meridien London, 21 Piccadilly, London W1V 0BH. Phone 1-800-543-4300 in the U.S. or 171 734 8000, fax 171 437 3574. Rates $450 and up. Wheelchair access.

There are over 300 large rooms in this magnificent palace, formerly the Piccadilly Hotel, which dates back to the 1910s and retains its best Edwardian-style decor. You'll enjoy the great health club in the basement, including its huge swimming pool. Other hotel facilities include two good, if not great, restaurants.

★★★ The Metropolitan, Old Park Lane, London W1Y 4LB. Phone 171 447 1047 or 1-888-272-3002, fax 171 447 1147. Rates $300 and up.

New, sleek, deluxe hotel, opened in 1997 with amenities galore. Well located, within walking distance of shopping, theater, and parks. The decor is strictly minimalist, so be warned, and the rooms are on the small side. Fully equipped gym and treatment rooms. The highlight is Nobu Japanese Restaurant, run by famed New York restaurateur

---

Off-Season Bargains at Le Meridien Hotels.

1999 was the fifth year of the "Le Passport" December through March promotion, so it may be offered again in 2000; be sure to ask. You can save up to 50 percent off the published rates. There is a two-night minimum stay, and tax and service charge (in lieu of tipping) are included. Advance reservations are required, must be guaranteed with a credit card and space is limited. Le Meridien hotels in London are: Le Meridien Piccadilly London, Le Meridien Waldorf London, Grosvenor House London, Strand Palace London, The Cumberland Hotel London. Gatwick and Heathrow airports also have Le Meridien or Cumberland hotels with the same savings. Call the 800 numbers for reservations. Rates are now available in GBP (pounds), USD (dollars) and the Euro. Reservations in the U.S., 1-800-543-4300; in the UK, 1-800 40 40 40, Web site http://www.lemeridien-hotels.com.

Drew Nieporent. There is also a private bar for guests of the hotel and members.

★★ Mornington Hotel, 12 Lancaster Gate, London W2 3LG. Phone 1-800-528-1234 or 171 262 7361, fax 171 706 1028. Rates $160 to $240.

Affiliated with the Best Western reservations system, the Mornington is, nonetheless, a Swedish hotel, in the sense that it is run by Swedes and has a lot of Swedish guests. The rates include a full Swedish buffet breakfast. Up near Lancaster Gate, the Mornington looks like a typical London town house on the outside; the rooms are very neat and Scandinavian in decor and comfort.

★★★ One Aldwych, 1 Aldwych London WC2B 4BZ. Phone 171 300 1000, in New York 212-223-2848; fax 171 300 1001. Rates $400 and up. Weekend rates (Friday to Sunday) start at $325. Wheelchair access.

This is a brand new hotel (1998), well located at the point where the City and West End meet, so that it is not far from theaters, shopping districts and the financial area. The hotel has all the amenities you would expect from a top new hotel, including three phones in the room, CD player, and so on. Facilities include two restaurants, business services and an excellent health club with a lap pool, gym, and steam, sauna and treatment rooms. Valet parking is available.

★★★ Park Lane Hotel, Piccadilly, London W1Y 8BX. Phone 171 499 6321 or 1-800-223-5652, fax 171 499 6321. Rates $300 and up. Wheelchair access.

This is an Art Deco hotel in the Mayfair section with period-style 304 rooms, all amenities. Facilities include a health and fitness center. Nonsmoker rooms. Restaurant, brasserie, and bar.

★ Regency Hotel, 19 Nottingham Place, London W1M 3FF. Phone 171 486 5347, fax 171 224 6057. Rates from $128 and up.

Note that this is not the hotel of the same name in Queen's Gate, Kensington, which is more expensive. Renovated earlier this decade, this is a straightforward hotel, with not many frills. The advantage of staying in one of the twenty rooms here is your proximity to Baker Street and other interesting sightseeing areas of London.

★★★★★ The Ritz Hotel, 150 Piccadilly, London W1V 9BG. Phone 1-800-525-4800 or 171 493 8181, fax 171 493 2687. Rates $400 and up.

This is a fun place to stay, for, despite the glamour its name evokes, the Ritz is like a big country house—over-decorated, of course, but with a caring and a nearly friendly staff. The 130 rooms are huge, as are the bathrooms, and everything is overlaid with gold trim in the style of Cesar Ritz's Paris establishment. Recently renovated, with a few rooms overlooking Green Park. The best place in all of London to have afternoon tea is in the Palm Court here, and the restaurant is excellent. Other facilities: business and fitness centers, hair salon, outstanding concierge service.

★★ Royal Lancaster Hotel, Lancaster Terrace, London W2 2TY. Phone 171 262 6737, fax 171 724 3191. Rates $350 and up.

Within walking distance of Marble Arch. Club Floors with special amenities, three restaurants, lounge, bar, business center. Nonsmoking rooms.

Ruskin Hotel, 23-24 Montague Street, London WC1B 5BN. Phone 171 636 7388, fax 171 323 1662. Rates $120 and up.

No frills in this neat but well-used place. There are only thirty rooms, a few with bath. And though the rooms are simply furnished, you do get a full English breakfast for the price. The hotel is near Russell Square and the British Museum; it's a bargain for this neighborhood.

★★★★ The Savoy, The Strand, London WC2R 0EU. Phone 1-800-63-SAVOY or 171 836 4343, fax 171 240 6040. Rates $408 to $528.

Despite its role as flagship of the luxury Savoy Group, the Savoy itself is not the chain's biggest hotel, having only 154 rooms and forty-eight suites. This is the quintessential English hotel in many ways, not only for its decor (recently renovated), but for its reputation—including its association with Gilbert & Sullivan, of course. The Grill Room here is one of the most famous restaurants in the world and worth more than one visit. For elegance and a view, try the River Restaurant upstairs, however. Health club (new) on top.

★★ Sheraton Belgravia Hotel, 20 Chesham Place, London SW1X 8HQ. Phone 171 235 6040 or 1-800-325-3535, fax 171 259 6242. Rates $400 and up.

This is a small hotel of eighty-nine rooms, well located near Knightsbridge, Buckingham Palace and theaters. Decorated in typical English country-home style. Nonsmoking rooms available.

★★★ Sheraton Park Tower Hotel, 101 Knightsbridge, London SW1X 7RN. Phone 171 235 8050 or 1-800-324-3535, fax 171 235 8231. Rates $425 and up. Wheelchair access.

Located opposite the Albert Gate entrance to Hyde Park in Knightsbridge. Executive rooms with fax machines, and nonsmoking rooms are among the choices here. Restaurants, bar, lounge, use of nearby health club.

★★ St. James's Court and Apartments, 45 Buckingham Gate, Westminster London SW1E 6AF. Phone 171 834 6655 or 1-800-888-4747, fax 171 630 7587. E-mail corveneb.sjc@stjamescourt.co.uk. Rates $264 to $376.

Located near Buckingham Palace, Knightsbridge and many sights, this place was renovated in 1997. The hotel offers rooms, suites, studios, and apartments of up to as many as three bedrooms. Apartments are serviced daily and include combined living-dining room and kitchen. Nonsmoking rooms are also available. Two restaurants, coffee shop, lounge, business center, health club, and valet parking are among the facilities.

★★ Sloane Hotel, 28 Draycott Place, London SW3 2SH. Phone 171 581 5757, fax 171 584 1348. Rates $225 and up.

The smallest place on our list, the Sloane is chosen for its location, just off Sloane Square, and its twelve beautiful antique-filled rooms. The rooms aren't huge, but the amenities in each are plentiful, and you'll love the decor.

★★★★   The Stafford, 16-18 St. James's Place, London SW1A 1NJ. Phone 1-800-525-4800 or 171 493 0111, fax 171 493 7121. Rates $328 to $392. Wheelchair access.

One of London's most charming hotels, all Edwardian elegance, the Stafford has long been a favorite of discerning travelers. It is just the right size for a hotel, with only sixty-five rooms and six suites, all recently renovated (1997). Taking tea in the cozy lounge is a pleasure; having a drink in the American Bar at back is practically an obligation. There's a nice restaurant, too. And though you may enter by the formal front door on St. James's Place, it's fun to exit through the bar onto Blue Ball Yard, a cobbled courtyard in back, through which you walk to luxurious accommodations in the former stables or past them to St. James's Street and the heart of London's West End.

★★   Twenty Two Jermyn Street, 22 Jermyn Street, London SW1Y 6HL. Phone 171 734 2353 or 1-800-682-7808, fax 171 734 0750. Rates $325 and up.

Edwardian-style townhouse hotel, nicely located in the West End near Piccadilly Circus, on a famous shopping street with beautiful men's shops. Only 18 rooms and suites, each with fireplace. No restaurant, but 24-hour room service is available. Small meeting room and business center.

★★★   The Westbury Hotel, Bond Street, London W1A 4UH. Phone 171 629 7755, fax 171 495 1163. Rates $300 and up. Wheelchair access.

Splendidly located in the heart of Mayfair, this 244-room hotel has nicely furnished rooms with all amenities. Rooms for nonsmokers, a restaurant, bar, lounge, shopping arcade, and best of all . . . free parking.

★★   Whites Hotel, Lancaster Gate, London W2 2NR. Phone 171 262 2711, fax 171 262 2147. Rates $280 and up.

From the outside, it looks like just another of those whitewashed hotels that Bayswater is full of, but this one is different. Many of its fifty-five large rooms overlook Hyde Park, and have balconies at that. There's also a nice restaurant with park views. You're near the Lancaster Gate subway station. What better place to live if you enjoy strolling (or jogging) in the park?

★★   Willbraham Hotel, 1-5 Wilbraham Place, London SW1X 9AE. Phone 171 730 8296, fax 171 730 6815. Rates $141 and up.

Located just off Sloane Street near Sloane Square, the Wilbraham is a favorite of some of our good English friends, who stay here when they come up from the country. In several old town houses joined together, there are about fifty rooms (a few of them suites). The rate includes a full English breakfast to get you ready for the world outside. The rooms are largish and nicely furnished, but without many frills. There is a decent restaurant on the premises, too.

Apartments for Sublet

Barclay International, a New York–based firm, has luxury apartments available from as low as $360 per week for a small studio in central London, with bigger flats and even houses available a bit farther out of the center. They have flats in the West End (Mayfair and Kensington) and even some in the prestigious Grosvenor House Hotel. For these, think $800 and up per week. Phone them at 1-800-845-6636.

---

9. Where to Eat in London

In the past decade or so, London has become an important culinary capital. It wasn't always so, but after World War II, the British began traveling (a lot), and when they came home, they longed for some of the good grub they had eaten abroad. Soon enough, foreign chefs began arriving in London and setting up in the restaurant business. Before long, the British began raising their own breed of food lovers, too. And now, you have outstanding chefs of both sexes behind (and often out in front of) the scene.

We want to tell you about our favorite restaurants, not just provide a list (which you can get from *Time Out*, if you like). We have eaten at these places and liked them, and don't want to be selfish about sharing the experience with you. They're based on our long experience of living and noshing in central London. Several are linked to historic London, such as the new restaurant in Karl Marx's old apartment house (he lived above another restaurant here in his own day). We also list some unusual pubs (crypts under the Cheshire Cheese, cobwebs in Dirty Dick's, the Mayflower Pub, from which the ship sailed on her famous voyage in 1620—with the passenger manifest here to prove it), and pubs with ghosts.

SMOKING: Some restaurants have smoking and nonsmoking areas. Request whichever you prefer when making a reservation. Many restaurants just mix smokers and nonsmokers and do not have special areas; if you want to go to that particular restaurant, you have to accept their rules.

SMOKING PROHIBITED: restaurants will permit smoking in their bar area, but not in the dining area. The rules in Europe are not as strict as in the U.S.

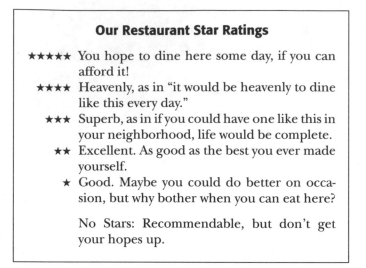

Our Restaurant Star Ratings

★★★★★ You hope to dine here some day, if you can afford it!

★★★★ Heavenly, as in "it would be heavenly to dine like this every day."

★★★ Superb, as in if you could have one like this in your neighborhood, life would be complete.

★★ Excellent. As good as the best you ever made yourself.

★ Good. Maybe you could do better on occasion, but why bother when you can eat here?

No Stars: Recommendable, but don't get your hopes up.

WATER: In the UK, water from the faucet is good to drink, but restaurants all serve " still" and "fizzy" bottled waters which are not too expensive.

WINE: There are wines from all over the world in England, so it is just a matter of taste. Most good restaurants have house red and white wines plus a wine list. Naturally, higher-priced restaurants serve higher-priced wines. **Beers** from around the world are sold in most restaurants, too.

★ Alastair Little, 49 Frith Street, W1 (Leicester Square). Phone 171 734 5183.

Expensive. The chef here and at his other place (see below) serves modern British cuisine, which means he fiddles with the food a lot, sometimes gilding the lily, as it were. We call it the "one-too-many-ingredients school of cuisine," but you may like that kind of thing more than we do.

★ Alastair Little at Lancaster Road, 136A Lancaster Road, W11 (Ladbroke Grove). Phone 171 243 2220.

Expensive. A branch of the Leicester Square eatery, less contrived decor, but quite similar modern British food. Very popular with the locals.

Our Listings & Price Categories

London restaurants, like all restaurants, can be categorized by food, price, popularity, neighborhood, atmosphere, and many other criteria. We are listing them alphabetically, and have tried to confine our listings to central London for your convenience.

Note on addresses: In our listings, we give the name of the nearest tube station in parenthesis, not only because you can use the Underground to get to the restaurant, but also to help you locate its neighborhood, a customary London way of finding your way around.

Our dinner price categories are:

Very expensive: £40 and up ($66 and up) for appetizer, main course, and dessert; no drinks, tip or taxes included.

Expensive: £30 to £39 ($50 to $65).
Moderate: £15 to £29 ($25 to $49).
Inexpensive: Under £15 (under $25).

★ Assaggi, 39 Chepstow Place, W2 (Notting Hill Gate). Phone 171 792 5501.

Moderate to Expensive. Italian cuisine here, above a pub named The Chepstow. Noted for traditional dishes, but especially for its salads.

★★★★★ Aubergine, 11 Park Walk, SW10 (South Kensington). Phone 171 352 3449.

Very Expensive. They used to call this kind of French cooking nouvelle cuisine, but now they just call it divine. Book well in advance for a marvelous evening.

★★ Avenue, 7-9 St. James's Street, SW1 (Green Park). Phone 171 321 2111.

Expensive. Modernized British cuisine in a trendy setting, in the most chic part of town. Somehow big and brassy, yet terribly British, being practically across the street from St. James's Palace.

★ Bank, 1 Kingsway, WC2 (Holborn). Phone 171 379 9797.

Expensive. The French food here has been Anglicized or modified or trendified, but all very nicely, thank you. Huge place, in an old bank building. Especially noted for its fish dishes.

★ Belgo Noord, 72 Chalk Farm Road, NW1 (Chalk Farm). Phone 171 267 0718.

Moderate. You have to be able to ignore the decor here (decor may be too kind a word), and concentrate on the Belgian cuisine, including the inevitable mussels, always a Belgian specialty, or wild boar, especially satisfying in winter.

★ The Belvedere, Holland House, Abbotsbury Road, W8 (Holland Park). Phone 171 602 1238.

Expensive. In the summer, this is a romantic place (formerly the orangery of Holland House itself), overlooking Holland Park, with modernized British cooking. Hard to find; ask for explicit directions even if going by cab.

★★★★ Bibendum, 81 Fulham Road, SW3 (South Kensington). Phone 171 581 5817.

Very expensive. Housed in the old Michelin tire repair garage ("Bibendum" is the name of the fat tire-man in the Michelin logo), in the trendiest possible part of London. This was one of the earliest of the greatest restaurants to come along a couple of decades ago and revolutionize the way the British (or at least, Londoners), eat. French cuisine without too many detours (think truffles or paté de fois gras), and a good-value-for-money Sunday brunch.

★★★ Blakes Hotel, 33 Roland Gardens, SW7 (Gloucester Road). Phone 171 370 6701.

Very expensive. The dining room here is enticing and entrancing in its decor, the food a marvel, the prices among the highest in London, even though you're dining in the basement here.

★ Bombay Brasserie, Courtfield Close, SW7 (Gloucester Road).
Phone 171 370 4040.

Expensive. One of London's best Indian eateries, with perhaps too
much emphasis on decor and not enough on simple cooking with the
right ingredients. They try to provide dishes from several regions of
the Indian subcontinent, including Kerala and Goa.

★ Café Nico, 90 Park Lane, W1 (Marble Arch). Phone 171 495 2275.

Expensive. Located in the Grosvenor House Hotel, and with
famed chef Nico Ladenis supervising; the café is but one of his several restaurants. French cuisine from a master who was one of the
early guides teaching Londoners how to enjoy really great food. This
place, a kind of glorified coffee shop in fact, may not be up to Nico's
usual standards.

★★ Canteen, Unit G-4, Harbour Yard, Chelsea Harbour, SW10 (Earl's
Court). Phone 171 351 7330.

Very expensive. You have to get a cab, and give very explicit directions, to get to this place where Mediterranean-style food is prepared
imaginatively. Ask for fish, and you won't go wrong.

★★★ Capital Restaurant, 22-24 Basil Street, SW3 (Knightsbridge).
Phone 171 589 5171.

Very expensive. One of London's oldest haute cuisine places, this
is in the Capital Hotel, itself a charming (but modern) hotel right
behind Harrods. The food is Franco-British. The best of both, in fact,
and worth the trip.

★★★ Chez Nico 90 Park Lane, 90 Park Lane, W1 (Marble Arch).
Phone 171 409 1290.

Very expensive. Located in the Grosvenor House Hotel, this is
their grand dining room, in fact. Traditional French cuisine, not too
many innovations, which many consider a blessing. Look for dishes
containing scallops or lobster.

★★★★ Claridge's Restaurant, Brook Street, W1 (Bond Street). Phone
171 629 8860.

Very expensive. One of the grandest dining experiences you can
have is in this impressive old room, with classic French cooking (as
the British understand it). If you want to dance after dinner, this is
the place to do it—in style, but only on Saturdays.

★★ Clarke's, 124 Kensington Church Street, W8 (Notting Hill Gate).
Phone 171 221 9225.

Very expensive. Trendy, almost twee, definitely a place for locals out to impress one another. Modern British food with California overtones, but few surprises.

★★★ Coast, 26 Albemarle Street, W1 (Green Park). Phone 171 495 5999.

Expensive. In a business area (the place was once an auto show room), this restaurant serves modern British cuisine and a little of everything else, but nicely. The chef is a protegée of famed chef Marco Pierre White.

★★ The Collection, 264 Brompton Road, SW3 (South Kensington). Phone 171 225 1212.

Expensive. Another huge, trendy spot, popular with young locals, The Collection attempts to serve food from all around the Pacific area, sometimes successfully, sometimes not so successfully. The meat dishes seem to appeal more than fish here.

★★★★ Connaught Hotel Grill, Carlos Place, W1 (Green Park). Phone 171 499 7070.

Very expensive. The pride of the Connaught Hotel (which also has an equally expensive restaurant), the Grill Room offers the quintessential British dining experience, matched only by the Savoy's Grill Room, perhaps. There are only a dozen tables in this splendidly dignified room, and reservations are always hard to get, but do try if you can afford the prices. Service doesn't get any better than this. May we suggest the mixed grill as the main course?

★★★★★ The Criterion—Marco Pierre White, 224 Piccadilly, W1 (Piccadilly Circus). Phone 171 930 0488.

Expensive. Formerly the Criterion Brasserie, this is another huge place the Cool Britannia people seem to adore so much. The star here is Britain's most famous chef, Marco Pierre White, who is rightly called the country's best, at least for the moment. His interpretation of French cooking garners only raves from every self-styled critic, and we think they're right. It's still a brasserie, so think of grills here, but consider also White's fabulous innovations—especially dishes like salmon risotto or pot-roast pork with spices. It's hard to ignore the overwhelming and gaudy decor, but try to concentrate on the food if you can.

★★★ Daphne's, 112 Draycott Avenue, SW3 (South Kensington). Phone 171 589 4257.

Very expensive. Mediterranean cuisine in a marvelous setting, resembling a conservatory. Look for chicken dishes in particular.

Deals, Broadway Centre, Queen Caroline Street, W6 (Hammersmith). Phone 181 563 1001.

Moderate. Part of a chain, with branches near Oxford Circus and down in Fulham. We don't ordinarily list burger places, but Deals is an exception, since it isn't aimed at kids, as are places like Hard Rock Café. If you must have a burger—and especially if you are driving to and from the airport or other points west of central London—you may as well stop by here.

★★ The Fifth Floor Café, Harvey Nichols Department Store, Knightsbridge, SW 1 (Knightsbridge). Phone 171 823 1839.

Expensive. Mediterranean cuisine (ask for fish), always popular with sun-seeking Brits. Elegant and comforting decor.

Fortnum's Fountain, 181 Piccadilly, W1 (Green Park). Phone 171 734 8040.

Moderate. Located at the Jermyn Street side of Fortnum & Mason, the famous department/food store that caters to the royal family, this is a time-honored spot for tourists and locals alike, with traditional British fare (like Welsh rarebit, or "rabbit" as Americans know it), and perhaps the best ice cream sundaes in London. This is a place for lunch or snacks, never for dinner (unless you're really not very hungry).

★★ Frederick's, 106 Camden Passage, N1 (Angel). Phone 171 359 2888.

Expensive. Tucked away out in an area of Islington best known for its street market, Frederick's has a lovely garden for spring and summer dining, and modern British cuisine, including lovely salmon or duck dishes.

★ Goode's, 19 South Audley Street, W1 (Bond Street). Phone 171 409 7242.

Very expensive. A restaurant in a china shop is about as expected as a bull in ditto, but at least this is a pleasant surprise, and no dishes go crashing. Traditional and modern British cuisine, nothing too imaginative.

★★ The Greenhouse, 27A Hay's Mews, W1 (Green Park). Phone 171 499 3331

Very expensive. High prices in a high-rent Mayfair neighborhood are not unexpected. You can't get more British in decor, or in the traditional cooking, either.

★ The Green Olive, 5 Warwick Place, W9 (Warwick Avenue). Phone 171 289 2469.

Moderate. Italian food, including good pizza, in an attractive setting out in the Maida Vale district, beloved of some local intellectual types.

★ Inaho, 4 Hereford Road, W2 (Bayswater). Phone 171 221 8495.

Moderate. Japanese food in a tiny, modest setting, in a relatively modest neighborhood not far from Notting Hill. Noodles and other cooked dishes are fine, sushi available only four days a week, so ask ahead.

★★★ The Ivy, 1-5 West Street, WC2 (Leicester Square). Phone 171 836 4751.

Very expensive. One of London's most famous, most beloved and long-lasting restaurants, the place for a pretheater dinner, and always consistent in its modern British cuisine.

★★ Julie's, 133-137 Portland Road, W11 (Holland Park). Phone 171 229 8331.

Expensive. The address "Holland Park" and the word "romantic" always seem to go together in London, and this elaborate dungeon-like place is no exception. The decor and food are veddy British.

★★ Kensington Place, 201-207 Kensington Church Street, W8 (Notting Hill Gate). Phone 171 727 3184.

Expensive. A very trendy place in a very trendy part of London, popular with the locals and verging on noisy at times. Ask for fish dishes and game in season.

★★★★★ La Tante Claire, 68 Royal Hospital Road, SW3 (Sloane Square). Phone 171 352 6045.

Very, very expensive. When a restaurant is one of London's best, it can charge high prices. When it's also impeccably French, it can double that. And so it goes at La Tante Claire, an old Gallic favorite, now boasting one of the country's most innovative chefs, Pierre Koffmann. Look for duck, venison, or terrines of all sorts.

★★ Launceston Place, 1A Launceston Place, W8 (Gloucester Road). Phone 171 937 6912.

Expensive. A sister restaurant to Kensington Place (see above), this is smaller (in a converted townhouse) and more relaxed. The menu is modern British, the decor very discreet.

★★ L'Aventure, 3 Blenheim Terrace, NW8 (St. John's Wood). Phone 171 624 6232.

Expensive. French cuisine (close to traditional) and the neighborhood make for a pleasant combination, comforting and charming.

★★★★ Le Caprice, Arlington Street, SW1 (Green Park). Phone 171 629 2239.

Very expensive. Long considered London's leading restaurant, it is one of several boasting that title these days. Neverthless foreign and domestic royalty continue to dine here, as well as big shots who like to be seen and who want prestige, not trendiness, wherever they go. Look for British produce such as salmon or, believe it or not, sausages. Just off Piccadilly.

★★★ Leith's, 92 Kensington Park Road, W11 (Notting Hill Gate). Phone 171 229 4481.

Very expensive. This spot has been around a long time, and deserves its continuing reputation as an outstanding place to dine well on modern British cuisine, of course, including pigeon and a nice vegetarian menu. There is also a branch in the City, if you happen to be down that way; it is an especially fun place for people-watching at lunchtime.

★ Lemonia, 89 Regent's Park Road, NW1 (Chalk Farm). Phone 171 586 7454.

Moderate. Slightly out of the way up at Primrose Hill (you might be able to see Parliament from the hill itself), but cozy, this is a Greek taverna with traditional Aegean cooking. As in many Greek places, we consider a meal of appetizers, salads, bread, and wine (and perhaps some cheese) to be as good as a main course.

★★★ Le Palais du Jardin, 136 Long Acre, WC2 (Covent Garden). Phone 171 379 5353.

Expensive. French cuisine (brasserie-style) and a trendy atmosphere are the foundations of this brasserie, a "garden palace" indeed, as it is almost as big as a royal residence.

★★★ Le Pont de la Tour, 36D Shad Thames, SE1 (London Bridge). Phone 171 403 8403.

Very expensive. It's fashionable to go down to the dock these days, and will be more so when the Millennium Dome is finished, making "down the river" a must-see venue. The "Tower Bridge" (the English translation of this place's name) is located in the Butlers Wharf Building, if that helps you or your cabby find it; and you do get great views of the Thames itself while dining. British food with some continental overtones. Try the fish anytime, and game in season.

★★★ L'Odeon, 65 Regent street, W1 (Piccadilly Circus). Phone 171 287 1400.

Expensive. French cuisine of the new and newish type is what you go here for, and maybe for the ample room in this barn-sized place.

★★ L'Oranger, 5 St. James's Street, SW1 (Green Park). Phone 171 839 3774.

Very expensive. A very attractive setting is the background for marvelous French cuisine, in a sister restaurant to Aubergine. (This used to be Overton's, a very clubby, longtime favorite of the "right people," whoever they might have been.)

Manzi's, 1-2 Leicester Street, WC2 (Leicester Square). Phone 171 734 0224.

Moderate. One of London's oldest restaurants, and a bit rundown, Manzi's is nonetheless popular for its good seafood. And you can't beat the location, so close to the West End theaters.

★★ Mezzo, 100 Wardour Street, W1 (Leicester Square). Phone 171 314 4000.

Expensive. If you want to meet the people, come here. It's such a big place, you'll feel like everyone in the whole wide world has come to have dinner in the same place as you and your party. The menu is . . . what? International, or eclectic—you name the genre, they probably have it. It can get noisy with the live music late in the evening, and you'll have to expect a certain amount of chaos, as Mezzo calls itself "Europe's biggest restaurant."

★★ Nico Central, 35 Great Portland Street, W1 (Oxford Circus). Phone 171 436 8846.

Expensive. Nico Ladenis, who now bounces around between several restaurants bearing his name, can be seen here from time to time, touching up his French dishes with some of that *je ne sais quoi.* The menu includes marvelous vegetable courses and main-course fish dishes.

★ Nicole's, 158 New Bond Street, W1 (Green Park). Phone 171 499 8408.

Moderate. Everyone is opening restaurants in the most unlikely places these days (such as in a china shop), so why not in a dress shop? This is in the basement of Nicole Farhi's dress shop. Modern British cuisine, of course—what else in this trendy shopping street?

★★★★ Nobu, 19 Old Park Lane, W1 (Hyde Park Corner). Phone 171 447 4747.

Very expensive. Located in the Metropolitan Hotel, this branch of the New York original is just as exciting and as mysterious, with its outstanding food and weird decor. To call the menu Japanese would be to call the United States a branch of England. There are some traditional Japanese dishes, but they are outnumbered by the many original inventions of owner Nobu himself. Co-owners are Drew Nieporent and Robert DeNiro.

★ Noor Jahan, 2A Bina Gardens, SW5 (South Kensington). Phone 171 373 6522.

Moderate. Even the address sounds Indian, as is the cuisine in this nicely decorated spot.

★ Odette's, 130 Regent's Park Road, NW1 (Chalk Farm), 171 586 5486.

Expensive. Up at Primrose Hill, in another trendy part of town (there are a lot of trendy neighborhoods in London, after all), Odette's offers modern British cuisine in a cozy setting. Fun for summer lunch, when you can sit outdoors; the set lunch is moderately priced.

★ 192, 192 Kensington Park Road, W11 (Notting Hill Gate). Phone 171 229 0482.

Moderate. What would you eat in the trendy Portobello district other than modern British cuisine, and in a refreshing (though yes, still, trendy) setting. Think pigeon, game, and fresh vegetables.

★ Orsino, 119 Portland Road, W11 (Holland Park). Phone 171 221 3299.

Expensive. Traditional Italian cooking, thank heaven, with consistently good results, especially in signature dishes based on risotto, or in the always-good pizzas. Pleasant and spacious decor.

★★★ Oxo Tower, Oxo Tower Wharf, Barge House Street, SE1 (Blackfriars). Phone 171 803 3888.

Expensive. The Oxo Tower is a famous London landmark, now turned into a restaurant on the "wrong" (or south) side of the Thames. You get marvelous views from here, whether you're dining in the restaurant or the brasserie, an eclectic menu, and a big kitchen that somehow produces nothing but fine meals. Owned by the Harvey Nichols department store people.

★★★ Quaglino's, 16 Bury Street, SW1 (Green Park). Phone 171 930 6767.

You can't find a better location in London, as will become clear when you visit this spot in the fashionable St. James's neighborhood, just off Jermyn Street. The menu is European, not British, but Sir Terence Conran has somehow made it a very English spectacle, in the manner of "Cool Britannia." This huge cavernous place is somehow big and brassy and subdued, all at once. The meat dishes tend to be better prepared than the fish, in our opinion.

★★★★ Quo Vadis, 26-19 Dean Street, W1 (Tottenham Court Road). Phone 171 437 9585.

Very expensive. This is a new incarnation of a once-famous (and very tired) Italian restaurant that was out of business for a while, but has been reborn through the efforts of leading chef Marco Pierre White, among others. So you will get modern British cuisine at its best when you dine here.

★ Red Pepper, 8 Formosa Street, W9 (Warwick Avenue). Phone 171 266 2708.

Moderate. Italian traditional is the theme here, including pizzas from a wood-fired oven.

Richoux, 172 Piccadilly, W1 (Piccadilly Circus). Phone 171 493 2204.

Moderate. One of four restaurants in a group, all in fashionable locations (the others are in Bond Street, Knightsbridge, and up in St. John's Wood), Richoux is really a place for tea or snacks, but does serve reasonably sized lunches, too. The place looks like it might have done in the 1930s, although in fact, it's been decorated many times since then and has just kept its old charm.

★★★★ River Cafe, Rainville Road, W6 (Hammersmith). Phone 171 381 8824.

Very expensive. Located on the Thames Wharf in this odd corner of London, the River Café has been famous for years, with royalty and prime ministers (Margaret Thatcher, for example), as well as presidents (George Bush, for one) coming here. Outstanding Italian cuisine in an extremely attractive setting.

★★ Rules, 35 Maiden Lane, WC2 (Charing Cross). Phone 171 836 5314.

Expensive. How long has Rules been here? Don't ask—a lady doesn't always want to give her age. (Well, okay, it opened its doors in 1798.) Yes, there are perhaps too many tourists, but if you're looking for Olde England, you couldn't do any better elsewhere. So just ignore those other tourists, or better yet, say hello to them—they're probably American or Canadian! As for food, think game and plum pudding, for English traditional the menu certainly is!

★ San Frediano, 62 Fulham Road, SW3 (South Kensington). Phone 171 584 8375.

Expensive. An old-timer by restaurant standards (it's been here since the early 1960s), this is a consistently good place for standard Italian cooking, in a friendly atmosphere.

★ San Lorenzo, 22 Beauchamp (pronounced "Beecham") Place, SW3 (Knightsbridge). Phone 171 584 1074.

Very expensive. This upscale Italian bistro has been around for at least thirty years, but has worn its age well.

★ Santini, 29 Ebury Street, SW1 (Victoria). Phone 171 730 4094.

Very expensive. You pay fancy prices in a not all that fancy neighborhood here, but the Italian cuisine is considered among London's best. The emphasis is on Venetian-style cooking.

★ Scalini, 1-3 Walton Street, SW3 (Knightsbridge). Phone 171 225 2301.

Expensive. Italian food in somewhat frenetic surroundings, perhaps too trendy for its own good.

★★ Scotts, 20 Mount Street, W1 (Bond Street). Phone 171 629 5248.

Very expensive. Scotts has been going since 1851 (it used to be in Piccadilly), yet the consistency of its seafood (the specialty here) has never wavered. Elegant decor makes dressing up a necessity.

★ Soho Soho, 11-13 Frith Street, W1 (Tottenham Court Road). Phone 171 494 3491.

Moderate. Basically, this is a brasserie, serving Mediterranean food to a busy Soho-type clientele. Think Provençal, and you'll know what to expect on the menu.

★★ The Square, 6-10 Bruton Street, W1 (Bond Street). Phone 171 495 7100.

Very expensive. This spot, just off Berkeley Square, serves French cuisine to the expense-account set for lunch or dinner. Very proper, but the restaurant welcomes new money as well as old.

★ Star of India, 154 Old Brompton Road, SW5 (Gloucester Road). Phone 171 373 2901.

Expensive. This is probably London's best Indian restaurant, and it's been a fashionable den for South Kensington's citizens for at least four decades. Traditional Indian cuisine, very good service, and an excellent vegetarian menu in addition to the meat and fish dishes.

Sticky Fingers, 1A Phillimore Gardens, W8 (High Street Kensington). Phone 171 938 5338.

Moderate. This is supposed to be an American diner, so we wonder why we're recommending it, unless you're homesick. Burgers and more.

★★ Sugar Club, 33A All Saints Road, W11 (Westbourne Grove). Phone 171 221 3844.

Expensive. This is a bit out of the way, but worth the trip if you like Asian cooking, which is part of the menu here. "Stylish" is the word for the decor, "friendly" the word for the service. An eclectic menu, with all sorts of nuances (the chef is from New Zealand).

★★★★★ Vong, Wilton Place, SW1 (Hyde Park Corner). Phone 171 235 1010.

Very expensive. Located in the swank Berkeley Hotel, Vong is a branch of Jean-Georges Vongerichten's restaurant in New York. You get a mixture of French and Thai here, in a stunning blend, and who would expect anything less from one of the world's best chefs?

Wodka, 12 St. Alban's Grove, W8 (Kensington). Phone 171 937 6513. Moderate. Polish food, and why not? It is a proud cuisine, and confident (who else serves pickles at breakfast?). The cuisine is not the heavy, traditional stuff, either, but nouvelle Polish if you please, even if blini and pirogi are still the favorites here.

★★ Zafferano, 15 Lowndes Street, SW1 (Knightsbridge). Phone 171 235 5800.

Expensive. Italian food in this part of town is easy to come by, but Zafferano serves, perhaps, the best in Knightsbridge. Ask for the seafood dishes; save room for the scrumptious desserts.

Zilli Fish, 36-40 Brewer Street, W1 (Piccadilly Circus). Phone 171 734 8649.

Expensive. Seafood and Italian cuisine are the stars here, in a nicely decorated Soho restaurant, complete with an aquarium.

Wheelchair-accessible Dining

Here are some places that definitely are accessible:

Expensive:

Aubergine, 11 Park Walk. Phone 171 352 3449, fax 171 351 1770. Lunch Monday to Friday, dinner Monday to Saturday. Closed two weeks at Christmas, first two weeks of August. All credit cards accepted.

Bibendum Restaurant, Michelin House, 81 Fulham Rd. Phone 171 581 5817, fax 171 823 7925, Lunch and dinner daily. Closed December 24–27. All credit cards accepted.

The Capital Hotel, Basil Street, Knightsbridge. Phone 171 589 5171, fax 171 225 0011. Open daily. All credit cards accepted.

Chez Nico, 90 Park Lane. Phone 171 409 1290, Lunch Monday to Friday. Closed ten days for Christmas, four days at Easter.

Le Gavroche Restaurant, 43 Upper Brook Street. Phone 171 408 0881/499 1826, fax 171 409 0939. Lunch and dinner Monday to Friday. Closed bank holidays, December 23–January 2.

The Restaurant, Hyde Park Hotel, Knightsbridge. Phone 171 259 5380. Lunch and dinner daily.

La Tante Claire, 68 Royal Hospital Road. Phone 171 352 6045, fax 171 352 3257, Lunch Monday to Friday. Closed three weeks in August, ten days for Easter and Christmas.

TEAS

Tea in England can be thought of in several ways. Tea is for breakfast, all meals, or that special time of day when you relax, have some delicious sandwiches or pastry, and listen to music. The following suggestions are for that "special tea," also called simply "afternoon tea" or just "tea," known only to England, Ireland, and Scotland. Always reserve ahead.

(Note: "High tea," a phrase frequently used in the U.S. to denote a fashionable afternoon of tea, pastries, and the like, in Britain is a term used for something like an American Sunday-night supper, and is a phrase frowned upon by "proper" Britishers. Some snobs there consider it a "working-class term," pointing out that "high tea" in Yorkshire means leftovers, sausages and other foods, washed down, of course, with tea (or, just as likely, with beer). Our advice—don't ever use the phrase "high tea" in London!

If you have a real English afternoon tea, you might want to skip either lunch or dinner. We list the top places to go for tea, but you can also have that afternoon tea at a department store or small tea shop; most hotels serve tea, too. There are many excellent afternoon tea places, but we cannot mention them all.

Brown's Hotel, 32 Albemarle Street. Phone 171 518 4121.
   Tea is served in the very traditionally decorated lounge.

Claridge's Hotel, Brook Street. Phone 171 629 8860.
   Beautiful dining room off the lobby with an expensive and delicious tea.

Fortnum & Mason, 181 Piccadilly. Phone 171 734 8040.
   They have a huge variety of teas at moderate to expensive prices. After or before tea, you can shop in the splendid food store for teas, candy, quail eggs, or almost anything special you might have in mind. They also have cookies packed in beautiful tins, which can be excellent gift items.

Grosvenor House, 90 Park Lane. Phone 171 493 3341.
   Excellent afternoon tea overlooking the park, with beautiful piano music in the background. Sit at small tables or on sofas, relax and enjoy the afternoon. The room is beautiful, the service excellent, and the food is quite good.

Harrods, Knightsbridge. Phone 171 730 1234.
   Harrods has at least ten restaurants, and tea can be had in many of them. Tea can also be served in the beauty parlor. Not outrageously priced. You can also buy tea or cookies in the Food Hall.

Lanesborough Hotel, 1 Lanesborough Place at Hyde Park Corner. Phone 171 259 5599.

Beautiful and absolutely "proper" afternoon tea is served in this gorgeous hotel. Very expensive.

Richoux, 172 Piccadilly. Phone 171 493 2204.
41A South Audley Street. Phone 171 629 5228.
86 Brompton Road. Phone 171 584 8300.
3 Circus Road in St John's Wood. Phone 171 483 4001.

We like all of these quite old-fashioned lunch and tea shops. The food is good, not great, the atmosphere very pleasant, and the afternoon tea, although not extensive, is quite suitable and reasonably priced.

Ritz Hotel, 150 Piccadilly. Phone 171 493 8181.

This is our all-time favorite—expensive, delicious, a beautiful place to splurge for afternoon tea. The service is excellent, the background music soft and restful, the atmosphere busy and fun, the room gorgeous, and the price out of sight. Don't say we didn't warn you.

CHILDREN'S FOOD OUT

Most restaurants have children's menus, or there is something on the menu that children like. The following are fun to take children to:

Deals.
Chelsea Harbour. Phone 171 795 1001. Monday to Saturday 11am–midnight, Sunday to 11:15. Burgers.
14-16 Foubert's Place. Phone 171 287 1001. Monday to Thursday noon to 11pm, Friday and Saturday until 1am. Burgers.

Bradmore House, Hammersmith Broadway. Phone 161 563 1001. Monday to Thursday noon to 3pm, 5pm, 11pm, Friday to Sunday noon to 11pm.

All three restaurants are wheelchair accessible; all three are casual dress, hamburgers, fries, and lots of fun. Sunday lunch at all three locations includes special fun for the kids: magicians, make-your-own sundaes, and all the Coke you can drink at no extra charge. Chelsea Harbour has the extra benefit of being on the water. You can watch the boats and walk along the pier.

Pizza Express.
There are at least ten Pizza Express restaurants in central London. The pizzas are good, the prices inexpensive. Most of the restaurants are wheelchair accessible. At least one is known as a good jazz venue.

Rainforest Café, 20 Shaftesbury Ave., Piccadilly Circus. Tel. 171 434 3111.
As soon as you are in the door the fun begins. Animals (fake and huge) swing their trunks, tails, and wings. You have a gift shop, thunder, rain, lightening, and a decent menu. Everyone can find something to eat. The menu includes burgers, salads, and the usual kid food that can be found in the U.S. Moderate prices.

Smollensky's Balloon, 1 Dover Street. Phone 171 491 1199.
Smollensky's on the Strand, 105 the Strand. Phone 171 497 2101. American fast food that is also good. steaks, burgers, and fries. Both restaurants open daily noon to midnight, Sunday until 10:30. Wheelchair accessible. Both have weekend activities for kids (1 to 3pm such as clowns, puppets, magic shows, and just plain fun.

Sticky Fingers, 1A Phillimore Gardens. Phone 171 938 5338. Daily noon to 11:30pm. Wheelchair accessible. Reserve ahead for Sunday lunch, as it gets very crowded. The usual kids' fare of burgers, ribs, fries, and fun. Coloring books are given to children as they arrive to occupy them while they wait for lunch or dinner. Moderate prices.

American Places

Burger King.
There are quite a few in central London, including one on Regent Street and one on Oxford Street. They do serve their purpose. Reasonable prices for quick service and decent, standard food.

Hard Rock Café, 150 Old Park Lane. Phone 171 629 0382. Daily 11am to 11pm, wheelchair accessible.
Located at Hyde Park Corner. People still queue up for this moderately priced hamburger restaurant, where the theme is rock and roll. Pete Townshend of The Who donated one of his guitars.

McDonald's.
There are at least ten McDonald's restaurants in central London, one on the Strand, one at Marble Arch, and one on Oxford Street.

They serve the quick, standard hamburger with fries and soda at a reasonable price.

Planet Hollywood, 13 Coventry St. Phone 171 287 0789. Daily 11am to 11pm. Wheelchair accessible.

Owned by popular Hollywood stars, this is another midpriced hamburger restaurant. Like Hard Rock Café, this restaurant is full of memorabilia from the stars.

10. Shopping in London

Shopping in London is very expensive, but if you are careful, you can find many things to buy. London is a wonderful shopping city, and, as in New York or Paris, every street is full of shops of all descriptions. Bargains are easier to find than you might think. Shop carefully, have fun and remember the VAT (Value Added Tax). Also remember that each person (including an infant) is permitted to bring $400 worth of goods into the U.S. duty free.

If you know what you want to buy when you arrive in London, be it china or a cashmere sweater, it is a good idea to know what it costs at home. Sometimes, even with the VAT refund, items are less expensive in New York than in London. English items are usually a better buy in England. American or European clothes are usually more expensive in England than in the U.S.

There are many shopping neighborhoods in London; in this chapter we will describe central London's main streets and what can be bought on each, plus the shops that we like for specific types of products. Feel free to keep exploring on your own. If you don't have the time or desire to wander in and out of small shops and streets, head directly for the department stores (also listed here). They are excellent for the most part, having almost everything you might possibly think of buying. (Anything you forget to buy can be purchased at the Duty Free shops at the airports.)

SHOPPING STREETS

With a good map, you can find other shopping areas, but we think this list should keep you busy for a long time.

Value Added Tax

If you are not a resident of the EC (European Community), you are entitled to a VAT tax refund when you leave the country. The VAT included in all purchases is 17.5 percent, so be sure to ask if the refund is available for what you are buying at the time. Some shops will allow a refund if you spend £50, others have a minimum of £75 or £100. Shop with your passport. The shopkeeper will ask to see it as proof that you are not a British subject; also, you will be required to give your passport information. If you qualify for the VAT refund, fill out the form and save it in the self-addressed (to the shop) stamped envelope provided by the shop.

When you leave Britain, you will have to go to the customs desk with your purchases (which you may have to show); the form will be stamped by the customs officer, and then you must mail the self-addressed and stamped envelope from your point of departure. If you forget, you forfeit the refund, which may be substantial. At London Heathrow airport, the VAT desk is to the right of the security entrance, and the mail box is right there, too.

The best way to shop if you are planning on getting a refund is with a credit card. Then the refund is credited back to your card and is easy to keep track of. You can also request a cash refund, which you will receive at the point of departure in whatever currency you desire. If you shop in Paris, Dublin, or Edinburgh, you are also entitled to the VAT refund. Purchases made in Ireland and Scotland can all be refunded in England. French purchases must be processed when you leave France.

Old and New Bond Streets

This is one continuous street with big-name boutiques plus department stores. One of the latter is **Nicole Farhi** at 158 New Bond Street. If you tire of shopping or are just hungry, stop at the excel-

Shop Where The Royal Family Shops

Four members of the royal family (the Queen, the Queen Mum, Prince Philip, and Prince Charles) are allowed (by the Queen) to grant royal warrants to certain shops or manufacturers. The shopkeepers are allowed to put up the appropriate coat of arms at the entrance to their shops, and to refer to the royal patronage in their advertising. If you're interested in shopping where these four persons "shop," look for the star * following the names of stores in our listings. The star indicates that the shop has a royal warrant. We should note that the four royals mentioned almost always have their shopping done for them, and they personally are seldom (if ever) seen in shops. There was a time when the Queen herself would shop at Harrods after they closed for the evening, but that hasn't happened lately, so far as we know.

lent restaurant on the lower level, open for breakfast, lunch, and dinner.

The other department store is **Fenwick** at 63 New Bond Street, which features Joe's Café. The restaurant is quite nice, takes reservations, and is a little less expensive than the one at Nicole Farhi.

A few of the shops on Bond Street are **Chanel, Versace, Hermes, Donna Karen, DKNY, Ferragamo, Lalique, Baccarat, Armani,** and **Smythson Stationery*** shop, **Church's Shoes**, and much more. You'll also find a wonderful sculpture of President Roosevelt and Winston Churchill sitting on a park bench together. You can sit between them and have your photograph taken. There is a lovely flower cart here, if you want or need some fresh flowers.

Umbrellas from **Swaine Adeney***, at 10 Old Bond Street, have been keeping Londoners dry since 1750. The shop now sells quality leather goods and horseback-riding gear, though umbrellas are still their forte. These are not the folding, ten-dollar kind. An umbrella from this shop starts at £125 and goes as high as £600, depending on the wood used for the handles and whether nylon or silk is used for the canopy. They also make travel umbrellas and oversized umbrellas that

won't turn inside out in heavy rain or wind. All umbrellas are guaranteed, and will be refurbished free of charge. They say that once you own
one of their umbrellas, you'll never need another (unless you lose it).

Size Conversion

If you plan to shop for clothing or shoes, you need to
know the British sizing system. It is best to try things on,
but if you are buying a gift, keep this chart handy.

Women

Clothing	American	4	6	8	10	12	14 etc.
	British	6	8	10	12	14	16
	Continental	34	36	38	40	42	44
Shoes	American	5	6	7	8 etc.		
	British	4	5	6	7		
	Continental	36	37	38	39		

Men

Suits	American	34	36	38	40 etc.	
	British	34	36	38	40	
	Continental	44	46	48	50	
Shirts	American	14½	15	15½	16	16½ etc.
	British	14½	15	15½	16	16½
	Continental	37	38	39	41	42
Shoes	American	7	8	9	10	11 etc.
	British	6	7	8	9	10
	Continental	39½	41	42	43	44½

Children

Clothing	American	3	4	5	6	6X etc.	
	British	18	20	22	24	26	
	Continental	98	104	110	116	122	
Shoes	American	8	9	10	11	12	13 etc.
	British	7	8	9	10	11	12
	Continental	24	25	27	28	29	30

Piccadilly

Piccadilly, at the bottom (south end) of Old Bond Street, is a wonderful venue for hotels, shops, restaurants, the **Burlington Arcade**, and **Sogo**, the Japanese department store, in addition to The Royal Academy Museum, and the entrance to Green Park. You can also pick up The Big Red Bus sightseeing bus on Piccadilly in front of the entrance to Green Park. The famous and wonderful Ritz Hotel is here, as is **Fortnum and Mason***, just down the street from the hotel. There you can buy teas, fancy jams, quail eggs, candy, and just about any other food item you wish. There is also a restaurant, which is open for breakfast, lunch, and dinner. Our all-time favorite book store, **Hatchards**, is nearby, too. You'll find children's books, new, old, autographed, travel, and art books, or any other type of book you could possibly want. There is also a large **Boots** Drug Store for developing film, and for buying the usual items one needs, such as the forgotten tooth brush or hair spray.

Regent Street

You can cover Regent Street by foot from Piccadilly to Oxford Circus. You'll see that it is full of shops. The kids won't complain if you take them shopping here. Regent Street has both the **Disney Store** and the largest toy store in Britain, **Hamleys***. **Libertys*** and **Dickins & Jones** department stores are on Regent Street. **The Scotch House** at 84 Regent Street is for cashmere sweaters, Scotch kilts and woolen items—plus, plus, plus. Just walk and you will find. One store we always stop at is the **British Air Travel Store**. If you fly British Air, you can reconfirm your reservations here. They have an outstanding travel book section, maps, travel bags, locks, and many other travel items. They also sell Concorde items such as souvenir planes, pens, and postcards.

Oxford Street and Oxford Circus

Both of these streets contain shop after shop of inexpensive stores for jeans and shoes, plus the **Virgin Megastore**, a huge **Marks & Spencer** with a food super market in the basement, the **Body Shop** with its soaps and shampoos, and one of the many **Boots** pharmacies to be found in London. There are discount bookstores on these streets, along with sweater shops, china shops and you name it, it's here. You'll also find **Debenhams** department store, **BHS** (British Home Stores) **D.H. Evans** department store, and **John Lewis** and **Selfridges** department stores. What cannot be found in the small shops can be found in these large department stores. These are not our favorite streets, but then again, we are not teenagers. If we were, we'd head straight here.

Covent Garden

This is a wonderful area that has been completely rehabilitated. You can walk for blocks and snoop in great little shops, buy something for your hair, or have a stuffed baked potato. It is just plain fun.

Jermyn Street

This is a lovely, short shopping street with fancy, expensive shops, a small hotel, restaurants, and hairdressers. Note **Alfred Dunhill*** and **Davidoff**'s for Cuban cigars. Remember to smoke those Cuban cigars in Europe where they are legal. You cannot bring them into the U.S. If the customs officer discovers them, they will be confiscated. **Turnbull & Asser***, **Hilditch & Key**, and **Harvie & Hudson** are the places to go for custom-made shirts, or those off the shelves. You can get a free map of the Jermyn Street shops in any shop or hotel lobby. The little hotel gem on this street is 22 Jermyn Street (see hotel listings).

Knightsbridge

The famous **Harrods*** and **Harvey Nichols*** department stores are here, very close to each other, in fact. Both stores have high-quality goods, excellent restaurants, good security, VAT desks, and anything else you might want. Harrods, of course, has even more than you could dream of wanting, including its justly famous food halls. Even if you need nothing, stop at the food hall. We can hardly pull ourselves away from the selections of meats, poultry, cheeses, breads, candy, patés, and caviars. Look at their wine department with its Harrods label wines, which are excellent. Harrods also has a travel agency and

Chinaware

London has beautiful china shops and gorgeous bone china. Most china shops usually sell bone china only, and first-quality only. It is less expensive than in the U.S. They will also ship any place you wish. Just watch the prices for shipping, and what the U.S. duty will be (It all adds up!). You can also buy lead crystal in most china shops, but if you are going to Ireland or Scotland, you can buy your crystal there at better prices, and also ship it home. Most china shops and department stores, like Harrods, have twice-yearly sales with excellent china and crystal prices. If you can wait for the sales, you'll achieve substantial savings.

Chinacraft, 98 The Strand.

Chinacraft sells both china and crystal, and all the best names. This shop sells first-quality only: Waterford and Baccarat crystal among others, and Spode, Royal Crown Derby, Wedgwood, Minton, and all of the others as well. You can buy a small crystal ring holder or a set of dishes in all price ranges. If you buy, a lot be sure to ask if they give a discount along with the VAT refund.

Reject China Shops at 134 Regent Street, 1 Beauchamp Place, and Covent Garden.

Owned by Chinacraft, they all carry seconds, but they carry first-quality, too, at the same prices as in all other china shops.

Thomas Goode*, 19 South Audley Street.

This is the most beautiful china shop we have ever seen in London or in any other city. They carry gorgeous china, crystal, silver, and accessories. Do not try to get a discount here; you won't! You can also have lunch here, with an exquisite table setting. The food is equally as good. The prices are high, but the surroundings are superb. See also Stoke-On-Trent, page 127.

theater-ticket desk. The neighborhood also has the main **Scotch House** shop, china shops, restaurants, hotels, **Boots**, and many low-end shops, too. The famous Hyde Park Hotel is across the street from Harvey Nichols and down the street from Harrods (see hotels).

ANTIQUES AND MARKETS

There are many antique and market areas in London, some better than others. We list the ones we like best. You can bargain in all of the markets, so don't accept the first price. You may eventually pay it, but try not to.

Portobello Road

Saturday is the big day here, but midweek is quieter, especially if you know what you are looking for. The street market is open on Saturdays from 6am to 4pm. The shops are open daily except Sunday. Don't ignore the streets that branch off from Portobello Road. The Saturday street stalls usually do not have the quality items that the shops have, but you could be lucky, and it is fun.

Grosvenor House Antiques Fair, Grosvenor House Hotel, Park Lane.

Usually in June. The best dealers in Britain exhibit at this fair. All items are over one hundred years old except paintings, and every item has been authenticated before being displayed.

Antiquarian Book Fair, Olympia.

Four days in the first week of June. This is one of our favorite fairs. You can find gorgeous books, prints, and illustrations. The prices are usually gorgeous too, but some reasonably priced books can be found.

Covent Garden Markets

There are three markets at Covent Garden: They are the Apple Market, Jubilee Market, and Opera Market. The Apple Market, open daily, is full of craft items. Antiques are sold on Mondays. The Jubilee Market, open daily, is geared toward the young, and as far as we're concerned is less exciting; it's also more difficult to find anything worthwhile. They also sell antiques on Monday. Opera Market is the low-end market, but again Monday is antiques day. This market sells cheap items, so it can be especially fun.

Camden Passage at Upper Street in the Islington area.

This area has well over two hundred antique shops, which are open from 10am to 5pm, Wednesday and Saturday from 8am to 4pm (closed Sunday).

Camden Lock, Camden High Street.

(Open Saturday and Sunday only from 10am to 5:30pm). Do not confuse this with Camden Passage. This is cheap old clothes, leather, and junk. We mention it only so you do not make a mistake.

Piccadilly Market, in the churchyard of St. James's Church, Piccadilly.

As you walk down Piccadilly, you can't miss this little market with many stalls selling clothing, crafts, candles, and the usual junk. It is fun to snoop if you have an extra twenty minutes, but that's all. Open Friday and Saturdays only.

Greenwich Markets

Get here by BritRail, car, or boat. The train takes fifteen minutes, the boat takes almost an hour and is a lovely trip on a nice day. There are loads of markets, which are held on Saturday and Sunday. Don't forget that Greenwich has museums, the dry-docked clipper ship, *Cutty Sark*, the Old Royal Observatory, the Royal Naval College, pubs, and much more. It makes for a splendid day trip and/or market outing.

The Crafts Market is held in the center of Greenwich and, as the name implies, the merchants sell crafts items. Bosun's Yard, near the Crafts Market on the waterfront, sells the same type of stuff that the

Crafts Market sells. The Greenwich Antique market sells more junk, with a few antiques thrown in. These are not your top-of-the-line markets, but they make for a fun day in London. Stop for lunch at the moderately priced Trafalgar Tavern, on Park Row, (closed Saturday lunch, Sunday dinner); or at The Yacht, at 5 Crane Street, which is inexpensive (open daily). See Greenwich in chapter 11, Day Trips from London, for more on this area.

We have just scratched the surface of antique areas, shops, and streets. If you want to see and know more, you can get further information from the London Tourist Office. There are truly fine antique shops all over London, but the ones we have mentioned are the fun, lively places.

SHOPPING FOR SPORTING GOODS AND CLOTHING

Lillywhites, Piccadilly Circus.
Six floors of sports equipment and accessories.

Olympus Sports, Oxford Street.
Great for sports and fitness equipment. They also stock various athletic team shirts (for rugby, soccer, and other sports), which make fun gifts.

Cobra, Oxford Street.
A huge assortment of clothes and shoes for all sports.

Children's Toys

As in any big city, there are many children's toy shops in London. If you are away from home, we think you might as well go to the best. You can always go to Toys "R" Us in your home town.

Hamleys*, at 200 Regent Street.

Hamley's is the largest toy shop in England, with an outstanding collection of dolls, British toy soldiers, double decker buses, stuffed animals, and anything else you might have in mind. Hamley's will ship all over the world and also refund the VAT. There is a gift shop on the main level and a snack bar on the lower level. Hamley's also has a small shop in Covent Garden and one at London Heathrow airport.

Harrods*, Knightsbridge.

The toy department, on the fourth floor, is excellent. Samples of the items for sale are available for kids to touch and play with before they buy.

Blacks, The Strand.

Equipment and clothing for walking, hiking, and camping, including tents, sleeping bags, and anything needed for the outdoors. Another shop with similar types of gear is YHA or Youth Hostel Association, located on Southampton Street in Covent Garden. (Phone 171 836 8541).

C&A at Marble Arch or Oxford Circus.

Beautiful ski clothing.

Farlow's of Pall Mall, near Piccadilly Circus.

Fishing equipment and clothing.

BRITISH SHOPS FOR TYPICAL BRITISH CLOTHING

Most of these shops have many branches. We are mentioning only a few of the traditional British shops. There are many more, such as

---

Boots, the Drug Store

Boots can be found on almost every street, it seems, and definitely in every neighborhood. There is almost nothing you cannot find in these excellent shops. You can have film developed in an hour, have a prescription filled, buy hair spray, toothpaste, makeup, lotions, creams, and even a sandwich and a cold drink. Anything you forgot to bring on your trip may be purchased at Boots.

Burburry's for raincoats and classic English clothing. You may like Simpson's of Piccadilly, which is a large department store full of British clothing and gifts. As the saying goes, look and you shall find—in London, the cliché can come true.

Aquascutum, Regent Street.
Known for classical clothing and raincoats.

Austin Reed, Regent Street.
Well-priced men's and woman's clothing.

Berk, Burlington Arcade.
Stocks gorgeous cashmeres in every color and style for men and women.

Jaeger's, Regent Street.
Classic British clothing.

Gieves & Hawkes, 1 Savile Row.
Beautifully tailored men's clothing.

Turnbull & Asser, Jermyn Street.
Known worldwide for its men's shirts and neckties. Although these can be bought in Harrods and stores in the U.S., try this pleasant and amusing shop first.

DEPARTMENT STORES

There are many more department stores in London than we list here, but we feel these will keep you busy enough. We picked the ones we felt were different from the ones you might find at home. The star * indicates that the establishment has a royal warrant (see our box, page 116).

Debenhams, Oxford Street.

Home furnishings, nondesigner clothing, designer fashions, cosmetics, and reasonable prices. This is a chain in the UK, so you can shop and exchange in other cities as you travel.

Dr. Martens, Covent Garden.

Doc Martens is not a doctor, but a brand of shoes. Now there is a fabulous department store, which has five floors of clothing, children's clothes, and accessories, and, needless to say, shoes and boots. This is London's newest department store.

Fenwicks on New Bond Street.

Fenwicks is an all-purpose department store. Its clothing departments have every price range, and you'll find here both a hairdresser and manicurist, as well as an excellent restaurant for lunch, called Joe's. They even take reservations; without one, you stand on line and wait.

Fortnum & Mason*, Piccadilly.

This is a gorgeous and expensive food shop on the ground floor of an expensive department store. There is also a restaurant where you can start the day with delicious scones, cream, jam, and tea.

Harrods* of Knightsbridge.

Harrods is, with Macy's, perhaps the most famous store in the world. It is decorated outside with lights twelve months a year and looks like a giant cake. We love it. You can find the most expensive, or sometimes reasonably priced things, depending on the department you visit. Also, there is a wonderful Harrods souvenir shop with gifts in every price range. Even if you buy nothing, it is worth a stop just to look.

Harvey Nichols*, Knightsbridge.

This shop is just up the street from Harrods, toward Hyde Park Corner. It specializes in top-quality fashion.

Marks & Spencer. Branches throughout England.

Marks & Sparks, as the British refer to the chain, can be found in almost every town in England. The Marble Arch store is the main London shop. M&S carries clothing, great sweaters, home furnishings, excellent prepared food (and food in general), and beautiful flowers. It is, no doubt about it, a British institution.

Stoke-On-Trent

This area is famous for its china and pottery. Before setting out on a side trip, call ahead to the factory you want to visit for directions and hours for museums, tours, and shops.

Portmeirion Potteries Ltd.
Here you can find beautiful cookware and tableware in the famous fruit and flower designs. There are shops that sell first-quality goods, and a seconds shop for slightly damaged items. London Road, phone 01782/411-756. No tours. Shop open daily 9am to 5:30pm, except Sundays 10am to 4pm.

Royal Doulton Company.
There are five factory shops in Stoke, all open to the public for bone china and gifts. Also factory tours and a museum of Minton China. Royal Doulton Pottery Factory, Nile Street in Buslem (a suburb), phone 01782/292 434. You must book in advance for tours Monday through Friday.

Royal Worcester.
Located south of Stoke, it produces beautiful bone china and porcelain. You can visit the Dyson Perrins Museum and tour the factory. Royal Worcester Porcelain Factory, Severn Street, Worcester, phone 01905/23221. Tours Monday through Friday. Book in advance (for same day, before 10am).

Wedgwood Visitor Centre.
Here, you'll see potters and decorators working on gorgeous Wedgwood China. Wedgwood Visitors Centre, Barlaston (a suburb), phone 01782/204 218. Open Monday through Friday, no factory tours on Friday, however. You must book in advance.

Liberty*, Regent Street.

Liberty is known for its printed fabrics and home furnishings. It's also the quaintest-looking department store you'll likely ever see; the façade is pseudo-Tudor and the old store, especially, has all sorts of nooks, crannies, and sloping floors. Until not too long ago, Mr. Liberty, the founder, inspected the place on a regular basis, even when he was confined to a wheelchair.

Nicole Farhi, New Bond Street.

Beautiful clothes for young people. High-styled, but not out-of-sight prices. Also an excellent restaurant called Nicole's, open for breakfast, lunch, and dinner. (If you forget anything in London, you can buy it at the new Nicole Farhi in Manhattan.)

Selfridges on Oxford Street.

This store has it all: clothing, home furnishings, cosmetics, and whatever else you might want to buy. The building itself is beautiful, so far as department stores go. The company was started by an American expatriate near the turn of the (last) century—in the early 1900s, that is.

11. Leisure Activities

COOKING SCHOOLS

There are many cooking schools in London, and within an hour's train or car trip of London. We have tried to list a variety of schools and courses, including vegetarian, baking, day schools, extended courses, degree courses, and just fun and interesting courses. We have not given prices, since these vary according to what you choose. Call, write, or fax for all information for these mostly off-season schools.

AGA Workshop, Watercroft, Church Road, Penn, Buckinghamshire HP10 8NX. Phone 1494 816535, fax 1494 816535.

Located twenty-nine miles from London, the school is easily reached by car or train from London's Marylebone Station. Overnight stays are available at local B & Bs. One-day programs include lunch and wine; two-day programs include lunch both days. Dinner on your own. Classes are held almost daily except in December. The emphasis here is on grilling, frying, holiday cooking and using fresh herbs and vegetables.

The Bath School of Cookery, Bassett House, Claverton, Bath, Avon BA2 7BL. Phone 1225 722498, fax 1225 722980.

Located seventy minutes by train from London's Paddington Station to Bath Spa Station. The courses available here are one-day, four-day, weekend, or four-week. Class size is kept to no more than ten students. Any student who completes a course of one week or more receives a diploma. Some of the courses available are: Introduction Course for beginners in the kitchen; One-Month Intensive Master Course; Four-Day Creative Cooking; Four-Day Gourmet Cooking; Four-Day Mediterranean Cooking. One-day courses are held from

9:30am to 3pm. Dishes include basic French, Italian, holiday cooking and ethnic menus.

Books for Cooks Cooking School, 4 Blenheim Crescent, London W11 1NN England, phone 171 221 1992, Fax 171 221 1517, e-mail info@booksforcooks.com.

This cooking school is held in a bookstore; the staff are cookbook authors. The cost of the class ranges from £10 for a children's class to £60 for a three-day course. The classes vary from bread baking, stir fry, vegetarian and holiday cooking to French bistro food.

Eileen Follows, Verity, Commonwood, Kings Langley, Herts WD4 9BA. Phone 1923 263104.

The trip from London to Chorleywood is twenty minutes via the Metropolitan Line from Baker Street. From the station it is a short taxi ride to the school. The cooking demonstrations take place in Eileen Follows's lovely kitchen, with no more than ten students at a time. Classes include coffee and biscuits upon arrival, demonstration and tasting, three-course lunch with wine, and an afternoon demonstration and tasting. Classes are held in the fall.

Hintlesham Hall, Hintlesham, Ipswich, Suffolk IP8 3NS. Phone 1473 652268 or 652334, fax 1473 652463.

Located four miles from Ipswich, which is a one-hour ride from London's Liverpool Street Station, and then a short taxi ride to the hall. The courses are held at this beautiful hotel, where you might want to overnight. Demonstration classes are held approximately once every six weeks for a day in the main hotel kitchen, and include a three-course lunch with wine. Courses might include Autumn Dinner Parties or Christmas Entertaining. Emphasis is on seasonal dishes, vegetarian, fish, and special entertaining.

Le Cordon Bleu L'Art Culinaire, 114 Marylebone Lane, London W1M 6HH. Phone 171 935 3503, fax 171 935 7621; toll free in U.S. 1-800-457CHEF; Phone in U.S. 914-426-7400, fax in U.S. 914-426-0104; e-mail info@cordonbleu.net; Web site http://www.t-mark.com/cordonbleu.

There are a variety of excellent courses available at this school: three-day, four-day, five-day, one-month and ten-week. The courses range in scope from bread baking and cake decorating to patisserie. The rates vary accordingly. This is one of the outstanding teaching schools for a culinary career.

Leith's School of Food and Wine, 21 St Alban's Grove, London W8 5BP. Phone 171 229 0177, fax 171 937 5257; e-mail info@leiths.com.

The courses range from fish, dinner parties, holidays, beginner's, advanced, and varieties of food.

This school is mainly for students interested in careers as chefs, or in catering, hotel restaurants, freelance work, and food styling, but there are a few courses for amateurs, too. The school owns Leith's Restaurant, whose chef teaches in the classroom. There are many holiday, weekly wine courses, and evening courses available.

Le Manoir Aux Quat' Saisons, Ecole de Cuisine, Great Milton, Oxford OX44 7PD. Phone 1844 278881, fax in U.S. 214-373-1162; toll free in U.S. 1-800-845-4274; e-mail lemanoir@blanc.co.uk.

Located one hour by car or train from London's Paddington Station, this cooking school offers a residential four-day, five-night stay. You arrive on Sunday and depart on Friday. The package includes accommodations, meals, wine with dinner, and a final-night champagne dinner. Classes are limited to eight and are held in the two-star Michelin kitchen. Courses are held between October and April, off-season.

Roselyne Masselin's Vegetarian Cookery School, P.O. Box 70, Bushey Hall Drive, Bushey, Buckinghamshire WD2 2NQ. Phone 1923 250099, fax 1923 250030.

You get here by train from London's Euston Station to Bushey Station. There are a variety of courses. Half-day demonstration courses include Dinner Party Cooking, Thai Cuisine, and other interesting courses. There are also full-day, four-day, weekend, and one-day London demonstration courses.

Squires Kitchen International, School of Cake Decorations, Squires House, 3 Waverly Lane, Farnham, Surrey GU9 8BB. Phone 1252 711 749, fax 1252 714714, e-mail school@squires-group.co.uk.

Located 50 minutes from London via train from Waterloo Station, this is a school for both beginners and advanced students of cake decorations. Group or individual classes are available. Classes are one-, two-, or three-day, and are held year-round. Some of the courses offered are Sugarpaste, Marzipan, Miniature Flower Making, Beginner Sugar Flowers, Novelty Cakes, Chocolate, and Christmas Ideas.

GARDEN TOURS

The English love their gardens, and for very good reason. The weather is perfect for green grass (lots of rain and mild weather most of the year). English gardens are known for their beauty, and if you love getting down on your knees with a trowel, gardens here can teach you a lot. Garden tours for a week or more explore sites in London and throughout the countryside. One-day local London garden tours are also available. The following are garden-tour companies.

Expo Garden Tours, 70 Great Oak, Redding, CT. 06896. Phone 203-938-0410 or 1-800-448-2685, fax 203-938-0427; e-mail garden trav@aol.com.

This outstanding company specializes in one-week or more air/land packages from the U.S. If you are already in England, you can join the tour there. They also have tours in Ireland and Scotland. All May tours include the Chelsea Flower Show. Tours include membership in the Royal Horticultural Society.

Gentle Journeys. Escorted Day Tours from London, Park House, 140 Battersea Park Road, London SW11 4NB. Phone 171 720 4891, fax 171 720 0250; toll free in U.S. and Canada 1-800-873-7145; e-mail tours@gentlejourneys.co.uk; Web site www:gentlejourneys.co.uk.

Tours start in May and run through October, and include deluxe air-conditioned buses, entrance fees, speakers, and professional guides. Extended tours can also be arranged with accommodations and meals. Chelsea Flower Show and Hampton Court Flower Show are included in day tours; membership in the Royal Horticultural Society is also included. RHS Wisley Gardens are a highlight. Private tours can be arranged, too. If you want to learn how to take care of your own garden when you get home, join Spadework, a special five-day course in the art of gardening.

12. London Sports

Yes, you can jog in Regent's Park or do your aerobics almost anywhere in London, especially in some of the posh hotel fitness centers. (A case in point for the latter is the Meridien's fitness center, with its fabulous swimming pool, in Piccadilly.) But aside from keeping in shape, you may want to just sit on the sidelines and see how the British like their spectator sports. A few are similar to those found elsewhere; some, like cricket, are unique to this island and its former colonies.

SPECTATOR SPORTS

For more information on sports events, call Sportsline (171 222 8000). To purchase tickets, ask your hotel concierge or call one of the ticket agencies, such as First Call-Keith Prowse (1-800-669-8687 in the U.S. or 171 836 9001 in London).

Cricket

For this most essentially English of sports, go to the fashionable Lord's Cricket Ground near St. John's Wood in northwest London, or the less swanky Oval Cricket Ground in southeast London. Summer is cricket season. Phone Lord's at 171 289 1611; Oval at 171 582 6660.

Horse Racing

Who doesn't love a day at the races? The excitement of the race, lunch, the bar, or perhaps buying a souvenir all add up to a fun day.

With luck, included in that day are some winnings, but if you are careful you can go home happy even if you don't go home rich.

The racing season for flat racing is from March to November. The steeplechase season is from August to June. You'll note that both of these are primarily off-season events. There are many courses within easy reach of London:

Ascot Racecourse. Phone 1344 22211.

Inaugurated in 1711 by Queen Anne, this is one of the greatest racecourses in the world. The four-day Royal Meeting in June is world famous.

Cheltenham. Phone 1 242 513014.

One hundred and five miles west of London, major steeplechase races take place here, with The National Hunt Festival held annually in mid-March, off-season. On the last day, the Gold Cup is awarded.

Epsom Racecourse. Phone 372 470 047.

For the last two-hundred years the same mile-and-a-half track has been used here. The two best-known races held here are The Derby and the Gold Seal Oaks. (The politically incorrect ads for the latter state that it is "a day for ladies, since this is a race for fillies.")

Kempton Park Racecourse. Phone 932 782292.

Very easy to reach from London; the train goes directly to the track, and it is a short walk to the entrance. There is a two-day Christmas Festival, and during the summer there are day and evening meetings, the most interesting of which is the Racal Meeting (June), which includes a fireworks display and military bands playing pieces such as the "1812 Overture."

Royal Windsor Racecourse. Phone 753 865234.

Especially famous for the summer races held in the evening. There are eleven days of flat racing held between April and August, while jump racing is held from December to March, off-season. Children under 16 are admitted free.

Sandown Park. Phone 1372 463072.

Famous for its Whitbread Gold Cup and Coral-Eclipse Stakes held in July, both jumping races. The racecourse is one of the most modern and yet one of the prettiest.

Aintree Race Course in Liverpool. Phone 151 523 2600. Not near London, but hosts Britain's famous Grand National steeplechase. The race is held every March or April, off-season, and can be seen on television throughout the country.

Soccer ("Football")

London has three teams, but the least rough audiences are at Chelsea Football Club (phone 171 385 5545). Games are played from August through April, off-season, that is.

For soccer tickets (all teams), phone in the U.S. to Hotelink at 1-800-683-0799.

Rugby

Twickenham, Rugby Road, Twickenham. Phone 181 892 8161.

This stadium hosts regular games, international as well as the national cup finals. Tours are conducted of the stadium and the museum (the latter telling the history of rugby). The museum is open Tuesday to Saturday 10:30 to 5:00, Sunday 2:00 to 5:00. Reserve well in advance for all Rugby matches, as tickets sell out very quickly.

Tennis

If you want to sit in the center court at Wimbledon during the championships in late June and early July, you have to get in the lottery by writing (no phone calls) between September and December of the previous year, to All England Lawn Tennis Club, P.O. Box 98, Church Road, Wimbledon, London SW19 5AE, with a self-addressed, stamped envelope (British stamps or International Postal Coupon). Tickets for other court seats are frequently available on the site on the day of play. Phone 181 944 1144 for recorded information.

PARTICIPATORY SPORTS AND OUTDOOR ACTIVITIES

Bicycles in and around London

The first rule is caution. London, like most major cities, has a lot of horrendous traffic, so if you value your life, follow the rules. Ride in the local parks such as Hyde Park, Richmond Park, Battersea Park, and Hampstead Heath. Regent's Park does not permit bike riding. There are also routes along the Thames. If you are riding outside the parks, buy a London Cyclist's Route Map so that you return home safely at the end of a day.

RENTALS: Dial-A-Bike, 18 Gillingham Street, SW1. Phone 171 828 4040.

Bikes can be rented by the day, week, weekend, or any other combination that suits you. You can purchase insurance, which reduces the deposit fee.

Boating

Boating is a lot of fun, especially with children, and can be enjoyed off-season with as much pleasure as on-season. Two parks in London have rentals and lovely areas for boating. There are also restaurants nearby, as well as walking paths.

The Serpentine in Hyde Park and Regent's Park both have rowboats, canoes, and pedal boats.

The Docklands, east of the city, has four marinas, and rentals of all kinds. Here you can rent canoes, small sailboats, windsurfing equipment, and rowboats. Also, you can take lessons.

Waterskiing

Royal Docks Water-ski Club, Gate 16, King George V Dock, Woolwich Manor Way, E16. Phone 171 511 2000.

The only place to waterski in all of London. Who would have thought it?

Golf

There are many public and private courses in London. If you plan to play, we suggest that you bring your shoes and clubs. Clubs can be rented at some courses, but check ahead. Also bring proper golf attire, such as a golf shirt and golf slacks. Do not plan to play in a T-shirt and jeans.

Private clubs usually require a letter of introduction from your home club with your handicap certificate. Some clubs restrict play to certain days of the week. It is best to make your plans before leaving home.

An excellent book that lists all the golf courses in England, Scotland, Wales, and Ireland (Republic of Ireland and Northern Ireland) is *Sun-*

day Express Guide to Golf Courses, published by AA Publishing, Norfolk House, Priestley Road, Basingstoke, Hampshire RG24 9NY, England.

In Britain, as in most places, off-season golf is just as good as on-season golf.

Fitness Centers

Most hotels now have fitness centers, which require that you be a hotel guest or member. Many fitness centers are simply pay-as-you-go—you'll find them in the local phone book.

Jogging

Like bike riding, jogging can be dangerous unless you know where to run. Because of London's mild weather, it's possible to jog throughout the year, off-season and on. The best places are Hyde Park, St. James's Park, Regent's Park, and Hampstead Heath in northern London.

Tennis

INDOOR TENNIS: Islington Tennis Centre, Market Road, N7. Phone 171 700 1370. Daily 8:00 to 10:00. Must reserve ahead.

Coolhurst Lawn Tennis and Squash Rackets Club, Coolhurst Road, N8. Phone 181 340 6611. Reserve ahead.

OUTDOOR TENNIS: Credit cards are not accepted for reservations at most courts.

Regents Park. Reserve ahead in person. No phone reservations or inquiries. Daily from 7:00.

Holland Park. Phone 171 602 2226. No reservations; first come, first served, and busy. Daily from 8am to 9pm.

Hyde Park. Phone 171 298 2100. Reserve ahead in person two days prior to play. Daily 9:00 to 5:00.

Lincoln Inns Fields. Reserve ahead. Phone 171 405 1393 between 11:00 and 3:00. Daily from 8am.

Islington Tennis Centre, Market Road, N7 phone: 171 700 1370. Reservations required, but no membership required for indoor play.

Paddington Sports Club, Castelain Rd, W9. Phone 171 286 4515.

There are over 2,000 public tennis courts in and around London. For a complete list of courts, contact your hotel concierge or the Lawn Tennis Association Trust, Queen's Club, Palliser Road W14. Phone 171 385 4233.

Horse Riding

Make reservations in advance at any of these stables, or ask your hotel concierge:
Richard Briggs Riding Stables, 63 Bathurst Mews, W2. Phone 171 706 3806. Near Lancaster Gate and Kensington Gardens.

Ross Nye's Riding Establishment, 8 Bathurst Mews, W2. Phone 171 263 3791. Near Lancaster Gate and Kensington Gardens.

Roehampton Gate Stable, Priory Lane, SW15. Phone 181 876 7089. Out near the suburb of Putney.

13. London for Children

London is probably one of the best cities in the world, if not *the* best, to take children for a vacation. There is no end to what you can do and see: toy-soldier guards in red jackets and bearskin hats, famous monuments with dungeons and gore, historical sights they've read about in school, real princes and princesses, accessible parks, theaters, museums, indoor and outdoor activities, zoos, kid-friendly restaurants, movies, and boat trips, just to mention some of the activities you can do with young people. The best part of it all is that it is equally wonderful off-season and on, so you can spend Christmas in London as comfortably as you can a summer vacation.

Some of the sights we mention in this chapter are described in other parts of this book, so we will not do so extensively again. Here, we list only our very favorite places for children. Of course, there are other interesting activities, so if you are in London for any length of time, check with the tourist office for brochures on what more to do and see.

To avoid disappointment, it is always a good idea to check ahead to insure the places you want to go to are open. We are giving up-to-date times as of this writing, but especially when you have children along, it behooves you to do your homework first.

SIGHTS WE LOVE AND CHILDREN LOVE, TOO.

Big Ben.
    Located in Parliament Square and looming over the Houses of Parliament, Big Ben (the name of the tower, not the clock itself) is known to every child. If you stand on the bridge spanning the River Thames

here, you can get a better view of Big Ben than if you stand too close to it. It was completed in 1859. You can't go into the tower, or up it.

Buckingham Palace. St. James's Park. Phone 171 839 1377. Palace: August and September, daily 9:30 to 5:30. Ticket office opens at 9am. Mews: check exact opening date. Usually March to September, Tuesday to Thursday noon to 4:00, October to March, Wednesday noon to 4:00.

This palace is the home of the royal family, especially Queen Elizabeth II and her consort, Prince Philip. Every August and September (for a fee), you can visit the State Dining Room, The Grand Hall, Music Room, Silk Tapestry Room, and Green Drawing Room, as well as several galleries. The royal mews are open if you wish to visit the Queen's horses and see the beautiful carriages used for all state occasions. Both the palace and mews are wheelchair accessible.

Cabaret Mechanical Theatre, 33 Covent Garden Market.

Automated toys and figures, moving models, and the like can be operated by push buttons.

Changing of the Guard.

Held every other day at 11am. See page 22 for details, but also check ahead.

Commonwealth Experience. Kensington High Street. Phone 171 371 3530, fax 171 610 5346; Web site www.commonwealth.org.uk. Daily 10:00 to 5:00, closed December 18–25.

This is great fun. Two floors of exhibitions, a simulated helicopter ride over Malaysia, and other adventures around the world.

Covent Garden.

In the middle of the theater district, this area is busy at all times with shops, food stands, restaurants, musicians, artists, and just plain fun. The main area consists of covered markets selling crafts, ribbons, and anything you can think of buying, at very reasonable prices. The first Punch and Judy show was performed in Covent Garden in 1662, so it's logical that there is a Punch and Judy festival held in May (check the date with the tourist office) at St Paul's Churchyard, Covent Garden (Phone 171 240 2255).

Cutty Sark. King William Walk, Greenwich. Phone 181 858 3445. Open Monday to Saturday from 10:00 to 6:00, off-season until 5:00, closed Christmas Day, Christmas Eve, Boxing Day. See page 202.

This last and famous clipper ship has figureheads, relics, and displays of the tall sail ships.

Davenport's Magic Shop. Charing Cross Underground Shopping Arcade, the Strand. Phone 171 836 0408.
Wonderful magic equipment.

Hamleys Toy Store. 188 Regent Street. Phone 171 734 3161. Daily Monday to Saturday 10:00 to 7:00, Thursdays to 8:00.
London's largest toy store, with every price range available. Just be prepared to spend a lot of time here. There are five floors stocked with items children love.

Harrods. Knightsbridge. Phone 171 730 1234. Saturday, Monday, Tuesday 10:00 to 6:00, Wednesday to Friday until 7:00.
The most famous store in London, with a fabulous toy and children's department. (See page 119).

HMS Belfast. Morgan's Lane, Tooley Street. Phone 171 407 6434. Daily 10:00 to 6:00, off-season until 5:00. Closed Christmas Day, Boxing Day. Tube: London Bridge or Tower Hill.
This is Europe's last big-gun warship (a cruiser) from World War II. All seven decks are open for visitors, including the bridge, the boiler room, and the engine rooms. You can also see the gun turrets, sick bay, and lots more.

Lego Land. Windsor Park, Windsor, Berkshire. Phone 175 362 6111, fax 175 362 6113. Daily 10:00 to 6:00 off-season, July and August until 8:00 (check ahead).
LegoLand is twenty-five miles from London and can be reached by train in half an hour. It can also be reached by car or bus. Allow five hours to see the entire park. One admission fee covers all park activities. If you book in advance (by credit card), you get into the park through a special gate without waiting in line to pay. Paying at the gate during the season usually means waiting on long lines. The entire park is wheelchair accessible. Wheelchairs, baby strollers, and cameras can be rented at the park. Just a small sampling of what to do for the day: an Imagination Center, a "Miniland" built with over 25 million Lego bricks, My Town Wild Woods, shops, restaurants, shows, and a circus. In short, fun all day long.

London Aquarium. County Hall, Riverside Building, Westminster Ridge Road. Phone 171 967 8000. Weekdays 10:00 to 6:00, weekends and bank holidays 9:30 to 7:30, closed Christmas Day.
This is a fun, educational, and exciting exhibit, with hundreds of varieties of fish and sea life from around the world. There is a beach

pier where you can pet certain forms of sea life that swim close to the shore, supervised by the aquarium staff.

London Bridge.

The new London Bridge (not to be confused with the Tower Bridge) was built in 1973. It is not a must-see, but interesting to know about, mostly because of the old children's song, "London Bridge is Falling Down." The funny thing is, it *was* falling down and had to be replaced, so some investors in Arizona bought the old one in 1973 and moved it there, where you can see it (reinforced) today. The Tower Bridge, which many people incorrectly think is called London Bridge, is far more beautiful.

London Dungeon, 28-34 Tooley Street. Phone 171 403 0606. April to September daily 10:00 to 5:30, October to March daily 10:00 to 4:30, closed Christmas day. Some "kids" love this touristy place. If you scare easily it is not for you. See page 70.

London Toy & Model Museum. (See Museums, page 66)

Pollock's Toy Museum. 1 Scala Street. Phone 171 636 3452. Monday to Saturday 10:00 to 5:00. Pollock's displays wonderful old toys, and sells beautiful new reproductions. On view in the museum are teddy bears, puppets (with scenery), dolls from around the globe, doll houses, a toy theater, and more. The outdoor garden has a large model railroad and a carousel, while the basement has model towns.

Royal Air Force Museum. (See Museums, page 67)

Russian Submarine, Long's Wharf, Thames Barrier.

A real Russian sub, once one of the Soviet Union's largest, is available for inspection here.

Segaworld. Trocadero, Piccadilly Circus. Phone 171 990 5040. Daily 10:00 to midnight, Friday and Saturday until 1am. Closed Christmas Day.

This is definitely the largest indoor theme park in London. There are six floors of rides and experiences (rides and video games are an extra fee above the entrance fee). See chapter 6, Inauthentic Alternatives, also.

Tower of London. Tel. 171 709 0765. March to October, Monday to Saturday 9:00 to 6:00, Sunday 10:00 to 6:00; November to February, Monday to Saturday 9:00 to 5:00, Sunday 10:00 to 5:00. Some wheelchair access, but not to the entire area.

One of London's greatest and oldest landmarks, described in full in chapter 4. This is a *must* for children of all ages. Take the guided tour if you have the time; it is well worth it, and explains everything in detail. Don't miss the Crown Jewels. The Yeoman or Beefeaters still guard the Tower and still wear the Tudor outfit. They are very willing to stand next to a child and have their pictures taken.

Tower Bridge. Phone 171 378 1928. Daily April to October 10:00 to 6:30, November to March 9:30 to 6:00.

Wonderful views from the walkway across the towers, which you can reach either by stairs or in an elevator. There are also a museum and the Victorian engine room exhibit, the latter demonstrating how the bridge used to be opened prior to the installation of the electrically powered hydraulic machines used today.

Virgin Game Center. 14 Oxford Street. Phone 171 631 1234.

Biggest selection of computer and fantasy games.

Windsor Castle. See Windsor Castle, page 227.

MUSEUMS FOR CHILDREN

There are many excellent museums for children—depending on the child's age or interests, you can decide what you want to see. Here are a few suggestions. Most of the major London museums mentioned in chapter five also have exhibits that children enjoy. Call ahead for exact exhibits and the age they are geared for.

Tower Bridge

Tower of London Modern Myths

The Tower has not always been a scene only of death. Ordinary people, the warders, lived there, too, and even in modern times, people are born there—though very few.

In a conversation we had not too long ago with the then Chief Yeoman Warder of the Tower of London, we asked a lot of questions about modern life inside the walls. We were intrigued, because a friend had been born in the Tower while his father was the governor there; we wanted to know if this happened very often. The Chief Yeoman Warder assured us it did not, pointing out that most governors (usually army generals) have wives past child-bearing age.

The Chief Yeoman Warder also implied that Rudolph Hess, contrary to popular belief, was not the last prisoner to be held in the Tower. He murmured vaguely something about "wartime and that sort of thing" when pressed for the identity of later inmates.

And our friend, who came into the world in the Tower? We asked him once whether there was any advantage to being born there, his mother having called in a midwife instead of going to a hospital. "Sure," he said, "I'm probably the only person most people will ever meet in their lives who can say he was born in the Tower of London!"

Ask a foolish question . . .

Bethnal Green Museum of Childhood. Cambridge Heath Road, Bethnal Green. Phone 181 980 3204 or 181 980 2415 (information). Monday to Thursday, Saturday 10:00 to 6:00; Sunday 2:30 to 5:15.

This museum houses the largest toy collection in the world. Included here are doll houses of every period, teddy bears, train sets, antique dolls, soldiers, marionettes, battle toys, children's clothing, and everything else to do with children and childhood.

British Museum. Great Russell Street. Phone 171 636 1555; wheelchair accessible.

This museum is huge and wonderful for kids, but can be taken in small doses. We love the museum's Quiz Trails, which you can get at the information desk. You can follow one trail or area of interest instead of wandering all over the place.

Greenwich National Maritime Museum. See chapter 14, Day Trips From London.

London Toy and Model Museum. 21-23 Craven Hill, Bayswater. Phone 171 402 5222; limited wheelchair accessibility. Monday to Saturday 10:00 to 5:30, Sunday and bank holiday Monday opens at 11am.

This is a "fun" museum, located in a town house converted into rooms full of toys, games, and dolls. The garden has a miniature electric railroad with trains you can ride on.

London Transport Museum. Covent Garden. Phone 171 379 6344. Daily 10:00 to 3:00, closed December 24–26.

This is an excellent museum for children interested in historic buses, trams, and trains, telling the story of London transportation. There are hands-on exhibits, which are always fun. Children can also sit in the driver's seat of a (nonmoving!) bus. There is a resource center for older children. Excellent gift shop with books, maps, and posters, all dealing with transportation.

Madame Tussaud's. Marylebone Road. Phone 171 935 6861; limited wheelchair access. October to March 10:00 to 5:30, April to September 9:00 to 5:30.

This museum is extremely popular, so it is a good idea to buy tickets ahead of time. Included in the museum are the wax figures of celebrities, presidents, rock stars, royalty, and sports figures. Kids love it, but . . . See also chapter 6, Inauthentic Alternatives.

Museum of the Moving Image, South Bank, underneath Waterloo Bridge, Waterloo. Phone 171 401 2636. Daily 10:00 to 6:00, closed Christmas Day and Boxing Day.

We love this museum, which features the history of film. You can audition to "star" in a film, or read the TV news as an announcer, and in general have a lot of fun. You also can see classic old films in the theater. Restaurant for lunch or dinner.

National Gallery. See chapter 5, Museums and Churches.

National Portrait Gallery, St. Martin's Place. Phone 171 306 0055; wheelchair accessible through Orange Street only. Monday to Saturday 10:00 to 6:00, Sunday noon to 6:00, closed January 1, Good Friday, May Day, December 24–26.

This museum has a wonderful collection of royals and politicians, as well as a few sports figures (cricketers among them!). You can also see portraits of present-day royals.

Natural History Museum. Cromwell Road. Phone 171 938 9123; wheelchair accessible. Daily 10:00 to 5:30, Sunday opens at 11am, closed December 23–26.

An incredible museum if your child loves dinosaurs, whales, stuffed animals, a rain forest, and a Discovery Center, the latter full of hands-on activities. Outside is a wildlife garden, opened in 1994.

RAF Museum, Royal Air Force, Grahame Park Way, Hendon. Phone 181 205 2266 or 181 205 9191(24-hour information). Daily 10:00 to 6:00, closed Christmas Eve, Christmas Day, Boxing Day, New Year's Day.

The national museum of aviation tells the story of flight, with seventy aircraft, including the Spitfire and the Harrier. There is also a flight simulator, so you can know what it feels like to fly through a tornado. Free parking, plus a restaurant and shop.

Science Museum: Exhibition Road. Phone 171 938 8000. Daily 10:00 to 6:00, Sunday from 11:00 to 6:00.

There are four excellent galleries devoted to the Garden, Things, the Network, and On Air. There is a Launch Pad space gallery, with experiments that can be done by children. You can experience test flights in the Flight Lab, which has twenty-four hands-on exhibits. Also: a Food For Thought Gallery about food, an Energy Bike exhibit, and the Apollo 10 capsule.

Victoria and Albert Museum. South Kensington. Phone 171 938 8500; wheelchair accessible. Monday noon to 5:30, all other days from 10:00.

This museum houses the largest collection of decorative art and design in the world. They have a fabulous dress collection. Part of this museum is the Bethnal Green Museum of Childhood, see previous listings.

RESTAURANTS THAT "KIDS" LOVE

See "Children's" Food Out in chapter 9, "Where to Eat in London."

PARKS FOR CHILDREN AND GROWNUPS, TOO

There are many more parks than those described below, but we think these are enough for a short visit to London. If you need more information on additional parks, contact the Tourist Office. Many parks have what is known as a One O'clock Club. This club is for preschool children accompanied by an adult. The activities are held inside and out, depending on the time of year and the weather.

Greenwich Park, Greenwich (see section on Greenwich in our "Sightseeing London" chapter for more information). Wheelchair accessible.

This park was built in 1433 by Henry VI.

Hyde Park. Wheelchair accessible.

This is a wonderful and beautiful park right in the center of the city, with loads of things to do. There are tennis courts, which can be reserved in advance. You can swim from May until the end of September in the Serpentine here, where there are also rowboats, paddle boats, and canoes for rent (at the boat house on the north side of the Serpentine). You can also ride horseback on the paths all year round. The Hyde Park stables are located at 63 Bathurst Mews (Phone 171 723 2813 or 171 706 3806). There are also playing fields and walking paths. After all of this activity, you may need a rest or a cup of tea. The Dell Restaurant is located at the Hyde Park corner of the Serpentine and is open daily from 9am to 6pm, off-season until 5:30pm. There are many kiosks serving refreshments throughout the park, too.

Kensington Gardens. West of Hyde Park. Wheelchair accessible.

Here you'll find a playground, a dog cemetery, the Round Pond for sailing model boats, and plenty of room just to run. There is also the stump of an oak tree with carvings of animals, fairies, and gnomes. This is a favorite place for parents and/or nannies to bring their children any time of the year.

Regent's Park. Wheelchair accessible.

The park has three playgrounds, the London Zoo, and lakes for boating. The excellent zoo, founded in 1829, has more than ten thousand animals, many of which can be petted (in the Touch Paddock), especially fun for young children. The main zoo has rare animals from around the world. Everyone always loves the penguins, which you can watch playing on slides and ramps. If you get hungry, you can stop at one of the two restaurants.

St. James's Park. Wheelchair accessible.

The highlight of this park are the pelicans, which live in a sanctuary here. You can watch them being fed at 3pm daily.

Hampstead Heath. Limited wheelchair accessible.

Hampstead Heath covers more than seven hundred acres, with beautiful woodlands, meadows, ponds, and views. There is plenty of running space here, and you can fish in the ponds. For athletes, there are cricket pitches, football fields, golf, horseback riding, tennis, and swimming. The village of Hampstead is fun to explore, too, with several lovely restaurants in all price ranges.

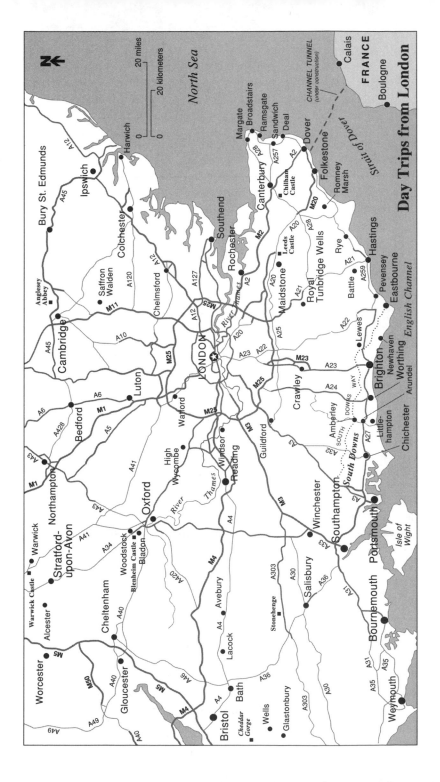

Day Trips from London

North Sea

English Channel

Strait of Dover

FRANCE

CHANNEL TUNNEL
(under construction)

20 miles

20 kilometers

Calais
Boulogne

Dover
Folkestone
Deal
Sandwich
Ramsgate
Broadstairs
Margate
Romney
Marsh
Canterbury
A2
A257
A28
Chilham
Castle

Hastings
Rye
Battle
A21
A259
Pevensey
Eastbourne
Leeds
Castle
A20
Royal
Tunbridge Wells
Maidstone
A20
A21
Rochester
A2
M2
Southend
A127
Chelmsford
A12
A120
Colchester
Harwich
Ipswich
A45
Bury St. Edmunds
Saffron
Walden
Anglesey
Abbey
M11
Cambridge
A10
A45
A6
Luton
A6
Bedford
A428
A5
M1
Northampton
M1
A43
Stratford-
upon-Avon
Warwick
Warwick Castle
Alcester
A41
A34
Woodstock
Blenheim Castle
Bladon
Oxford
A40
Cheltenham
Worcester
M5
Gloucester
M50
M5
A49
A40
A46
A40
Bristol
Bath
A4
Lacock
A46
M4
Cheddar
Gorge
Wells
Glastonbury
A303
A30
Salisbury
A36
A303
Stonehenge
A30
A30
A303
Avebury
A4
High
Wycombe
Windsor
Reading
M4
M40
Thames
River
A4
A329
Guildford
M3
A3
Winchester
A31
A33
Southampton
A3
Bournemouth
A31
A35
A31
Weymouth
A35
A354
Portsmouth
Isle of
Wight
Chichester
Littlehampton
Arundel
Worthing
Newhaven
Brighton
A23
M23
A24
Crawley
A22
A23
A25
A22
Lewes
South Downs
SOUTH DOWNS WAY
Amberley
A27
A259
London
M25
A12
A1(M)
River Thames
A20
Watford
Leeds
North Sea

14. Day Trips From London

When you arrive in any city, town, or village, you should take a bus tour if one is available, to get an overview of where you are and what you want to see. This is especially important for one-day trips. On a single day you cannot possibly see everything. Even a one-hour bus tour from the center of town will point out the highlights, and then as time permits, you can go back to see what interests you most. Day trips are an excellent way to see the countryside, but if time allows, stay more than a day in the places that have more to see. Read on and discover the highlights of visiting some of the wonderful towns within a two-hour radius of London.

Even Paris, Dublin, and Edinburgh are included, because—especially if you are visiting Europe for the first time—you can see one of these remarkable places on a day trip by air, train, or ferry.

Each day trip included in this section has been picked because it is special. Remember, stay longer than a day if you can.

A reminder when calling any of the British sights, hotels, or restaurants in this section:

If calling from the U.S: dial 011 44 plus city code and phone number. Omit any zero (0) appearing before the city code.

If calling from the UK: dial 0 plus city code and phone number.

ALDEBURGH, SUFFOLK COUNTY

Aldeburgh (pronounced "Ald-burrah") is a charming seaside town and summer resort on the North Sea. Its High Street, the main street in town, has dozens of interesting cottages and shops, while the beach is only a street away. On the beach, a lifeboat is always at the ready.

Fishermen sell their fresh fish daily here. Two miles up the road is Thorpeness, another seaside village, and smaller yet.

Tourist Information Center: The Cinema, High Street, Aldeburgh, Suffolk IP1 5 5AU. Phone 172 845 3637.

How to get to Aldeburgh (and Snape, where the concerts are held)

BY CAR FROM LONDON: Get directions to the A12, on which you bypass Ipswich in the direction of Lowestoft. Take the A1094 Aldeburgh Road off the A12. For Snape, turn right at Snape Church.

BY TRAIN FROM LONDON: The train from London's Liverpool Street Station to Ipswich takes 1 hour, 10 minutes. From Ipswich, you can rent a car or change trains to Saxmundham station. There, take a taxi, which you can reserve ahead by calling 172 860 2344 or 604090.

Rental cars. Europcar: Phone 147 321 1067; Hertz: Phone 147 321 8506.

Aldeburgh is famous for its festivals and concerts, held throughout the year. Its most famous resident was the composer Benjamin Britten, who lived here from 1947 until his death in 1976. Many of his works were first heard in Aldeburgh, including the most famous of his operas, *Peter Grimes*, in 1945. The opera is based on a poem by George Crabbe, a local writer. The Festival celebrated its fiftieth anniversary in June 1997. Each year, there are lunchtime concerts, touring-company concerts, operas, and Christmas concerts, plus, of course, the highlight—the annual Benjamin Britten concerts.

You should reserve tickets ahead if possible. Aldeburgh can be a day trip or an overnight; there are lovely places to stay in the area.

The address for Festival tickets is: Aldeburgh Festival Box Office, High Street, Aldeburgh, Suffolk IP15 5AX, England. Phone from the U.S.: 011 44 1 728 453543. Tickets may be paid for with all major credit cards. Although the festival is called the Aldeburgh Festival, the concert hall is in nearby Snape.

There are many options, so write ahead for a program. Discounts, standby tickets, and a special Sunday offer are all available. Disabled patrons are accommodated at all events; inform the box office by mail when you reserve your tickets. There is wheelchair space, as well as parking space and headsets for the hearing impaired.

Where to stay if you overnight in the area

Some suggestions: Please realize that some of these hotels are small, local places. Some have as few as two bedrooms, so be sure to call ahead so as not to be disappointed. If you call for reservations, be sure to ask all the questions, such as, whether there is a bathroom and shower in the room, whether they serve breakfast, if you can walk to the concert hall or how do you get there.

The other alternative if you have come by car is to overnight in Ipswich, which is a large town with much to do and see. See Ipswich, later in this chapter.

There is a central booking service for local hotels and bed and breakfast places. Phone 172 845 3637.

Adnams Hotels has three hotels in the Southwold area: the Swan. Phone 1502 722186; the Crown. Phone 1502 722275; the Cricketers, Phone 1502 723603. All three have nice accommodations, good restaurants, and wine lists.

Kiln Farm, Benhall. Phone 1728 603166, fax 1728 604401.
B & B, children and pets welcome.

Brudenell Hotel, Aldeburgh IP15 5BU. Phone 1728 452071, fax 1728 454082; Toll free in U.S. 1-800-225-5843.
At the southern end of town, overlooking the sea. Rooms with hair dryer, radio, TV, phone. Facilities include an elevator, restaurant, and bar.

Earl Soham Lodge. Phone 1728 685473.
B & B serving evening meals. Rural area.

Grange Farm, Dennington. Phone 1986 798388.
B & B serving dinner. Beautiful fourteenth-century moated house, with gardens and tennis court.

Ocean House. Phone 1728 452094. Sea-front house in Aldeburgh.
All rooms with TV and sea view. Breakfast served.

Seckford Hall, Woodbridge IP13 6NU. Phone 1394 385678.
Country-house hotel with indoor heated pool, eighteen-hole golf course. Dinner served.

Sternfield House, Saxmundham. Phone 1728 602252, fax 1728 604082.
Beautiful house, with swimming pool and tennis court, two miles from concert hall.

Theberton Grange Hotel. Phone 1728 830625.
Country house on beautiful grounds, ten minutes from Snape.

The White Lion Hotel, Aldeburgh, IP15 5BJ. Phone 1728 452720, fax
1728 452986; toll free in U.S. 1-800-528-1234.
This is a small, sixteenth-century hotel overlooking the sea. Rooms
with bath, TV, phone, room service. Facilities include two restaurants
and bar. Pets allowed.

The Wentworth Hotel, Wentworth Road, Aldeburgh, Suffolk IP15
5BD. Phone 1728 452312, fax 1728 454343.
Located on the beach, the Wentworth is considered Aldeburgh's
best hotel. The hotel boasts thirty-eight beautifully furnished rooms,
most with bathrooms and sea views. All rooms have TV, radio, and
direct-dial phones. Restaurant with excellent English and French
food and good wines; local fish is a highlight. If you want to play golf,
there are two excellent courses nearby, and the hotel staff will
arrange tee times.

Restaurants

152 High Street, Aldeburgh. Phone 1728 454152.
Open 10am for breakfast and lunch and preconcert dinners.

Adnams Hotels. Phone, see Where to Stay.
Three good restaurants and wine lists.

Butley-Orford Oysterage. Phone 1394 450277.
Seafood restaurant, open daily for lunch and dinner.

Captain's Cabin Restaurant, Aldeburgh. Phone 1728 452520.
Lunch, tea and preconcert dinner.

Concert Hall Restaurant at Snape Maltings. Phone 1728 688130.
Open before and after concerts.

The Lighthouse, Aldeburgh. Phone 1728 453377.
Lunch and dinner served.

Plough and Sail, also the South Bar Restaurant, both at Snape Maltings Concert Hall. Phone South Bar 1728 688130. Reserve ahead.
Open before and after concerts.

Regatta, 171-173 High Street, Aldeburgh. Phone 1728 452011, closed
Monday, Tuesday off-season. Wheelchair access.
Specialties are local fish and local game in season.

The Wentworth Hotel Restaurant. See address and phone number listed in Where to Stay, above.

Be sure to try the local fish, lobster, and crab. Good wine list.

Sightseeing in and around Aldeburgh

Aldeburgh Bookshop.

Good selection for such a small town.

Aldeburgh Moot Hall and Museum. Tel. 1728 452871. Call ahead for opening times.

A sixteenth-century town hall and museum containing items of local interest. Photographs show life in Aldeburgh and its fishing industry, its lifeboat and crews.

River Trips from Snape Quay, depending on the tide. Phone 1728 688303.

Snape Maltings Riverside Centre.

Six shops and galleries, open daily all year. The Christmas shop is open from September to December. Granary Tea shop serves home-cooked food. The River Bar and Plough and Sail Pub are also open daily all year, 10am to 6pm, winter until 5pm.

Tudor House Gallery, High Street, Aldeburgh. Phone 1728 454280.

Paintings based on Benjamin Britten's music. Call ahead to be sure when they are open.

The Church of St. Peter and St. Paul.

Overlooking the town, it has memorials to famous Aldeburgh residents. Benjamin Britten is buried here, as is Elizabeth Garrett Anderson, the first woman in England to become a physician. She was also the first woman mayor of Aldeburgh.

BATH, SOMERSET COUNTY

Bath is 107 miles, and one hour and twenty minutes by train from Paddington Station. The town is a wonderful day trip if you are short of time, but if possible, you should give yourself a treat and spend a few days here. There is a lot to do and see, with beautiful hotels and excellent restaurants. We think Bath is a must if you have just enough time for one out-of-London day. There won't be time to rest, so get ready for a full, exciting day.

Bath offers rolling hills, beautiful architecture, shopping, dining, wonderful atmosphere, and plenty of walking if you have good shoes for that—a must, in our opinion.

If you are in Bath for just a day, be sure to take a double-decker bus tour for an hour to see the highlights, then continue on your own. Most sights of major importance are around the Roman Bath area. You might also like to take a free guided walking tour of the city. Ask at the tourist office for the location where the walks begin.

Tourist center: Abbey Chambers, Bath BA1 1LY. Phone 1225 477101 or 1225 462831. Not all sights are wheelchair accessible. Ask at the tourist center.

Roman Baths and Pump Room. Daily 9:00 to 6:00, off-season until 5pm.

The baths were discovered in 1879 by the borough engineer while digging sewers. The Roman baths are probably one of Britain's major tourist spots, and people come from all over the world for the waters, which you can sample in the Pump Room. Take the tour to understand fully the history of the baths. The Great Bath is a wonderfully preserved pool that is open. Then there are small baths; the Kings Bath and the Circular Bath. The baths were reserved by the Romans for men only. The water is always 112 degrees Fahrenheit. Just do not try to put a finger in the water today, even if you are a man. After the tour of the baths, continue to the Pump Room, where you can sample the spa water.

Roman Baths Museum, Stall Street. Daily except December 25–26.

This museum is next to the Baths and worth a visit. Here you will get a good overview of the history of the Baths.

Bath Abbey. Daily.

The Abbey was begun in 1499 and completed in the seventeenth century. It is next to the Baths, Pump Room, and Museum.

Assembly Rooms and Museum of Costume, Bennett Street. Daily March to October. 9:30 to 6:00; off-season 10:00 to 5:00. Closed December 25–26.

Built in 1769 by John Wood, these rooms were the center of the elite social life of Bath. The museum displays clothing from the sixteenth century up to the present time.

Royal Crescent.

Designed in 1767 by John Wood the Younger, this is a gorgeous street with thirty houses joined together with 114 Ionic columns. It is considered the most beautiful street in Britain.

No. 1 Royal Crescent. Tuesday to Sunday 11:00 to 5:00; mid-December to February 11:00 to 4:00; closed Good Friday.
Restored interior of eighteenth-century house.

The Circus, Brock Street.
The Circus, a circular group of Georgian houses, is considered the best work of John Wood the Elder.

American Museum, Claverton Manor. Phone 1225 460503. April to October; off-season, call them, because it has been under consideration to keep the museum open daily throughout the year.
Founded in 1961, the museum has an exhibit showing George Washington's Mount Vernon garden of 1785. Also on display are Shaker American furniture and Native American Art.

Holburne of Menstrie Museum, Great Pulteney Street. Daily Tuesday to Saturday 11:00 to 5:00, Sunday 2:30 to 6:00. Closed mid-December to mid-February.
Paintings by British artists such as Gainsborough, and displays of silver, porcelains, and twentieth-century craft works.

Pulteney Bridge.
Built in 1774, it spans the Avon River, and is one of the few remaining bridges in Europe that is still lined with shops.

There are other splendid sights in Bath, such as the medieval Covered Market, which is still being used today.

If you come by car and are staying for more than a day, there are some nice side trips after you have seen and enjoyed Bath. Castle Combe near Bath has old stone houses and a babbling brook, and once was cited by the English Tourist Board as "the most beautiful village in England." Wells, near Bath, is famous for its cathedral. East of Bath is Salisbury, with its magnificent cathedral, and Stonehenge, famous for its prehistoric stone circle right in the middle of Salisbury Plain.

HOTELS

Expensive

Bath Spa Hotel, Sydney Road, Bath BA2 6JF. Phone 1225 444424, fax 1225 444006; toll free in U.S. 1-800-225-5843.
Restored Georgian mansion set in beautiful gardens, a ten-minute walk from the center of Bath. Beautifully decorated bedrooms with

private bath, TV, radio, phone, minibar. The hotel is wheelchair accessible, and has an indoor pool, spa pool, gym, outdoor tennis, and croquet. Free parking.

The Priory Hotel, Weston Road, Bath BA1 2XT. Phone 1225 331922, fax 1225 448276.

Located one mile from Bath in a residential area, this is a Gothic setting, not the typical Georgian setting of the area. Bath Golf Course is next door, so if you are interested in golf, ask all the right questions when you book. Beautiful rooms with flowers and books to make you feel at home. Wheelchair accessible, excellent restaurant.

Royal Crescent Hotel, 16 Royal Crescent, Bath BA1 2LS. Phone 1225 739955, fax 1225 339401.

Located in two Georgian townhouses in the famous Crescent, with lovely views of the city and countryside. Beautiful rooms with bath, TV, four poster beds, antique furniture, room service. Facilities include a garden and croquet. Excellent French restaurant called Dower House.

Moderate

The Queensberry Hotel, Russell Street, Bath BA1 2QF. Phone 1225 447928, fax 1225 446065. Closed Christmas week.

Located in three Georgian townhouses, this has been a very popular hotel for many years, and rightfully so. Lovely garden, close to the center of Bath, TV, phone, flowers, bottled water in very pretty rooms. Room service twenty-four hours per day; tea served in drawing room. The Olive Tree Restaurant, located in the hotel, is very popular with locals as well as guests.

TEA

The Canary Restaurant, 3 Queen Street, Bath. Phone 1225 424846; wheelchair accessible. Open daily.

Located near Trim Bridge on a cobbled street.

RESTAURANTS

There are many excellent and not so excellent restaurants of various price ranges in Bath. We offer just a few to get you started. Most hotels we have suggested also have restaurants.

Expensive

Vellore, at the Bath Spa Hotel, Sydney Road. Bath Phone 1225 444424. Dinner only except for Sunday lunch.

Excellent food, service and wine list. Considered one of the best restaurants in Bath.

Moderate

Hole in the Wall, 16 George Street. Bath Phone 1225 425242. Closed Sunday, and December 25–26.

Typical excellent British food. This is a well-known restaurant and an old-time favorite.

Moon and Sixpence, 6A Broad Street. Bath Phone 1225 460962.

Popular local restaurant with good value.

BLENHEIM PALACE (LOCATED IN WOODSTOCK, OXFORDSHIRE)

Tourist Office, Hensington Road, OX20 1JQ. Woodstock, Oxfordshire Phone 1993 811038 (summer only).

If you do not visit Blenheim Palace at the same time you visit Oxford, it can be done on another day. Depart from London's Paddington Station for the one-hour trip to Oxford, then change to a local bus. There is also bus service from London's Victoria Coach Station to Oxford, from where you take the local bus to Woodstock.

Blenheim (pronounced "Blen-um") Palace is only eight miles north of Oxford, so when visiting Oxford check ahead to see if the Palace is open, too. This outstanding "home" is one of England's greatest stately mansions, with 200 rooms and 2,000 acres of parkland. Blenheim was built in the early eighteenth century for the first Duke of Marlborough. Sir Winston Churchill, grandson of the seventh duke, was born here in 1874 while his mother (an American) was visiting. There is a very interesting display of his belongings. Churchill and his family are buried in Bladon village, which is near the palace, in which the eleventh duke presently lives. Open: Mid-March to October, daily 10:30–5:30pm daily. Last admission 4:45.

What to do and see at Blenheim Palace

Be sure to get a map of the Palace and grounds when you pay to enter. You can spend the day exploring if you wish.

The Triumphal Arch is your first sight at the palace, which has been continuously occupied by dukes of Marlborough since it was built. The Arch was a monument to the first duke.

In order to see the gorgeous interior, it is best to take one of the guided tours, which last about an hour. The Long Library, planned as a picture gallery, is one of the highlights. The Green Drawing Room has a full-length portrait of the fourth duke. Note also the Red Drawing Room, Green Writing Room, state rooms, and the Winston Churchill memorabilia. After enjoying the inside, be sure to explore the outside. Boat rides are available on the lake, or you can rent a rowboat and get your exercise. The Butterfly House has tropical butterflies living in an almost natural habitat. The Marlborough Maze, (extra charge), the world's largest hedge maze, is great fun.

If time permits, visit the village of Woodstock before heading back to London. You might want to stop for lunch or dinner in town. Park Street, the main drag, has a County museum (open daily), the town stocks, and the local church.

Local restaurants

There are a number of restaurants at the Palace open for lunch.

The village of Woodstock also has a few inns, pubs, and restaurants.

Feathers, Market Street. Phone 1993 813158, fax 1993 813158. Open daily.

Located in the town center, the restaurant (it's also a small hotel) is attractive and boasts good food. Local game is popular during the season. Other dishes are lobster, grilled tuna, and chicken. The hotel is nicely furnished.

The Chef Imperial, 22 High Street. Phone 1193 813593, fax 1193 813591. Open daily except December 25–27.

This is a Chinese restaurant on the main street in Woodstock. The menu features Peking and Szechuan dishes.

BRIGHTON, EAST SUSSEX COUNTY

Brighton Station is 55 minutes by train from London's Victoria Station.

Brighton is a seaside resort, but it has much more to offer the visitor than the water, which is usually cold. Brighton started as a fishing village known as Brighthelmstone. The town became fashionable in 1786 when the Prince Regent (later to become George IV) came here to live with his mistress, Maria Fitzherbert, who later became his wife.

Tourist Office: 10 Bartholomew Square. Phone 1273 323755. Pick up the Visitor's Guide with a map and list of the sights to see in Brighton.

The Royal Pavilion on the Steine (or waterfront). Daily off-season 10:00 to 5:00, June to September to 6:00. Phone 1273 603005. Tearoom (in the Pavilion on the 2nd floor) October to May 10:00 to 5:00, June to September 10:00 to 6:00.

The pavilion was built in 1815 for the Prince. When Queen Victoria came to see the pavilion, she was horrified and wanted it demolished. The people of Brighton saved it by purchasing it from the Queen in 1850. Since restored to its original splendor; the pavilion is fully furnished. The Pavilion has many different styles of architecture and decor, including (realistically or in fantasy form) Chinese, Egyptian, Oriental, and a variety of other styles that you will have to try and figure out by yourself. It is marvelous and weird at the same time.

Other sights in Brighton worth seeing

Brighton Museum and Art Gallery, Church Street, on the grounds of the Pavilion. Daily except Wednesday 10:00 to 5:00, Sunday 2:00 to 5:00.

The collection consists of 19th- and 20th-century art. Free to public.

In May the annual Brighton Arts Festival is a highlight. Check the dates with the tourist office.

Horse racing is another attraction in Brighton. Check with the tourist office for the racing schedule.

The Lanes is an area in the center of Brighton and is the oldest part of town. On its narrow streets, fishermen's cottages have been turned into pretty shops, restaurants, antique shops, jewelry shops, and boutiques. It has become a pedestrian area, making it ideal for wandering and snooping. You might stop for lunch at one of the seafood restaurants or pubs in the area.

The Brighton Marina is one of the largest in Europe. There is now a village in the marina with homes, cinemas, shops, seaside restaurants and pubs. During the summer there are boat shows.

Volk Electric Railway. Daily from Easter to Labor Day.
Built in 1883 and still running, this is a ride along the sea front.

The Brighton Sea Life Centre. Phone 1273 604234. Daily 10:00 to 6:00 off-season, open later in the summer.
Wonderful for children.

Walking Tour: Guided tours of Brighton's old town are held daily during the summer. The tours start at the information center.

Near Brighton is Glyndebourne, famous for its excellent summer opera season (see chapter 2, the Calendar).

Lunch

Browns, 3-4 Duke Street. Phone 1273 323501. Daily 11:00 to 11:30.
Located near the Lanes, this is an excellent family bistro. Food is served all day—Brunch, lunch, tea, or dinner. Specialties include pasta, salads, salmon. Moderate price.

One Paston Place, 1 Paston Place. Phone 1273 606933. Lunch Tuesday to Friday and Sunday, dinner Tuesday to Saturday.
Mostly French food, featuring homemade soups, salads, fish, and lovely desserts. Moderate price.

CAMBRIDGE, CAMBRIDGESHIRE COUNTY

Cambridge is a one-hour train trip from King's Cross Station or Liverpool Street Station, both in London. If you come by car, you must park and walk. Drivers are barred from the town center daily from 10am to 4pm. You can also come by bus from London's Victoria Bus Station. The bus takes approximately two hours.

We think Cambridge requires more than one day to see it all, but if this is a day trip, do the best you can. Staying overnight makes it a memorable visit. There is a lot to do and see.

Tourist office: Wheeler Street. Phone 1223 322640, fax 1223 463385 Summer, Monday to Friday 9:00 to 6:00, Saturday 9:00 to 5:00, Sunday 10:30 to 3:30. Winter Monday, Tuesday, Thursday, Friday, 9:00 to 5:30, Wednesday 9:00 to 9:30.

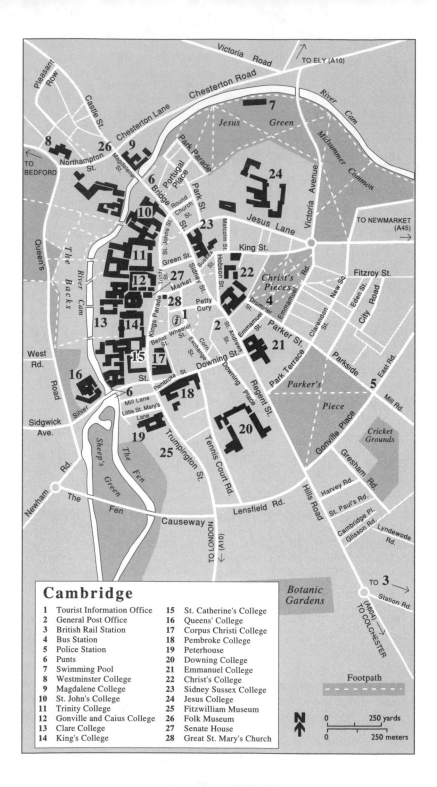

Cambridge

1 Tourist Information Office
2 General Post Office
3 British Rail Station
4 Bus Station
5 Police Station
6 Punts
7 Swimming Pool
8 Westminster College
9 Magdalene College
10 St. John's College
11 Trinity College
12 Gonville and Caius College
13 Clare College
14 King's College
15 St. Catherine's College
16 Queens' College
17 Corpus Christi College
18 Pembroke College
19 Peterhouse
20 Downing College
21 Emmanuel College
22 Christ's College
23 Sidney Sussex College
24 Jesus College
25 Fitzwilliam Museum
26 Folk Museum
27 Senate House
28 Great St. Mary's Church

Botanic Gardens

Footpath

N

0   250 yards

0   250 meters

At the tourist office you can book a tour of Cambridge's colleges and also buy tickets for the Guide Friday open-top hop-on-hop-off buses. Here you can also buy the Cambridge Mini-Guide, which has all of the information needed for touring the colleges and museums, as well as a good street map. Join a walking tour, accompanied by a Blue Badge Guide. Tours leave daily year round from the tourist office. For information call 1223 322640 or 463290,

Travelers with Disabilities: Cambridge is very easy for the disabled. Free scooters and wheelchairs can be borrowed from the Shop-mobility Centre at Lion Yard car park, 9th floor, Monday to Saturday 10:00 to 4:00. To reserve ahead, call 1 223 46 33 70. The disabled can get an orange badge which allows for free parking at meters as well as at pay-and-display parking spots and other parking areas. These can be obtained at the tourist office.

Cambridge is an excellent all-season city to visit. Note that the colleges may be closed during exams from May to mid-June, and museums are usually closed on Mondays.

Start your visit to Cambridge with Market Square, where an outdoor market is held daily except Sunday. Great St. Mary's Church here is the University Church. You can climb to the tower for an overview of the city.

Continue on to King's College, founded in 1441 by King Henry VI and finally completed in 1536. Visit the chapel with the carved coats of arms of King Henry VIII. It took 70 years to complete the structure, with its magnificent, stone fan-vaulted roof. The impressive stained-glass windows tell stories of the Old and New Testaments. Also see the *Adoration of the Magi* by Rubens, which hangs behind the altar (traditionalists had a fit when this work of "profane" art was first placed there a few decades ago.) If possible, return for Evensong, held daily except Mondays during the school year.

Trinity, the largest college, was founded in 1546 by King Henry VIII. The Great Gate here leads to the Great Court, one of the most magnificent in Europe. Visit the gorgeous Wren Library, built by Sir Christopher Wren in 1676. It houses some early works of Shakespeare and an original manuscript of *Winnie-the-Pooh*.

A tour of the city by boat is also a real treat. The River Cam can be navigated by punt, rowboat, or canoe. Also, walk along the Backs, which are the gardens alongside the river, from which you get an entirely different view of the colleges and their gardens and lawns.

Punting on the Cam

Punting is not as easy as it looks. You steer and propel the light punt with the same long pole. The difficulty comes when you jam the pole too deep into the muddy bottom of the river, push to propel the boat, then find you can't pull the pole out in time. The result: You have to make a split-second decision—hang onto the pole and let the boat glide gently away from you, or let go of the pole and stay with the boat, but without further means of propulsion or steering. Most first-timers who find themselves in this predicament hang onto the pole for dear life, and end up getting wet when they finally splash down into the water. This all makes for great fun, and even greater photos if someone snaps the punter in this dilemma.

See also

St. John's College, with its Bridge of Sighs connecting the two halves of the college.

The Round Church, built in 1130, one of very few medieval churches remaining in England.

Magdalene (pronounced "Maudlin") College, founded in 1428, famous for its Pepys Library. Magdalene Street is beautiful, with restored houses from the sixteenth and seventeenth centuries.

Queens College, founded in 1449 by the wives of English kings. Behind the college is the famous Mathematical Bridge, built in 1749, with no nails holding it together.

If you only get to one museum, make it the Fitzwilliam on Trumpington Street. It is considered one of the most important in Britain, with its collections of Impressionist art, silver, porcelains, medieval and Renaissance art and armor, and much more. The museum is open daily except Mondays from 10am to 5pm and Sunday from 2pm to 5pm.

If you have time, also visit: Peterhouse, the oldest college; The Botanic Gardens; The Scott Polar Research Institute with mementos of Captain Scott's trip to the South Pole; The Cambridge Festival, held in July with music, theater, dance, and more.

The American Military Cemetery, four miles from Cambridge, contains the graves of more than 3,000 Americans who flew from British bases during the war.

A Side Trip from Cambridge to Duxford

If you come to Cambridge by car or bus, try to save some time to visit Duxford Airfield, eight miles south of Cambridge. The Imperial War Museum here is worth a visit. Allied aircraft flew from Duxford during World War II. There are twenty aircraft on display, eleven of which are from the war (including a Boeing B-17 Flying Fortress). The museum is open daily from 10am to 6pm through October 25. Off-season, it is open from 10am to 4pm. For information in the U.S., call 1-800-233-4226.

Hotels

There are no deluxe hotels in Cambridge. The few we list below are first-class and tourist hotels, and are lovely.

Arundel House, 53 Chesterton Road, Cambridge CB4 3AN. Phone 1223 367701, fax 1223 367721. Rates $50 to $100 including tax and service.

The hotel has 105 rooms, but be sure to ask for a low floor if you have luggage, since there is no elevator. Not all rooms have full baths, so ask in advance. The hotel overlooks the river and park; it has a bar and restaurant. The restaurant is closed December 24–26.

University Arms Hotel, Regent Street, Cambridge CB2 1AD. Phone 1223 351241, fax 1223 315256. Rates $150 to $225.

Beautiful Edwardian building overlooking Parker's Piece (with its cricket pitch). Located on a main shopping street , one mile from the train station. All rooms have bath, TV, phone, and radio. Wheelchair accessible. The rooms could use a little updating, but are comfortable. Children under fourteen stay free in parents' room. Nice dining room with buffet breakfast, and bar room.

Garden House Hotel, Granta Place, Mill Lane, Cambridge CB2 IRT. Phone 1223 63421, fax 1223 316605. Rates $175 to $250.

Two restaurants: Le Jardin, which is more formal; and the Riverside Lounge for snacks and drinks. Tea is served on the lawn in good weather. This hotel is beautifully located on the banks of the River Cam. Nicely furnished bedrooms (request a river view). Children stay free in parents' room.

Restaurants

Midsummer House Restaurant, Midsummer Common. Phone 1223 369299, fax 1223 302672. Daily, no dinner Sunday and Monday; closed Christmas season.

Located on the River Cam. The service and food are excellent; risotto, scallops, halibut, roast duck, and delicious desserts. Expensive.

Le Paradis Restaurant at Duxford Lodge, Ickleton Road in Duxford. Phone 1223 936444, fax 1223 832271. Daily except December 26–30 and Saturday lunch.

This is a small country hotel and restaurant located in the village center. Price-fixed menu as well as à la carte, with excellent fish, game in season, chicken, and desserts. Nice wine list, atmosphere, and service. Expensive.

CANTERBURY, KENT COUNTY

Canterbury's East Station is one hour and twenty-five minutes from London's Victoria Station; or travel from from London's Charing Cross and Waterloo stations to Canterbury's West Station. Although most sights are open daily, some are closed on Sundays, so be sure to check ahead.

Tourist Office: 34 St. Margaret's Street. Phone 1227 766567; train information 1732 770111. Tourist office is open Monday to Saturday off-season, daily during the summer. If you want to take a city tour, which we highly recommend, note that they depart from the tourist office.

Canterbury is the seat of the Anglican Church. St. Augustine came here in 597 to convert King Ethelbert of Kent, and became the first Archbishop of Canterbury as a result. The original Canterbury Cathedral was built in 602, and burned down in 1067. Its reconstruction began in 1070 and was finally completed in 1503. You enter the cathedral area through the magnificent Christ Church Gate. The cathedral has two large towers which lead you into the nave, which was rebuilt in the fourteenth century. There is a marking in the floor where Archbishop Thomas Becket was murdered on December 29, 1170. *The Canterbury Tales* by Chaucer describes the murder, as does T. S. Eliot's play, *Murder in the Cathedral.*

Note the Bell Harry Tower, whose bell rings every evening, and also whenever a king, queen, or archbishop dies. There is also an elevated choir, the longest in all of England. Trinity Chapel is where Thomas Becket was buried and lay until Henry VIII had the tomb demolished and the bones scattered. Henry IV is the only king buried in the chapel. The Corona is a circular chapel with a marble chair in the center, which is used for the coronation of archbishops. The Crypt, which dates from Norman times, is the oldest part of the cathedral. Services in French are still held in the Huguenot chapel in the crypt. The Cloisters were built in the fifteenth century.

Continue on to St. Augustine's Abbey, founded in 598 and destroyed by Henry VIII after the Reformation. Today there are only ruins left. It is open daily all year, but check the times before making the trip. Next, see St. Martin's Church, supposedly the oldest church in England still in use.

During World War II Canterbury was badly bombed, but the city has been rebuilt. It now has plenty of shops, hotels and restaurants, as well as the 1,000-seat Marlow Theatre, which presents performances of opera and theater. In the fall, Canterbury hosts an International Arts Festival.

Other sights if time permits: The Roman Museum; the Royal Museum; The Weavers House (settled by Huguenot weavers in the seventeenth century and now a gift shop); the Canterbury Heritage Museum, once the Poor Priests Hospital, built in the fourteenth century.

Lunch

Sullys, High Street, located in the County Hotel, not far from the cathedral. Phone 1227 766266, fax 1227 451512. Daily for lunch and dinner.

Both à la carte and price-fixed meals are available. Excellent Dover sole. Moderate price.

Ristorante Tuo e Mio, 16 the Borough, opposite the King's School. Phone 1227 761471. Closed Monday, Tuesday lunch, last two weeks of February and last two weeks in August.

Family-run trattoria with good veal and chicken dishes.

COVENTRY, WEST MIDLANDS COUNTY

Ten miles from Warwick, twenty miles from Stratford, and seventy-five minutes by train from London's Euston Station.

Tourist Office: Bayley Lane. Phone 1203-8323034. Daily 9:30 to 6:00. Here, buy the City of Coventry Tourist Guide. It has a city map and information on all of the city sights. There is also a Saturday walk which departs from the tourist office at 2pm. Train information 1203 555211.

You go to Coventry primarily for its bombed-out old cathedral and its new one, consecrated in 1962. The thousand-year-old cathedral was destroyed by the Nazis during World War II, and the shell has been left standing. This should be your first stop prior to visiting the new cathedral. In the ruins are whatever remained after the bombing, plus new sculpture and dedications. The fourteenth-century tower still stands, and can be climbed for a view of the city. At the eastern end of the old cathedral is an alter with a cross made of two roof timbers salvaged from the bombing. Behind the cross is a broken stone wall with the words "Father Forgive." The devastation itself is a deeply emotional sight. If you arrive on a Sunday morning, you will hear the most beautiful melodies being played by two men ringing the bells in the bombed-out cathedral. That alone is worth the trip.

The new cathedral is directly across the street and is gorgeous, with its engraved glass, tapestry, stained-glass windows, and beautiful sculptures. The engraved-glass screen is by John Hutton, the stained-glass windows by John Piper, and much of the sculpture by Sir Jacob Epstein. The Baptistry is on the right. Here you can see a charred cross from the old cathedral, and Graham Sutherland's *Christ in Glory* tapestry, said to be the largest tapestry in the world. An eighteen-minute movie, *The Spirit of Coventry*, is shown in the new cathedral— well worth the time. A donation is requested. There is a visitors' center with information in various languages, and the history of both cathedrals. There is also a gift shop located between the cathedrals, selling religious articles and post cards.

Other sights in Coventry are: The Guildhall of St. Mary, a medieval building; the Herbert Art Gallery and Museum, open daily; the Museum of British Road Transport, with cars dating from 1897 (some Coventry-made cars are Daimler, Jaguar, and Triumph). Open daily 10am to 5pm except December 25 and 26.

Lady Godiva was a resident of Coventry. She supposedly rode through the streets naked, with only Tom "peeping"—thus the story.

There is a statue of Lady Godiva in Broadgate Park; Tom peeps at her on the hour from Broadgate Clock.

Tea

Mr. Pickwick's Tea Room, Brookfarm, Stoneleigh Road. Phone 1203 693547. Open daily, wheelchair accessible.

This little tea room is slightly out of the way, but different. It is located in a converted tractor shed on a farm beside a brook and waterfall. The pictures on the walls are from Dickens's *Pickwick Papers*. Afternoon tea includes a delicious scone with jam and cream, fruit cake or strawberries and, of course, your choice of tea. If you prefer cake instead of a scone, try the apple cake, pies, or pudding—all excellent.

Bed & Breakfast

Old Mill, Mill Hill, Coventry CV8 2BS. Phone 203 303588.

This is a converted mill with twenty attractive rooms, dining room, moderate price.

Lunch

There are many small restaurants, tea shops, and lunch places in the center of Coventry. But for something special, try the following hotel and restaurant, for which you'll need a taxi or car:

Brooklands Grange Hotel, Holyhead Road. Phone 1203 601601, fax 1203 601277. Daily for lunch and dinner.

Nicely prepared fish dishes and salads. A la carte and price-fixed meals. Moderate price.

DUBLIN, REPUBLIC OF IRELAND

Dublin is known as *Baile Atha Cliath* in Gaelic, meaning "town of the fords." The English name comes from Dubh-linn which means "black pool." The pool was the overflow of the River Liffey, where Dublin Castle is now located. Dubh-linn was founded by the Ostmen of the territory of Fingal, which is now north County Dublin.

The capital of Ireland is over one thousand years old and is a treat to visit any time of the year, but off-season is the best. After seeing

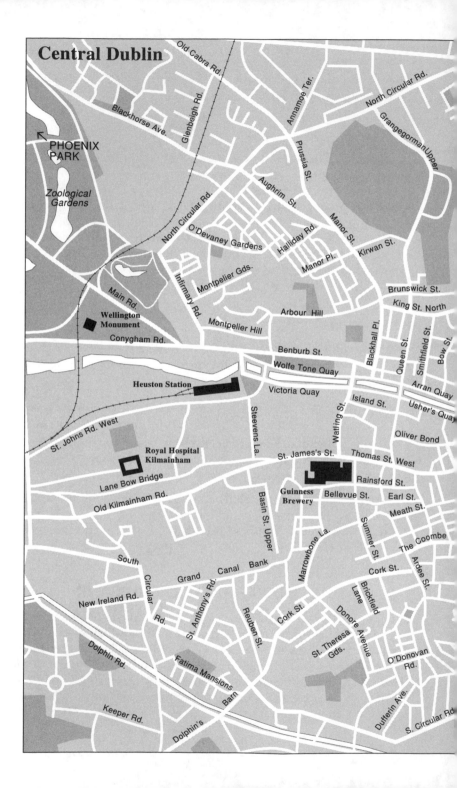

Central Dublin

Old Cabra Rd.

Blackhorse Ave.

Glenbeigh Rd.

Annamoe Ter.

North Circular Rd.

GrangegormanUpper

PHOENIX PARK

Zoological Gardens

Prussia St.

Aughrim St.

Manor St.

North Circular Rd.

O'Devaney Gardens

Halliday Rd.

Kirwan St.

Manor Pl.

Infirmary Rd.

Montpelier Gds.

Arbour Hill

Brunswick St.

King St. North

Main Rd.

Wellington Monument

Montpelier Hill

Blackhall Pl.

Queen St.

Smithfield St.

Bow St.

Conygham Rd.

Benburb St.

Wolfe Tone Quay

Arran Quay

Victoria Quay

Island St.

Usher's Quay

Heuston Station

Steevens La.

Watling St.

Oliver Bond

St. Johns Rd. West

St. James's St.

Thomas St. West

Royal Hospital Kilmainham

Rainsford St.

Lane Bow Bridge

Guinness Brewery

Bellevue St.

Earl St.

Old Kilmainham Rd.

Meath St.

The Coombe

Basin St. Upper

Marrowbone La.

Summer St.

Ardee St.

South

Grand   Canal   Bank

Cork St.

Circular

St. Anthony's Rd.

Brickfield Lane

New Ireland Rd.

Reuben St.

Cork St.

Donore Avenue

Rd.

St. Theresa Gds.

O'Donovan Rd.

Dolphin Rd.

Fatima Mansions

Barn

Dufferin Ave.

Keeper Rd.

Dolphin's

S. Circular Rd

and villages on the coast with lots to see, restaurants for lunch, and paths to walk or hike, plus golfing, fishing, and exploring. We describe here only the highlights of Dublin and nearby day trips. If you stay longer than three days, contact the Irish Tourist Board for further information.

Irish Tourist Board: 345 Park Avenue, New York City, N.Y. 10154 Phone 212-418-0800 or 1-800-223-6470.

Bord Fáilte (Irish Tourist Board), Baggott Street Bridge, Dublin 2, Ireland. Phone 1 602 4000, fax 1 602 4100. Web site www.ireland.travel.ie.

Tourist Offices

Suffolk Street. Dublin. Phone 850 230330 (From outside Ireland 669 792 083. This is the main Dublin Tourist Office, with information, accommodation reservations, a money exchange office, tour schedules, and a ticket office for concerts and theaters. The Dublin Tourist Office Web sites www.dublins-fair-city.com and www.visit.ie/Dublin. The phone service operates Monday to Friday 8:00 to 8:00, Saturday and Sunday 8:00 to 5:00.

Dublin Airport. Phone 01 844 5387.

Dun Laoghaire ferry port (pronounced "done leary"). Phone 280 6984.

In London; 150 New Bond Street. Phone 171 493 3201. Gulliver is a computerized tourist information and reservation system that operates from tourist offices. The computer can tell you of hotel availability, theaters, concerts, places to visit, and more. From Ireland call Gulliver at 605 7777.

Currency

The currency is the Irish pound or punt, which is made up of 100 pence. Punts can be purchased at U.S. banks, Irish banks, and ATM machines. Visa, MasterCard, PLUS, and CIRRUS debit cards are also acceptable, as are American Express cards.

Entrance Requirements

A valid passport for American and Canadian tourists.

Electric Current

The current is 220 AC. An adapter and converter are required for American appliances. If you have dual-voltage appliances, you only need a plug adapter. Plugs are three square pins.

Pets

As in England, there is a quarantine (six months!), so leave Fido at home.

Shopping

Start at the Powerscourt Townhouse Centre just off Grafton Street. This is where the crafts council is located. In the gallery and shop are wonderful Irish handicrafts from around the country. Grafton Street and Henry Street have many shops for Waterford hand blown crystal, Tipperary crystal, Beleek china, and tweeds. The Kilkenny Centre in Nassau Street also has excellent shops; buy a beautiful Aran sweater or tweed cap. Walk down Temple Bar, "the left bank of Dublin," and you'll note that the streets are lined with shops for knits, glass, antiques, and beautiful clothes. (Temple Bar also is the location for Dublin's Viking Adventure and the Arc, a cultural center for children.) You can find crystal in all price ranges. Many articles are sold in Ireland that cannot be found abroad. Dublin has many excellent book shops offering the new best sellers, as well as books on Ireland and by the many great Irish writers. There are many old book shops with both new and old wonderful Irish books that cannot be found at home. You can search for a crystal *Cinderella's Slipper* in the U.S. and never find it, but it can be found in Ireland. If your budget is limited, you can still have fun shopping. There are knit hats, sweaters, gloves, scarves, and small crystal objects. No matter what your budget, you do not have to go home empty-handed.

Value Added Tax Refunds

As a visitor from outside the European Community, you can get the tax refunded at the end of your trip. Be sure to ask for the refund form, shop with your passport, and follow the directions. And be sure to be at the airport or ferry in enough time to go to the customs desk prior to departing the country. Also, if possible, use a credit card when shopping so that the VAT can be refunded directly to your credit card. It is easier to keep track that way. If you are visiting the UK after Ireland, you can take care of the VAT when you leave England.

Car Rental

To rent a car, you must be at least twenty-one years old and no older than seventy-five. A valid U.S. or Canadian license is required. Cars must be returned with a full tank. Traffic drives on the left. Seat belts are a must. Also, do not drink and drive; there are strict laws.

If you are going to Dublin for a day or even a few days, you do not need a car. But if you want to take day trips out of Dublin, a car is the best way to travel.

How to Get Around Dublin

ON FOOT: Dublin is not a big city, so you can get around on foot; wear good walking shoes and remember to look in both directions before crossing streets. As in London, the traffic comes from the direction opposite to what we are used to in the U.S.

BUS: Bus stops are located every few blocks. If you are headed for the city center, your bus will say "An Lar." which is Gaelic for "to the center." Buses run quite frequently, and the fares are reasonable. If you require bus information from Dublin Bus (Bus Atha Cliath), phone 873 4222. The Central Bus Station (Bus Eireann) number is 836 6111.

Bus Eireann also has guided tours throughout Dublin and Ireland, which can be booked through the tourist office on Suffolk Street, or from the bus company directly. Any hotel concierge can also arrange for bus tour tickets.

RAIL: Irish Rail (Iarnrod Eireann). Phone 836 6222.

DART: Dublin Area Rapid Transit links the city center with the suburbs and seaside. You can travel to Howth in the north and Bray to the south and many places in between, including Dun Laoghaire, where the ferry from Wales comes in. DART information 703 3504. There is an all-day Adult Rambler ticket for only I£3.50.

Taxi: Taxis line up at hotels, bus stations, train stations, and on main streets. They can also be called: All Fives Taxi at 455 5555; Blue Cabs at 676 1111.

Telephones

Telephones are located on streets and in shopping malls, pubs, and restaurants throughout the city and countryside. Some take coins, but most now require a card which can be purchased in shops or post offices.
　　Dialing: Dublin to Dublin, no prefix of 01 or 1.
Dublin from Ireland, 01 plus number.
Ireland from the U.S., 011 353 plus city code plus number.
Dublin from the U.S., 011 3531 plus number.

Travelers with Disabilities

For information on hotels and sights that have wheelchair accessibility, contact the National Rehabilitation Board of Ireland, the Square Shopping Centre, Dublin 24. Phone 462 0444.

The Irish Wheelchair Association, 24 Blackheath Drive, Clontarf, Dublin 3. Phone 833 8241. Will loan wheelchairs at no cost, but they do like you to make a donation.

Theater

Abbey Theatre, founded by W. B. Yeats, is a world-famous repertory stage, with the Peacock Theatre in its basement. The Gate Theatre is also a wonderful repertory theater, second to the Abbey in prestige. The Olympia and the Gaiety theaters have touring companies, musicals and opera, and also rock concerts. The Point Theatre has rock concerts and boxing matches.
　　The National Concert Hall is a gorgeous new building with a huge organ at the back of the stage. If you are not in Dublin to hear a concert, at least visit the hall. There is a restaurant for lunch, preconcert dinners, and intermission drinks (Phone 478 5005).

Golf

There are more than two hundred and fifty golf courses in Ireland. Ask at the Irish Tourist Office for golf packages or one-day availability. It is all possible.

There is also a free golf reservations service:

Golfing Ireland, 18 Parnell Square, Dublin 1. Phone from Dublin 850 423 423, from Northern Ireland or other countries 353 1 8726711; fax 353 1 8726632. e-mail golf;caiol.ie. 9:00 to 5:00 Monday to Friday. Credit cards accepted.

A few reminders when going to Ireland:

Off-season is wonderful. There are fewer tourists, hotel rates are reduced, and the people are always friendly to North Americans. The staff in hotels, pubs, restaurants, shops, and museums have more time to help without the tourist rush. You can play golf twelve months a year due to the mild climate. The only thing to watch off-season is the opening hours of museums and sights, which may be shorter than during the summer months. Always check ahead when planning a day's outing.

Bring an umbrella, and also a raincoat if you have the space in your luggage. Definitely an umbrella!

Try not to go on a public holiday. The Irish are serious about them and just about everything is closed. Holidays are New Year's Day, St. Patrick's Day (March 17), Good Friday, Easter Monday, May Day Holiday, June Holiday (date varies), August Holiday (date varies), October Holiday (date varies), December 25 and 26. Always check the exact dates before your trip.

Don't be insulted if an Irishman says "get away"; they don't really mean it. It means, "I don't believe it."

Safety: Like every other city, Dublin has its share of pickpockets and crime. Do not leave your car unattended if it has luggage showing. Wear a money belt or fanny pack if you plan on carrying your passport and cash. Be alert in crowded shopping areas and public places. It is best to travel without jewelry or cash, in any case. Credit cards are accepted everywhere.

Do Not Carry More Cash Than You Can Afford to Lose

One of the authors of this book was taking a walk along the sea in Sandycove, near Dublin, on a lovely sunny afternoon, when two boys pulled up alongside, snatched her handbag, knocked her down, got back into what turned out to be a stolen car, and fled. A woman in another car saw what happened, followed the thieves' car, got the license number, and returned to take the author to the police station. After a few hours, the car and handbag were found, minus the cash. The moral of the story: Don't carry more cash than you'll need for the day, wear a fanny pack, and always be aware of where you are and who or what is around you. Don't worry—the author enjoyed the rest of the trip!

Getting There

Dublin has become one of Europe's major tourist cities, and luckily it is close enough to London to make it ideal for a day trip or a a longer stay. If you fly, it is a perfect day trip. If you take the ferry, you must make it at least a three-day stop. It will not be a hardship.

If you fly, the airlines are British Air, Aer Lingus, British Midland Air, and Ryanair. There are at least twenty flights a day to Dublin from three airports in London, starting at 6:55am and leaving almost every hour during the day. The last flight from Dublin is at 8:45pm, arriving back in London at 9:55pm.

Crossing the Irish sea by ferry can be done at any time of year, and it is a very easy trip. The only thing to remember (as always when traveling) is to "go light" with luggage if possible. Porters are nonexistent. When you arrive in the Republic of Ireland, you go through customs on either the "declare" or "nothing to declare" lines. There are duty-free shops on the ferries, the best buys being alcohol and tobacco.

To travel from London to Dublin by ferry, go first to Euston Station in London. Take the train to Holyhead in Wales, and then the ferry to Dun Laoghaire in Ireland. Dun Laoghaire is a suburb of Dublin. The ferry trip takes three-and-a-half hours. Duty-free shops and food and drink services during the trip help to make it a fast and enjoyable one. The ferry has both first- and second-class service. Getting from Dun Laoghaire to Dublin is accomplished by DART train, bus, car rental, or taxi, all available at the pier.

If the ferry is too slow for you, try the Stena catamaran service, which only takes an hour and a half to and from the same ports.

Tickets can be purchased ahead of time from BritRail. Both the Eurailpass and the BritRail Pass + Ireland pass are accepted on the trains in the Republic of Ireland. Check the fares with BritRail, as they do vary according to the type of ticket you buy. There are discounts for seniors, advance ticket purchase, and so on.

Apartment Rentals

If you plan to stay more than a day, and do not want to stay in an expensive hotel, you can rent an apartment in the center of Dublin for a few days at very reasonable rates. It is fun to become part of a neighborhood.

The brochure *Ireland Self-Catering Guide* is available for I£10 from Cork Kerry Tourism, Tourist House, Grand Parade, Cork, Ireland. Phone 011 353 21273251, fax 011 353 21273504. Credit cards are accepted for payment.

Bachelor's Walk is one of the properties rented on a nightly or weekly rate. Nightly, the rate is $92.00; weekly, $385. The price includes TV, washer, dryer, and linens. The telephone is an extra charge. Bachelor's Walk is wonderfully located at the Liffey River and Ha'penny Bridge.

Hostels of Ireland

If you prefer a hostel, which is much less expensive than a hotel or rental, you can obtain a free guide from Independent Holiday Hostels of Ireland, 57 Lower Gardiner Street, Dublin 1. Phone 836 4700, fax 836 4710; e-mail ihh;caiol.ie. The hostels are open daily, with no curfews and no required membership. Kitchens and private or family rooms are available.

What To Do and See in Dublin

Dublin is divided by the River Liffey. The city is packed with wide streets, cobblestoned alleys, spacious squares, riverside quays, open markets, and beautiful Georgian doorways. It has medieval churches and castles, old bridges, elegant parks and gardens, fine galleries and museums, and a busy nightlife.

IF YOU ONLY HAVE ONE DAY: There are two options for this day:

You might want to start with an overview bus tour. The Dublin City Tour leaves from 59 Upper O'Connell Street (phone 873 4222) and lasts one hour and fifteen minutes. It is a hop-on hop-off bus with ten stops. As the driver describes a sight or area, you can get off, see what you wish, and get the next bus to continue on. This is an ideal way to see the main attractions of the city without getting too exhausted. The Gray Line Tour Company also has tours of Dublin and Ireland (phone 605 7705, fax 670 8731). They offer half-day, full-day, and weekly tours—whatever fits your needs. They have a hop-on hop-off city tour as well. The hop-on hop-off tour departures start at 9:30am and continue all day. They leave from 14 Upper O'Connell St, or Suffolk Street. Call for reservations. They also have half- and full-day trips to the day-trip locations recommended, below. Credit cards are accepted for all tours.

The other option is to walk. Dublin is a surprisingly compact city that can be walked with ease (if you have good walking shoes).

Start the day in the medieval area around Christ Church and St. Patrick's Cathedral. Then continue on to High Street. From there go on to Dublin Castle, Trinity College (with its famous *Book of Kells*), then over the river to O'Connell Street. Someplace in here be sure to stop for lunch in a pub. If you like strong beer, have a dark, thick, foamy Guinness, brewed here. Since there is no time to waste on a day trip, walk past the historic General Post Office, as there is little to see inside. If time and your feet permit, you might want to do a little shopping.

IF YOU HAVE MORE THAN ONE DAY: See the above sights and those below, The Highlights of Dublin.

The Highlights of Dublin

Trinity College.

The college was founded by the order of Queen Elizabeth I in 1592. Until 1956 the Catholic Church did not permit its followers to attend the school, considered to be a Protestant college. Today it is open to everyone.

The beautiful Old Library is a must. There are two levels of shelves in the gorgeous Long Room with over two hundred thousand books. Old manuscripts are in glass cases. Open daily except for the ten days of Christmas through New Year. The *Book of Kells*, dating from 800, is on display in the Colonnades Gallery. In order to preserve it, one page is turned per day. This is a 340-page book that was handwritten and illustrated by monks in the ninth century. It contains the New Testament (written in Latin). Monday to Saturday 9:30 to 5:00; October to May, Sunday noon to 4:30. June to September Sunday 9:30 to 4:30.

The Dublin Experience gives an audio-visual story of the city from Viking times to the present. It's located in the Arts Building on the Trinity campus. Open daily May to October 10am to 5pm.

Christ Church Cathedral. Daily, closed December 26 and January 1.

The cathedral was founded in 1038 by King Sitric and is the oldest building in Dublin. The tomb of the Earl of Pembroke, known as Strongbow, the first Norman conqueror of Ireland, is here. On view in the Synod House, part of the cathedral, is Dublinia, a history of Dublin in medieval times. Dublinia shows how the common folk lived in the medieval city; there are Viking exhibits and an audio-visual show (the latter in five languages). You can also climb the seventeenth-century St Michael's Tower for a view of Dublin. Gift shop open daily. Dublinia is open daily except December 24–26.

St Patrick's Cathedral. Daily from 9:00 to 6:00.

Within walking distance of Christ Church, the cathedral is dedicated to St Patrick, Ireland's national saint. The cathedral was built in 1192, and is the largest in the country. Handel's *Messiah* was performed here in 1742 when Handel himself was in Dublin. The writer Jonathan Swift is buried in the church. He was also the Dean of St. Patrick's from 1713 to 1745. Daily and Sunday services are held here.

Both St. Patrick's and Christ Church cathedrals are Protestant, even though Ireland is a predominantly Roman Catholic country; Dublin does not have a Catholic Cathedral. This is due, of course, to the fact that the structures were erected by the British conquerors of Ireland, whose church under Henry VIII changed from being Roman Catholic to Protestant. Today, the cathedrals are the property of the Church of Ireland, which is what Protestants in this country call their religion, though they are affiliated with the Anglican Church in England much as Episcopalians are in the United States.

Dublin Castle. Monday to Friday 10:00 to 5:00, Saturday, Sunday, and Bank holidays 2:00 to 5:00.

This thirteenth-century Norman castle holds a genealogical office, handy if you want to find your Irish ancestry. England's King John built the castle as his Irish seat of power. One of Queen Victoria's thrones is here, made for her visit to Dublin. Not much remains of the original castle, but it is still worth seeing. It was rebuilt in the eighteenth century. The beautiful little Church of the Most Holy Trinity with the sculpted heads of English kings and queens is worth a visit. A restaurant and crafts shop are open to visitors.

Guinness Brewery Centre. Daily except December 25, 26, January 1.

This is Europe's largest brewery, originally opened in 1759. There are no tours of the brewery, but there is a visitor's center located at James's Gate (phone 1 453 6700). Here there is a World of Guinness exhibition, an audio-visual show, a souvenir shop, and a bar for tasting the beer.

The National Gallery of Ireland. Daily 10:00 to 5:30, Thursdays until 8:30pm, Sunday 2:00 to 5:00.

Opened in 1854, the National Gallery, located on Merrion Square West, has some of the world's greatest artists represented, among them Titian, Rubens and Goya. Free tours are held daily.

The National Library, Kildare Street. Phone 661 8811, admission free. Monday 10:00 to 9:00, Tuesday and Wednesday 2:00 to 9:00, Thursday and Friday 10:00 to 5:00, Saturday 10am–1pm.

The library has all of the first editions and writings of Irish writers, as well as every book published in Ireland. You can also find all Irish newspapers and magazines. The main reading room was opened in 1890.

The National Museum of Ireland, Kildare Street and Merrion Row. Tuesday to Sunday 10:00 to 5:00

Full of Irish antiquities, it tells the story of Ireland from 6000 B.C. There is also a gorgeous Irish Gold exhibit from the Bronze Age. An exhibit called "Ar Thoir na Saoirse" tells the story of the Irish battle for independence from 1916–21.

The Irish Museum of Modern Art, at The Royal Hospital Kilmainham. Tuesday to Saturday 10:00 to 5:30, Sunday from noon.

The museum exhibits the works of Irish artists of the twentieth century. The royal hospital was built in 1684. There is a coffee shop and gift shop.

Irish Jewish Museum, 4 Walworth Road, Off Victoria Street. Phone 676 0737. Off-season October to April, Sunday 10:30 to 2:30; summer Tuesday, Thursday, Sunday 11:00 to 3:00.

Opened in 1985 by Chaim Herzog, who was born in Dublin and

later became the president of Israel, the museum was once a synagogue. The history of Irish Jews goes back to the 1800s.

The General Post Office, O'Connell Street. Daily 8:00 to 8:00, Sundays and bank holidays 10:00 to 6:30.

The GPO still has bullet holes from the 1916 Easter uprising. Note the plaque commemorating the event, written in both English and Gaelic. The Irish flag was raised here to proclaim the nation's independence. The GPO opened in 1818 and was rebuilt after the 1916 uprising. It's the only post office open on Sundays. It also has a currency exchange desk.

The James Joyce Centre: 35 North Great Georges Street. Phone 878 8547, fax 878 8488, e-mail Joycecen;caiol.ie. April to October Monday to Saturday 9:30 to 5:00, Sunday noon to 5:00, November to March Tuesday to Saturday 10:00 to 4:30, Sunday 12:30 to 4:30.

Dedicated to the works of James Joyce and his life, with daily walks, tours and an audio-visual center. Also a library, book shop, and coffee shop.

Phoenix Park.

The President of Ireland lives in a residence in the center of this three-square-mile park, which is the largest city park in Europe and which is in the center of Dublin. Also living in residences in Phoenix Park are the American ambassador and the Papal Nuncio. The Dublin Zoo is also located here.

St. Stephen's Green.

The green is right in the middle of the city, surrounded by houses and hotels. Inside the park you'll find a man-made lake, paths, monuments, and statues. One sculpture is of the Countess Constance Markievicz, who defended the square in the 1916 uprising and was later elected to the British House of Commons.

Ha'penny Bridge.

The only pedestrian bridge over the Liffey River. It was built in 1816.

O'Connell Street.

The main street of Dublin was named for Daniel O'Connell, who brought about Catholic Emancipation in 1825. Prior to that Catholics had no vote. This thoroughfare is a beautiful, wide street with four monuments on it. Once there were five, but on March 8, 1966, the statue of Lord Nelson was blown up. Quess what? No one knows who did it. Also on O'Connell Street is the GPO. Just up from the GPO is a fountain fondly referred to as "the floozie in the jacoosie." Opposite the post office is Clery's Department Store. In New York City people once met under the Hotel Biltmore clock; in Dublin, you meet under the Clery's clock.

Molly Malone statue.

Everyone knows the song about Molly Malone, who "wheeled her wheelbarrow through streets broad and narrow." It seems she did that during the day, and did other things at night, so Dubliners call her "the tart with the cart." Her statue (with cart and all) can be found right on Grafton Street, and at night, because it is life-size and right down on the sidewalk, you might even run into her before you notice she's made of bronze.

Merrion Square.

This was one of the first gorgeous Georgian squares, with its magnificent tall, narrow town houses, complete with colorful doors (red and blue dominate). There is now a deluxe hotel in the square occupying a number of attached town houses.

Temple Bar. Information Center: 18 Eustace Street. Phone 671 5717, fax 677 2525; e-mail info;catemple-bar.ie.

The bohemian area of the city, with art galleries, musical pubs, restaurants, and a hotel owned by the musical group U2. The area is located near the river Liffey and the city center, between Trinity College and Christ Church Cathedral. Within the area: the Irish Film Center, The Children's Cultural Center, The Photography Centre, and much more. Just wander, and you will discover narrow streets and some interesting sights.

Dublin's Writers Museum: 18-19 Parnell Square. Phone 872 2077. Monday to Saturday 10:00 to 5:00, Sunday and holidays 11:30 to 6:00, summer months until 7pm.

This museum is located in an eighteenth-century mansion. It was opened in 1991 to celebrate great Irish writers, with displays, talks, and readings, as well as a story hour for children. The Irish love to tell stories. Four of their writers are winners of the Nobel Prize, so they must be doing something right! On display are books, letters, paintings, and personal items connected to the authors. The best-known writers honored here include Jonathan Swift, who wrote *Gulliver's Travels*; Oscar Wilde, who wrote *The Picture of Dorian Gray* and *The Importance of Being Earnest*, among other great works. Two excellent books about Oscar Wilde include one written by his son, and one by his grandson. Other authors represented are George Bernard Shaw, who wrote *Pygmalion* (which became the musical *My Fair Lady*); Sean O'Casey, who wrote the famous *Juno and the Paycock* and many lyrics to songs such as "Nora"; James Joyce, author of *Ulysses*, which was banned in Ireland while he was alive, and *Dubliners*; William Butler Yeats, who was a founder of the Abbey Theatre and winner of the Nobel Prize after writing dozens of poems about his beloved Ireland; and Oliver Goldsmith, who wrote *She Stoops to Conquer*. Tours are available in several languages. There is a restaurant and book shop.

Dublin Walks

The following are group walks:

Literary Pub Crawl. 35 Heytesbury Street. Starts at the Duke Pub, Duke Street. Off-season, November to March, Thursday to Saturday evenings; summer, nightly at 7:30, Sundays all year at noon.

Actors read the works of great Irish writers, and you visit the best-known pubs.

Historical Walking Tours of Dublin. phone 845 0241. Meet at the front gate of Trinity College. Saturday and Sunday at noon.

The two-hour walk includes Trinity College, Parliament House, Temple Bar, Dublin Castle, City Hall, Christ Church, and more.

Revolutionary Dublin Tour. Phone 662 9976. Meets at Fusilier's Arch, Stephens Green, at the top of Grafton Street. Weekdays at 2:30, weekends at 10:30am or 2:30.

The walk takes two hours and includes information on the period from 1916 to 1923. It includes the Ha'penny Bridge, Dublin Castle, Crow Street, Stephens Green, Trinity College, and O'Connell Street.

Horse Racing

The Irish love horse racing, and there is plenty of it. Off-season racing is very popular, Christmas and Easter being the times for big events. Leopardstown is only six miles from Dublin, and offers a big race the day after Christmas (St. Stephen's Day). At Easter, the races are at Fairyhouse. In May, the three-day meeting races are held at Punchestown. The summer races are held at Curragh, about thirty-five miles from Dublin. The tourist office has an *Irish Racing Calendar*, published annually.

Irish Horseracing Authority, Leopardstown Racecourse, Foxrock, Dublin. Phone 289 2888, fax 289 8412.

Tea

Bewley's. Open daily.
Opened in 1840. After a day of sight-seeing and walking, you might want to stop for a cup of tea at this famous tea shop/restaurant. You can also start your day with a big Irish breakfast, or have lunch here. The main restaurant is Bewley's of Grafton Street.

Some Places Worth Visiting Within Easy Reach of Dublin

The best and easiest way to sightsee outside of Dublin is by car. The roads are good, the sights interesting. Just remember which side of the road you are on. You can also travel by DART, bus, or train; but you cannot do or see as much, stop for lunch at a restaurant or pub a little out of the way, or linger over some beautiful spot if you don't have a car. You can go north or south, but not both in one day.

NORTH OF DUBLIN

MALAHIDE CASTLE. You can get to Malahide by train, but not to the castle. It is best to drive. Castle. Phone 846 2516; gardens, 846 2456. Year round Monday to Friday 10:00 to 5:00, weekends afternoons only.

One of Dublin's oldest private estates, it was bought by the state in 1976, after it had been inhabited continuously by the Talbot family since 1185. The oldest part of the castle is the tower, which dates from the twelfth century. The medieval hall is preserved in its original state. The interior is full of beautiful furniture, paintings, and decorations, the castle itself surrounded by gorgeous gardens.

Visit the Fry Model Railway on the grounds of the castle, with its collection of handmade models of Irish trains built by Cyril Fry in the 1920s and '30s. Phone 845 2758. Monday to Thursday (summer months Monday to Friday) 10:00 to 1:00 and 2:00 to 5:00; Friday to Sunday 11:00 to 1:00 and 2:00 to 6:00.

Lunch or dinner: Bon Appetit, 9 St. James's Terrace, Malahide. Phone 845 0314. Excellent fish, which is a house special, but the menu also includes Irish and French food. A beautiful Georgian building beside the sea. Lunch Monday to Friday 12:30 to 2:30, dinner Monday to Saturday 7:00 to 11:00. Moderate to expensive.

Grand Hotel, Malahide. Phone 845 0000. After sight-seeing you might want to stop at the ground-floor Matt Ryan bar for a cup of tea or a drink.

HOWTH: Both Howth and Malahide can be seen on the same day. Howth can be reached by DART train and is only eight miles northeast of Dublin.

The name Howth is derived from the Scandinavian "Hofud" or "Hoved," meaning a "headland" or "promontory." Victorious Norsemen set up Howth as a port over eleven hundred years ago (in 897), after conquering the local Celtic inhabitants. The first stone of the present Howth harbor was laid in 1807, and it long served as the main route from Ireland to Holyhead in Wales.

The name of Ireland's Eye comes from the Scandinavian *ey*, meaning an "island." The island is a mile offshore from Howth and has a Bird Sanctuary, which can be reached by boat in twenty-five minutes, costing I£4 round-trip.

Howth it self is a fishing village and seaside resort. It has lovely views, walks, and seafood restaurants. The author H. G. Wells called the view from Howth Head one of the most beautiful in the world. A sight to see if you are here in May or June is the Howth Castle Gardens, planted in 1875, and world famous for its 2,000 varieties of rhododendrons. The castle itself is not open to visitors. It has been the home of the St. Lawrence family since 1177, when they landed in Howth and defeated the locals at the Battle of Evora. The present building dates from 1564.There are lovely walks available on the grounds, and a public golf course. Phone 832 2624. Open daily, no admission fee.

Howth Transport museum, also at Howth Castle. Phone 847 5623.

On view are double-decker buses, fire engines, trucks, bread-delivery trucks, and the last tram to Dublin. Open weekends 10:00 to 5:00.

Lunch or dinner, expensive: Abbey Tavern, Abbey Street. Phone 839 0307, reservations required, credit cards accepted. Daily except Sunday October to March, no lunch April to September.

Located in the heart of the village, this tavern specializes in fish dinners and Irish cuisine. A highlight is Sole Abbey. Each evening year-round, traditional Irish music and songs are performed here.

Next to the Abbey Tavern is the Old Abbey. In 1038, Sitric Mac Aulaffe, the Danish high king of Dublin, gave land to build the Abbey, one of the few Gothic buildings remaining in the Dublin area.

King Sitric, East Pier. Phone 823 6729, credit cards accepted. Monday to Saturday except bank holidays, Christmas Day, Easter.

Well-known fish restaurant on the harbor front. Beautiful sea views from the informal upstairs dining room, wonderful ambiance. Don't come here unless you love seafood and fish, which are beautifully prepared. Featured: fried squid, lobster, crab, and freshly caught fish such as turbot, trout, and salmon. The favorite dessert is Meringue Sitric, a meringue filled with vanilla ice cream and covered with chocolate sauce.

Lunch or dinner, moderate: Adrian's, 3 Abbey Street. Phone 839 1696, credit cards accepted. Open daily.

Lovely little seaside bistro on Howth Hill. The menu features fish risotto or rabbit casserole.

Dee Gee's Wine and Steak Bar, Harbour Road. Phone 839 2641.

Across from the DART station, this place serves snacks during the day and dinner at night. The food is mainly steaks, hamburgers, pasta, and seafood.

SOUTH OF DUBLIN

DUN LAOGHAIRE (Pronounced "Dunleary") is a town on the DART line only six miles from Dublin.

Dun Laoghaire is named after a fifth-century king who built a fort here. It was a fishing village until the early 1800s when the East and West piers were built. After that it became a port for shipping fleets. There is also a car ferry service. Dun Laoghaire is your first sight of Ireland if you come by ferry from Holyhead in Wales, three-and-a-half hours away.

There are four yachting clubs in Dun Laoghaire, three for members only. In 1997 the Cunard Line's QE2 made its first visit to Ireland, stopping here.

The National Maritime Museum. Haigh Terrace. Phone 280 0969. Tuesday to Sunday 2:30 to 5:30.

The museum is in a former mariners' church. The collection features maritime pictures, documents, stamps, cards, flags, and more.

Upper and Lower George Street are the main drags in Dun Laoghhaire, liberally lined with shops, boutiques, and restaurants. See also Moran Park, with gardens and a bowling green.

Follow Promenade Street to the Joyce Tower at Sandycove Point in Sandycove. Phone 280 9265. April to October, Monday to Saturday 10:00 to 1:00 and 2:00 to 6:00.

This is a must for lovers of James Joyce, and is within walking distance of Dun Laoghaire. James Joyce lived here for part of his life. The tower is the setting for the first chapter of his novel, *Ulysses*. Inside you will find photographs, letters, and first editions of Joyce's work.

Restaurants, moderate: Brasserie na Mara, 1 Harbour Road, Dun Laoghaire. Phone 280 0509, credit cards accepted. Monday to Saturday except bank holidays, Good Friday, and Christmas week.

This excellent restaurant overlooks the harbor. The Irish name na Mara means "of the sea," so fish and seafood are the highlights here. You can get poultry, too. The fish specialty is seared tuna with a salsa sauce. Many desserts are "flaming."

De Selby's, 17-18 Patrick Street, Dun Laoghaire. Phone 284 1761 or 284 1762, credit cards accepted. Dinner daily, and lunch Sunday. Closed December 24 and 25 and Good Friday.

Located in the center of town, this is a very popular restaurant. Fish is excellent here, along with Irish dishes like stews and mixed grills.

South Bank, 1 Martello Terrace, Dun Laoghaire. Phone 280 8788. Dinner Monday to Saturday.

Within walking distance of the James Joyce Tower at Sandycove. Located on the seafront; request a harbor-view table when reserving. Irish food and fish are excellent here.

Bray. On the DART line, but better to go by car if you plan to see the south side in one day.

Bray is a resort with a beach and boardwalk. Go to Bray only if you plan to continue on to the very small village of Enniskerry and the most magnificent park and estate of Powerscourt.

Powerscourt Estate and Gardens, Waterfalls, in Enniskerry in County Wicklow. Powerscourt is only twenty miles south of Dublin. You can drive on your own (which we suggest) or take a bus tour.

The estate is located at the foothills of the Wicklow mountains. There are gardens, paths to wander, lakes, terraces, statues, and a restaurant and gift shop. The mansion is located at the top of the driveway; the gardens, lakes. and paths below. It is simply gorgeous. There is also an interesting pet cemetery at Powerscourt, with sad little headstones. In the American Garden, the plants are indigenous to America (catalog available in the gift shop). The famous waterfalls, the highest in Ireland, are five miles south of the gardens, so use your car. You might want to walk the nature trail surrounding the water-falls. The waterfalls are open all year from 9:30 to 7:00, off-season from 10:30am to dusk. The mansion and gardens are open daily from 9:30am to 5:30pm, but check ahead before making the trip. There is a disabled route that covers the pet cemetery and all of the gardens.

Enniskerry is a tiny village with a few restaurants. You might want to stop for lunch at Poppies in the village center. (Poppies Country Cooking, Enniskerry, Co. Wicklow. Phone 282 8869.)

Hotels in Dublin

Like any major city, Dublin has many hotels and restaurants in every price range. If you are staying more than a day, try to reserve ahead. Dublin is a busy city, with one of the most booming of European economies. If you have a car, it is a good idea to check that the hotel you are staying at has a secure parking area. When making a reservation, always ask if there is an off-season rate, weekend rate, mid-week rate or a rate that includes breakfast—Irish breakfasts are wonderful; they include eggs, bacon, and cheese, and if you indulge in one you may not want to eat again until dinner time. Many discounts are only available when booking, not when you arrive, so ask all these questions ahead of time.

If booking in a Bed and Breakfast, be sure to ask if the room has a toilet and bath or shower in the room. You don't want to discover it is down the hall.

EXPENSIVE

Berkeley Court, Lansdowne Road, Dublin 4. Phone 660 1711, fax 661 7238.

This deluxe hotel is located in Ballsbridge, a lovely residential area just a ten-minute taxi ride from the center of Dublin. The hotel exterior is modern, but the interior is filled with beautiful antiques and carpets in the large, well-furnished rooms (with modern bathrooms).

There are 169 rooms, twenty suites, two restaurants (one formal). The hotel has an indoor pool, beauty shop, barber, tennis, and shops.

Clarence Hotel, 6-8 Wellington Quay, Dublin 2. Phone 670 9000, fax 670 7800.

This hotel on the banks of the Liffey River in the Temple Bar area reopened in 1996 after extensive renovation. The fifty large rooms are beautifully decorated with king beds, oak furniture and excellent amenities. The rooms also have a TV, VCR, minibar, safe, fax connection, bathrobes, and beautiful toiletries. Three rooms are handicap accessible. The public areas are also beautiful, with business and party facilities. Valet parking. The U2 rock group is a part owner. All credit cards accepted.

Conrad Dublin International, Earlsfort Terrace, Dublin 2. Phone 676 5555, fax 676 5424.

This hotel is well located opposite the National Concert Hall. You can walk to all downtown sights, such as St. Stephen's Green and Grafton Street. This is a large hotel, with 190 rooms and suites, two restaurants, a bar, and a large business center. The pub Alfie Byrne's is located in the hotel. There are no views. The rooms are small, but well furnished with large beds, AC, phones in the bathrooms, minibar, fax available and 24-hour room service. Valet parking, hair dresser, gift shop.

Killiney Castle, Killiney, County Dublin. Phone 284 0700, fax 285 0207.

If you have a car and don't mind the ten-mile drive to Dublin center, this hotel is an ideal spot. The hotel has 88 rooms, two restaurants, a bar overlooking the water, indoor heated pool, sauna, health club with treadmills and bicycles, tennis and squash courts, and beautiful walks to nearby villages. The best rooms face the front of the hotel, with gorgeous views of Dublin Bay. All credit cards accepted.

Merrion Hotel, Upper Merrion Street, Dublin. Phone 603 0600, fax 603 0700.

This is a super-deluxe, 145-room new hotel, in the heart of Dublin near the Parliament building. It is housed in four eighteenth-century Georgian townhouses joined together, plus a new building overlooking a garden. The hotel is completely air conditioned, and has a garage, spa, indoor swimming pool, and Ireland's only two-star Michelin restaurant. The restaurant's chef, Guillaume LeBrun, is superb with local fish and local produce. The rooms are beautiful, with king beds, beautiful Frette linen, and separate tubs and showers. Rates $400 and up.

Shelbourne Hotel, St. Stephen's Green, Dublin 2. Phone 676 6471, fax 661 6006.

Here you'll find 142 rooms, twenty-two suites, two restaurants, two bars, free parking. All credit cards accepted. The Horseshoe Bar and the Shelbourne Bar are very popular with local people as well as hotel guests. Deluxe rooms face the front of the hotel with views of St. Stephen's Green and the mountains. The back rooms have no view, but compensate by giving you a good, quiet night's sleep. All rooms are large and well furnished with three phones. The lobby is always busy, as is the lovely lounge adjacent to the lobby where you can have lunch, tea, a drink, or a late night snack.

Westbury, Grafton Street, Dublin 2. Phone 679 1122, fax 679 7078.

The hotel is located right in the city center near the major shopping streets and sights, and has its own shopping mall. The 220 rooms and suites are very well furnished. The large lobby is a local gathering place, partly due to the popularity of its Seafood Bar and Terrace Bar. Try the afternoon tea here, too.

MODERATE

Blooms Hotel, 6 Anglesea Street, Temple Bar, Dublin 2. Phone 671 5622, fax 671 5997.

Located near Trinity College and Dublin Castle. The hotel's name comes from James Joyce's hero in *Ulysses*. The ninety-seven rooms are very nice, although not luxurious. There is a bar, and a terrace for good weather. Credit cards accepted.

Stephen's Hall, Earlsfort Centre 14-17 Lower Leeson Street, Dublin 2. Phone 661 0585, fax 661 0606.

Located just off St. Stephen's Green, this hotel has thirty-seven suites, no rooms. Each suite has a lobby, sitting room, kitchen, bathroom, and one or two bedrooms. The rooms are well furnished. The restaurant serves three meals a day, or you can have the hotel do your market shopping and do your own cooking. Free parking. All credit cards accepted.

BUDGET

Jurys Christchurch Inn, Christchurch Place, Dublin 8. Phone 454 0000, fax 454 0012.

Well located near Christ Church Cathedral and the city center. Some rooms have a view of the cathedral. Some will accommodate four people. Children under fourteen stay free in parents' room. Parking for a fee nearby. Rooms are nicely decorated and have phone and TV. All credit cards accepted.

B & B

The Bed and Breakfast concept is very popular in Ireland. Get the book *Bed and Breakfast Ireland.* (Town and Country Homes Association, Ltd., Beleek Road, Ballyshannon, Co. Donegal, Ireland. Phone 072 51377, fax 072 51207. I£2.50 plus postage.) All of the counties of Ireland are represented in this book, each B&B with a picture and full description of the property. You must ask all the right questions when making reservations because homes vary. Some have one or two rooms, some do not have private bath, TV, tea maker in the room or meals in the cottage except for breakfast. Rates are very reasonable, and all properties in this book have been approved by the Irish Tourist Board. Each county has a local representative listed at the front of the book. If you have any problem, call the representative.

Restaurants in Dublin

Don't be afraid to try a restaurant that looks nice, even if it is not listed here. There are many good pubs, cafes, bistros, and restaurants. You cannot go wrong with local fish and Irish food.

EXPENSIVE

The Commons, Newman House. 85-86 St. Stephen's Green. Phone 475 2597, fax 478 0551. Lunch Monday to Friday 12:30 to 2:30, dinner Monday to Saturday 8:00 to 11:00. Closed Christmas, bank holidays. Reservations suggested.

This is a beautiful restaurant, located in an historic Georgian townhouse. Starters of choice are terrine of foie gras, steamed red mullet, or a delicious salad. Excellently prepared main courses feature fish and game in season. Wicklow lamb is also a favorite. Good wine list. Wonderful homemade petits fours and coffee will complete a tasty dinner. Don't leave without trying a delicious rice pudding tart.

Roly's Bistro, 7 Ballsbridge Terrace, Ballsbridge. Phone 668 2611, fax 660 8535. Daily except Good Friday, and Christmas Day, and December 26. Reservations a must.

Delicious breads, and starters such as Clonakilty black pudding and herb sausage or Dublin prawns. Salads also are scrumptious. Roly, the host, has a Michelin-starred chef who deftly prepares local fish, roast hen, rabbit, mussels, and Wicklow lamb. Desserts include crème brûlée, mousses, and excellent Irish cheeses. We suggest Irish coffee to finish.

Oisin's Irish Restaurant, 31 Upper Camden Street. Phone 75 34 33. Dinner Tuesday to Saturday 7:00 to 10:30.

The menu is both in Gaelic and English, and features traditional Irish food. Excellent local fish. The local music is also a highlight.

Les Frères Jacques, 74 Dame Street, next to the Olympia Theatre. Phone 679 4555, fax 679 4725. Open daily except lunch Saturday, Sunday, bank holidays, December 25–31. Credit cards accepted. Dinner daily except Sunday, bank holidays, and Christmas week.

There is a piano player to entertain you during the evening meal. The menu changes along with the seasons. Game (including domesticated ostrich) is served in season as are fresh seafood and fish. French specialties such as escargots (snails), veal, and poultry are excellent. Desserts are delicious, and the dinner can be completed with Irish coffee.

MODERATE

Elephant and Castle, 18 Temple Bar. Phone 679 3121. Closed Good Friday, December 25 and 26. Open daily. No reservations.

This is an informal, New York–style restaurant with salads, pastas, stir-fry chicken and fish, sandwiches, and burgers.

Imperial Chinese Restaurant, 12a Wicklow Street (near Grafton Street). Phone 677 2580. Daily, except for December 25 and 26.

This is basically a Cantonese restaurant, but delicious fish is also available. Dim sum is featured for lunch daily and on Sundays until 5:30pm.

DUBLIN PUBS

Dublin has more pubs than we can possibly mention. We'll describe a few, but try any that look interesting to you. You won't be disappointed.

Brazen Head, Bridge Street. Phone 677 9549.

This is Dublin's oldest pub, dating from 1688. Popular for its traditional music and singing sessions on Sunday nights.

Davy Byrnes, 21 Duke Street. Phone 677 5217. Closed Good Friday and December 25, 26. Bar food served daily noon to 10:00, Sunday noon to 3:00, 4:00 to 10:00, off-season until 9:00.

Popular with Dubliners as well as tourists. Well located near Grafton Street. Excellent food at reasonable prices. No children under seven.

Kitty O'Shea's Bar, 23-25 Upper Grand Canal Street. Phone 660 8050. Daily 10:30 to 11:30, Sat. until 12:30am, Sunday 12:30pm–11pm. Closed Good Friday, December 25, 26.

This is one of Dublin's best known and most popular pubs. Outdoor dining. Typical Irish food such as stew, Connemara lamb, Ballycastle crab claws, and Kitty's hamburgers. Traditional Irish music nightly.

O'Dwyer's, Mount Street. Phone 676 3574. Monday to Friday 11am to 11:30pm, weekends from 5pm. Closed Good Friday, December 25, 26.

Very popular for lunch as well as dinner, the late-night club is popular with young people for the music as well as the pizza.

The Old Stand, 37 Exchequer Street. Phone 677 5849. Monday to Saturday 10:30am to 11:30pm, Sunday 12:30pm to 3pm, 4pm to 11pm. Closed Good Friday, December 25, 26.

Popular with locals and tourists. Good, moderately priced food such as sirloin steak, roast lamb, chicken, cod, fresh vegetables, smoked salmon, and sandwiches.

EDINBURGH, SCOTLAND

Edinburgh (pronounced "Ed-in-bur-uh") is four hours from London's Kings Cross Station, and is a beautiful city well worth the trip for a day or longer. We think Edinburgh is lovely most times of the year, but off-season spring and fall, are the best. The days are longer during the summer, but that does not make them drier. The same umbrella you take to London and Dublin is a must for Edinburgh, too.

Tourist Offices

Main Office: Princes Street. Waverly Station, city center. Phone 0131 557 1700, fax 0131 557 5118. Open May, June, September Monday to Saturday 9:00 to 8:00, Sunday 10:00 to 8:00; July, August Monday to Saturday 9:00 to 9:00, Sunday 10:00 to 9:00; October to April Monday to Saturday 9:00 to 6:00, Sunday 10:00 to 6:00.

Edinburgh Airport: Phone 0131 333 1000. Open daily. London: Scottish Tourist Board, 19 Cockspur Street, London SWIY5BL. Phone 171 930 8661. New York: British Tourist Authority, 551 5th Avenue, Suite 701, New York, NY 10176. Phone 212-986-2200 or 1-800-462-2748, fax 212-986-1188

Travel From London to Edinburgh

There are many ways to get from London to Edinburgh. We think you need at least two days in Edinburgh, but if you fly round-trip, you can see the highlights in a day.

AIR: Edinburgh Airport is only seven miles from the city center. (Phone 131 333 1000.) From the airport to the city takes approximately twenty minutes by car, bus, or taxi. There is no train service from the airport. By air, you can fly in an hour from Heathrow Airport on British Air or British Midland. From Gatwick Airport, take Air UK or British Air. From Stansted, it's Air UK or Ryanair.

TRAIN: From King's Cross Station, London. (Phone 171 278 2477.) The most direct train is the Flying Scotsman, which departs from King's Cross Station and arrives four hours later at Waverly Station in Edinburgh. The round-trip fare is $271 first class and $161 second class.

The trains are air-conditioned and have full restaurant or buffet service. There is also sleeper service from London to Edinburgh if you want a full day in London and a full day in Edinburgh.

The fares vary according to the type of ticket and service. Be sure to ask about advance fare purchase, senior and child fares, and any other discounts. If you have a BritRail Pass, it is good for use in Scotland. From the United States, call BritRail at 1-800-551-1977 or 212-575-2667. BritRail passes must be bought before leaving the U.S.

BUS: It is possible to take a bus from London to Edinburgh, but we do not recommend it, mainly because the trip takes eight hours.

Driving in Scotland

Driving is on the left hand side, as it is everywhere in Britain and Ireland. The only requirement for renting a car is a valid drivers license (you must be between twenty-one and seventy years of age). Seat belts are a must.

Travelers with Disabilities

Write to these organizations, which produce guides describing all of the available facilities in Edinburgh: Disability Scotland, Princes House, 5 Shandwick Place, Edinburgh EH2 4RG; Phone 0131 229 8632. National Trust for Scotland, 5 Charlotte Square, Edinburgh EH2 4DU; Phone 0131 226 5922. Call the Tourist Office in Edinburgh for additional information.

Money Matters

The currency in Scotland is the same as in London. The pound sterling is used, as are Scottish notes which have the same value as English notes. They are interchangeable in Scotland, but not in the UK. When you leave Scotland, exchange your Scottish notes for English ones if you are headed back to the UK. Money can be exchanged at the airport, train station, banks, and the *bureau de change* at the tourist office.

Telephone

Emergency number: 999. No coins required from pay phone. This number can be used for fire or ambulance.

The country code: 44; the city code: 0131. From the U.S., dial 011-44 plus 131 plus the phone number.

Electricity

If you bring a shaver or hair dryer from home, you must have an adapter and converter. The electric current in Scotland is 220 volts AC. Wall outlets take plugs with 2 round prongs and plugs with 3 prongs.

National Holidays

January 1, 2; March 28, 31; May 27; August 26; December 25, 26.

Senior Citizen Discounts

Don't be afraid to ask. They do exist for museums, theaters, etc. You must show proof of age. Men must be over sixty-five and women over sixty.

Shopping

The British VAT sales tax is 17.5 percent, which you are entitled to get back if you do not live in a European Community country. See page 115 for a full description.

What to Do and See in Edinburgh

Wear good walking shoes; most of the major sights are within walking distance of one another.

BUS TOURS: We like to start any short stay in a new city with an overview bus tour.

Guide Friday Bus Tour. Phone 0131 556 2244. Buses depart from the Waverley Bridge Reception Centre, Waverley Station.

Once you have seen the highlights, you can return to what interests you most. Just take a one-hour tour. Then walk.

Lothian Regional Transport. Phone 0131 555 6363.

This company offers a variety of options. They offer tours to St. Andrews and Fife, or the Trossachs and Loch Lomond. They also have a hop-on hop-off bus that we love. This enables you to sightsee for one fare; if something looks wonderful to you, hop off, visit, and wait for the next bus to continue on. Tours depart from the Waverley Bridge at the Waverley Station. They also pick up at all the hop-on hop-off stops.

Scotline Tours. Phone 0131 557 0162 between 8am and 11pm.

This is a great tour if you don't want to walk, but you do want to see all of the sights. It takes over four hours to see everything; including Edinburgh Castle, the High Kirk of St. Giles, and the Palace of Holyroodhouse. The guide points out all the interesting sights (both in the old and new towns). Try to reserve ahead. This is a very popular tour.

EDINBURGH CASTLE: If you just have a short time here, start with Edinburgh Castle in the old town. Located on top of an extinct volcano overlooking the city, it was a royal residence from the eleventh century and the last stronghold of Mary, Queen of Scots. You can actually spend a few hours in the castle because there is so much to see. St. Margaret's Chapel, the oldest building in Edinburgh, honors Queen Margaret, who died in 1093. The Royal apartments include the room where Mary, Queen of Scots gave birth to James VI, who became James I of England in 1566. The Crown Chamber includes the Honours of Scotland (the ancient crown, scepter, and sword). Great Hall has a beautiful hammer-beamed roof. It was built in 1502 and is still in use for official meetings. The Cannon is fired daily at 1pm. The Castle also has the Scottish War Memorial and the Scottish United Service Museum. The Castle Esplanade is the spot where the annual Military Tattoo is held each August. Open all year.

Hands Off My Rod, Scepter & Crown!

On the first visit one of this book's authors made to Edinburgh Castle, some years ago, he found himself alone, on a cold January day, in the Regalia Room with a shivering custodian. Although he believed he already knew what the answer would be, the author asked the guard, "Were these regalia used in the coronation of the present Queen?"

"Ahhrrgg," snarled the warder, "She cum oop here and took a look at 'em," he said, pausing significantly. Then, drawing himself up proudly, he continued, "But we dinna let 'er touch 'em."

P.S. Whether or not the regalia were used in Westminster Abbey back in 1953, the sacred (to the Scots) Stone of Scone (pronounced "skoon") has been used in every coronation of a British monarch for nearly seven centuries, and was kept in the abbey. After having been liberated by Scot patriots, then returned to London, it was finally given back to the Scottish people on St. Andrews Day 1996.

The Royal Mile

The most famous walk in Scotland runs from Edinburgh Castle to the Palace of Holyroodhouse. It consists of a number of streets, lined with shops and intersected with quaint lanes and squares. You could easily spend a day wandering this interesting mile.

Holyroodhouse Palace

Located at the bottom of the Royal Mile (Edinburgh Castle is at the top). Queen Elizabeth II and Prince Philip stay here when they visit Edinburgh, and it is closed when they are in residence. Mary, Queen of Scots' rooms have been completely restored. The Royal Apartments are also on view, as is the Great Picture Gallery, 150 feet long with 111 portraits of Scottish monarchs. Charles II commissioned the portraits to show his Scottish roots.

Hotels

If you arrive without a reservation (a bad idea, since the city is usually busy), try DIAL-A-BED. Phone 0131 556 3955 or 0131 556 0030, fax 0131 556 2029. This is a free service for booking hotels in all categories.

Balmoral Hotel, Princes Street, Edinburgh EH2 2EQ. Phone 131 556 2414, fax 131 557 3747. Toll free in the U.S. 1-800-225-5843. Rates $194 to $413. Wheelchair accessible.

This moderately deluxe hotel was reopened after extensive renovations in 1991. The Balmoral now has regained its rightful reputation among frequent travelers as the best hotel in the city. It overlooks Edinburgh Castle and gardens. Facilities include business center, health club with indoor pool, gym, and beauty salon. An imposing hotel in the grand manner, its 189 large rooms and suites are all elegantly furnished, and have every mod con (the British for "modern convenience") you could think of, including air-conditioning and all amenities. The best address for anyone visiting Scotland's capital.

The Caledonian Hotel, Princes Street, Edinburgh EH1 2AB. Phone from the U.S. 011 44 131 459 9988, toll free 1-800-727-9818, fax 011 44 131 225 6632. Rates $211 to $405 and up.

This is a marvelous old pile, with the best hotel location in town. Thoroughly modernized inside (in 1997), it vies with the Balmoral as most prestigious hotel, usually losing if only because it is, sniff some, next door to the train station. It is quite elegant, with 246 very large rooms for the most part, outstanding service, and three restaurants. Almost on top of Waverley Station, Edinburgh's most important rail terminus, at the opposite end of Princes Gardens from the Balmoral Hotel and Edinburgh Castle. Rooms for nonsmokers. Wheelchair accessible.

George Inter-Continental, 19 George Street, Edinburgh EH2 2PB. Phone 131 225 1251, in the U.S. 1-800-327-0200; fax 131 226 5644. Rates $227 to $275.

If you don't like the big, ugly Victorian piles that make up the Balmoral and Caledonian, try the George, which blends in nicely with the Georgian buildings around it. (It blends in because this is an eighteenth-century building, having been extensively renovated not so long ago.) There are nearly 200 rooms with all amenities, but the place has a small, country-house feel about it, almost. Two restaurants, nearly equal in elegance and service. Not far from Princes Street. Free parking.

Howard Hotel, 34 Great King Street, Edinburgh EH3 6QH. Phone from the U.S. 011 44 131 557 3500, toll free 1-800-322-2403, fax 011 44 131 557 6515. Rates $200 and up. Wheelchair accessible.

This fifteen-room, first-class hotel with all amenities is located in the heart of Edinburgh near the castle. It is built within three converted and renovated Georgian townhouses. One restaurant. Free parking.

The King James Thistle Hotel, 107 Leith Street, Edinburgh EH1 3SW. Phone 011 44 131 556 0111, toll free 1-800-847-4358, fax 011 44 131 557 5333. Rates $186 and up (corporate rates are available).

This 143-room first-class hotel is located in the city center, not far from Edinburgh Castle. Rooms for nonsmokers. Recently renovated, with all amenities. Free parking.

Conveniently located right on Princes Street, the main drag of Edinburgh, the Mount Royal has about 150 rooms, with great views of the castle and Princes Street Gardens, across the street. Nice restaurant, too.

Old Waverley, 43 Princes Street, Edinburgh EH2 2BY. Phone 131 556 4648, fax 131 557 6316. Rates $154 to $259 and up.

On Princes Street and facing the gardens, the Old Waverley has slightly smallish rooms, but enough ambiance to turn your kilt a different color (a Scottish mock threat) if you don't keep moving!

Restaurants

The Balmoral and Caledonial hotel restaurants are excellent, expensive, and beautiful. Jacket and tie required for their main dining rooms.

L'Auberge, 56 St. Mary's Street. Phone 131 556 5888.

Expensive. Thoroughly French in cuisine and ambiance, this is the place to go when you tire of even the best Scottish cooking.

Channing's Brasserie, South Learmonth Gardens. Phone 131 315 2226.

Expensive. They've put together several Edwardian townhouses here, and made them into a kind of club, or so the ambiance feels. Ask for the fish dishes, especially salmon.

Jackson's, 2 Jackson Close, 209-213 High Street, Royal Mile. Phone 0131 225 1793. Closed Sundays.

We love this restaurant in the historic old town. It is expensive, but well worth the cost. The food is Scottish, with Angus steaks and what they call "Border" lamb. The wine list is extensive, with over fifty malt whiskies and Scottish wines.

Pierre Victoire, 10 Victoria Street. Phone 131 225 1721.

Moderate. One of a chain, this is a bistro-style French restaurant, with especially good-value lunches.

Skippers Bistro, 1A Dock Place, Leith. Phone 0131 554 1018.

Moderate to expensive. A favorite of ours, this is located in Leith (a suburb of Edinburgh). It's a warm, cozy place with fine seafood (their fishcakes are the best). Menus change daily, according to what fish is available.

GREENWICH

Located very near London (and a part of Greater London), Greenwich (pronounced "gren-itch") is an ideal short trip. Only five miles east of Trafalgar Square, it can be reached by car, boat, train, or bus.

Tourist Office: 46 Church Street. Phone 0181 858 8376. Open all year from 10:15 to 4:45. They give away the excellent *Greenwich Visitors' Guide*.

Getting to Greenwich

BOAT: It's only a 45-minute trip from London's Westminster Pier, Charing Cross Pier, or Tower Pier. The boats depart frequently to and from Greenwich. Phone, Westminster Pier departures 171 930 4097; Charing Cross and Tower Piers departures 171 987 1185. Riverbus Boats depart daily from Chelsea Harbor, Charing Cross Pier, and other piers. Phone 171 987 0311.

BritRail: Depart from Charing Cross, Waterloo East, or London Bridge stations. The train ride takes 15 minutes. Train information 171 928 5100.

Bus: Take bus 177 or 188 from London to Greenwich.

Car: Five miles from central London on local streets.

Sights of Greenwich

You could spend an entire day here. If you are coming on a weekend for the markets, see our section on Greenwich Markets, page 122. If you are coming to sight-see, read on.

Henry VIII and Elizabeth I were both born in the Royal Palace of Greenwich. Sir Francis Drake was greeted here by Elizabeth I in 1580 upon his return from sailing around the world. Elizabeth II knighted Sir Francis Chichester at the Royal Naval College after his solo sail around the world nearly 400 years later.

Greenwich Pier area: Monday to Saturday 10:00 to 6:00, Sundays from noon, off-season to 5pm.

The nineteenth-century clipper ship *Cutty Sark* is in dry dock here. Take the tour of the ship, which first set sail in 1869. The *Cutty Sark* was one of the world's fastest sailing ships, and was used for many purposes, but ended its career as a World War II training ship.

Docked next to the *Cutty Sark* is the *Gipsy Moth IV*, a 53-foot ketch in which Sir Francis Chichester circled the globe in 1967. Open Easter through September only.

National Maritime Museum. Monday to Saturday 10:00 to 6:00, Sunday 2:00 to 6:00, closes at 5pm off-season.

This is the world's largest maritime museum. It includes the Royal Observatory, the Queens House, and Flamsteed House. The Museum is a must with its exhibits of boats (including a paddle steamer), galleries of information about Lord Nelson and Captain Cook, the Barge House with royal barges, and exhibits about the French and American revolutions. The Queens House was built by Inigo Jones as a summer palace for Queen Anne of Denmark, wife of James I. The Queen's bedroom on the second floor can be visited, and the house is full of beautiful things to see, such as magnificent furniture and exquisite silks. Eliza-

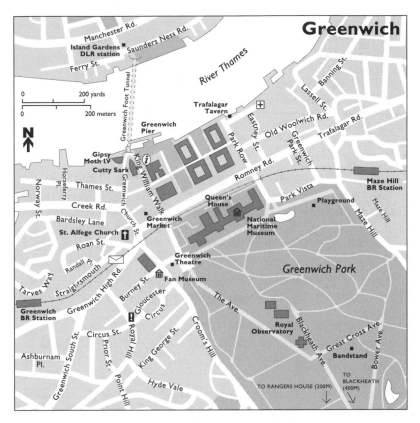

beth II reopened this house to the public in 1990. Flamsteed House was built by Sir Christopher Wren in 1675. The old Royal Observatory houses a museum of astronomical instruments and clocks. The Prime Meridian which divides the eastern and western hemispheres is marked by the line of zero degrees longitude on which Greenwich Mean Time (GMT) is calculated. At this point you can stand with one foot in the eastern hemisphere and one foot in the western. Set your watch here. It will definitely be correct. Phone 181 858 4422.

Royal Naval College: Daily except Thursdays 2:30 to 5:00. Phone 181 858 2154.

Built on the site of the old Tudor Palace at Greenwich during the seventeenth century, it became the Royal Naval College in 1873. The Painted Hall and Chapel are open to the public. The Painted Hall is now the officers' mess hall of the college. Don't miss Benjamin West's painting in the chapel of the shipwrecked St. Paul.

Ballast Quay
A riverfront area for lunching, for people-watching, shopping in the markets, and resting your feet.
St. Alfege's Church
Built in 1714 on the site of a twelfth-century church. Henry VIII was baptized in the earlier church.

Fan Museum. Tuesday to Saturday 11:00 to 4:30, Sunday noon to 4:30pm.
If you are a fan of fans, this is *the* place to be.

Thames Barrier. Ask directions at the tourist office.
This barrier was completed in 1982 to protect London from tidal flooding. The Visitors' Center has an audio-visual show and working models of the barrier. If you ever get a chance to see this man-mademonster rise up out of the water, or move about in any manner, you will be impressed—we guarantee it.

The Millennium Dome

See page 53 in our Sightseeing Chapter.

Restaurants

Treasure of China, 10-11 Nelson Rd. Phone 181 858 9884. Open daily.
Peking, Szechuan food.

Spread Eagle, 1-2 Stockwell Street. Phone 181 853 2333. Daily except Sunday dinner and Christmas day.
English pub food.

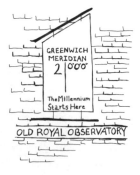

Plume of Feathers, 19 Park Vista. Phone 181 858 1661. Open daily.
English pub food.

Bosun's Whistle, west wing of Maritime Museum. Phone 181 858
7090, Open Museum hours.
Tea, lunch.

Trafalgar Tavern, Park Row. Phone 181 858 2437. Daily except Saturday lunch, Sunday dinner.
This is the most expensive restaurant in the area. English food in a
restaurant setting (as opposed to a pub).

HAMPTON COURT PALACE

Thirty minutes by train from London's Waterloo Station or a gorgeous three-hour boat ride from London's Westminster Pier to
Hampton Court. (You can also go by bus or car.) The boat operates
from April to September. Phone 171 930-2062.

The palace is open daily from 9:30 to 6:00, but closes at 4:30 from
mid-October to mid-March. Closed December 24–26. Phone 181
781 9500.

It is best to go on a nice day since there is a lot of walking outside
in the maze, gardens, gift shop, and back to the boat or train or however you arrived. Allow an entire day for this great treasure, and wear
good walking shoes: There is a lot to see and it is all on foot. There
are a number of restaurants on the grounds plus a gift shop, so your
full day can be very pleasant.

Hampton Court was built by Cardinal Wolsey in 1514 and given to
Henry VIII in 1529. Queen Victoria opened it to the public in 1838. It
is still the residence of royal favorites, who live here in "grace-and-
favor" flats.

What to see

You enter through the Trophy Gates, built for William III, buy your
ticket, walk across the moat where you will see the "King's Beasts"
sculptures, take your photographs, and continue into the palace.
There are six routes you can choose to follow. If possible, try all
six.

ROUTE 1: Start at Henry VIII's Tudor Royal Lodging. Continue on to

Henry's Great Hall, with its beautiful sixteenth-century tapestry relating the story of Abraham. Then on to the Great Watching Chamber. This is where the guards stood watch. Next is the Haunted Gallery, where the ghost of Catherine Howard, one of Henry VIII's wives, is said to lurk. Next is the Royal Chapel.

ROUTE 2: Starts with the Queen's State Apartments, with their Audience Chamber, Drawing Room, Bedroom, and Queens Gallery. The apartments, designed by Sir Christopher Wren, were built for Queen Mary in 1690, but she died before they were completed.

ROUTE 3: Begin at the Georgian Rooms, used by George I and George II, who were the last kings to live in Hampton Court. The Cartoon Gallery is next, although the original pieces that hung there are now at the Victoria and Albert Museum in London. Next comes the Communication Gallery, with portraits of Charles II's court.

ROUTE 4: Start at the King's Apartments, built in 1680 for William III and restored after a fire in the 1980s. Continue through the Guard Chamber, which has more than three thousand arms on the walls, and to the Presence Chamber, with its throne. Then on to the Great Bedchamber and the Little Bedchamber, where the king slept. Finally, take a look at William III's private suite.

ROUTE 5: Begin with the Wolsey Rooms from the early sixteenth century. Continue onto the Renaissance Picture Gallery, with paintings on loan from Queen Elizabeth II.

ROUTE 6: The Tudor Kitchens, which prepared food for over eight hundred people in Henry VIII's court.

After you finish viewing the interior, it is time to see the outside. First, see the Privy Garden, nearby which are the Pond Garden and the Banqueting House, built in 1700 by Sir Christopher Wren. The Great Vine was planted in 1768 and still has grapes growing on it. Continue on to Hampton Court Park if your feet are still holding up. It is a long walk, but the view is beautiful. The last stop of the day is Queen Anne's Maze, built in 1714. It is great fun, and you can't get lost. Finally, you get your chance to visit the gift shop, after which you return to London.

Restaurant

Le Petit Max, 97a The High Street, Vicarage Road, Hampton Wick. Phone 181 977 0236. Reserve ahead if possible. Open daily for lunch and dinner.

Excellent food, the chef buying only the freshest ingredients in season. Grilling and roasting is very popular here. Desserts are excellent. No wine list, but you can bring your own bottle (corkage fee).

IPSWICH, SUFFOLK COUNTY

One hour ten minutes from London's Liverpool Station. Tourist Office: St. Stephen's Church, St. Stephen's Lane. Phone 147 325 8070. Open Monday to Saturday 9am to 5pm.

The tourist office has some excellent maps and guides for a small fee.

Ipswich is one of England's oldest Anglo-Saxon towns. In the thirteenth century, it was the port for the Suffolk wool trade. After the Industrial Revolution, Ipswich exported coal, too. During World War II, the town was surrounded by at least sixty air bases of the U.S. Eighth Air Force, from which over three thousand bomber raids against Germany were launched. After the war, Ipswich developed into an industrial and commercial center; it is still a major port.

Sights

Christchurch Mansion. Tuesday to Friday 10:00 to 5:00. Closed December 25, 26, January 1, Good Friday.

Contains the best collection of Constable and Gainsborough paintings outside of London. Both artists were from Suffolk. The mansion was built in 1548, and Elizabeth I stayed here in 1561.

Ipswich Museum. Tuesday to Saturday. Closed December 24–27, January 1, Good Friday.

The museum has a Roman Villa display, with costumed figures in a Roman setting. Also on exhibit are replicas of locally excavated artifacts. The originals are in the British Museum, London.

St. Stephen's Church, St. Stephen's Lane. Phone 01473 258070.
This is one of twelve other medieval churches in town.

The Tolly Cobbold brewery has daily guided tours.

Ancient House, also known as Sparrowe's House, is a sixteenth-century timber building with beautiful carvings. It is now a store selling kitchen equipment.

Hotels

Courtyard by Marriott Ipswich, The Havens, Ransomes Europark, IP3 9SJ. Phone 01473 272244, fax 01473 272484.

Just over three miles from Ipswich. Modern, moderately priced hotel with 60 rooms (some nonsmoking), bar, and restaurant. Wheelchair accessible.

The Marlborough Hotel, Henley Road, Ipswich IP1 3SP. Phone 01473 257677, fax 01473 226927.

Moderate price. This lovely hotel, situated in a residential area, is comfortable, clean, and welcoming, with a beautiful garden. The restaurant serves well-priced and very good meals. The young chef offers an excellent three-course price-fixed dinner which might include duck, rabbit, or monkfish. He also serves excellent vegetarian meals. Good wine list.

Hintlesham Hall, Ipswich IP8 3NS. Phone 01473 652334.

Five miles from Ipswich. Deluxe hotel. Twenty-four pretty rooms in a sixteenth-century house in a park a short distance from Ipswich. Good restaurant, plus tennis, croquet, fishing, and riding. See also our section on cooking schools in chapter 11.

Great White Horse Hotel, Tavern Street. Phone 01473 256558.

This is a hotel to stop and have a drink at, not to stay in. It can be traced back to 1571. This hotel has been host to Charles Dickens, George II, Louis XVIII, and Lord Nelson, among others. Dickens wrote his great novel *The Pickwick Papers* while living here.

Station Hotel, opposite the train station. Phone 01473 602664.

This is a nice place to stop for lunch, dinner, tea, or a drink while waiting for a train.

Afternoon Tea

Sue Ryder Coffee Room, Hadleigh Road. Phone 01473 287999. Tuesday to Sunday from 10:00.

Serves tea, coffee, and homemade pastry.

Restaurants

Dhaka, 6 Orwell Place. Phone 01473 251397. Daily except December 25, 26.
Indian food at its best. Moderate price, credit cards accepted.

Kwok's Rendezvous, 23 St Nicholas Street. Phone 01473 256833. Closed Saturday lunch and Sunday.
Excellent Peking and Szechuan food in a seventeenth-century town house. Moderate price, credit cards accepted, wheelchair access.

Marlborough Hotel Restaurant, see Hotels above.

Mortimer's on the Quay, Wherry Quay. Phone 01473 230225, fax 01473 761611. Closed Saturday lunch, Sunday, last two weeks of August, December 24 to January 4 and bank holidays.
This restaurant has a lovely setting and very good seafood. Moderate to inexpensive.

St. Peter's Restaurant, 35-37 St. Peter's Street. Phone/fax 01473 210810. Tuesday to Saturday.
Very popular bistro with pub food as well as main courses such as lobster, chicken, and fish. The pub meals include pizza, pasta, and salads. For dessert, try the delicious homemade ice cream. All credit cards accepted.

OXFORD, OXFORDSHIRE COUNTY

One-hour train ride from Paddington Station.

Tourist Office: Gloucester Green. Phone 01865 726871. Open daily.
There are excellent walking tours that leave the tourist office daily throughout the year. The walk takes two hours and includes the highlights of the city plus the colleges that are open on the day you take the tour. After the tour, you can continue on your own.

Oxford has the oldest university in England. Its colleges, both new and old, are located throughout the city; there is not one campus. Most of the colleges are open to visitors. Be sure to check opening times for the college you wish to visit, as the times vary.

Magdalen (pronounced "Maudlin") College, founded in 1458, is the richest college at Oxford. But the most impressive, architecturally, is Christ Church College (1525), with its splendid dome. You should see the chapel here, if nothing else. Other important colleges are

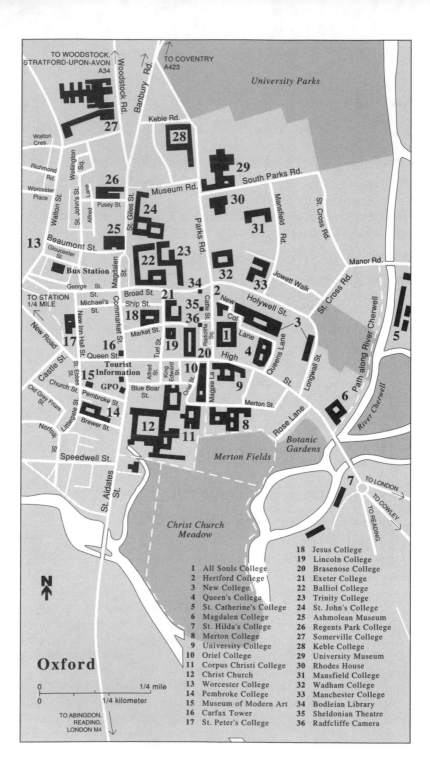

TO WOODSTOCK, STRATFORD-UPON-AVON A34

TO COVENTRY A423

University Parks

Woodstock Rd.

Banbury Rd.

Keble Rd.

Walton Cres.

27

28

29

South Parks Rd.

Richmond Rd.

Worcester Place

Wellington Sq.

Walton St.

St. John's St.

Alfred Lane

Pusey St.

St. Giles St.

Museum Rd.

26

30

Mansfield Rd.

St. Cross Rd.

24

31

Parks Rd.

Manor Rd.

13

Beaumont St.

Gloucester St.

25

23

22

32

33

Jowett Walk

St. Cross Rd.

Bus Station

Magdalen St.

George St.

34

New Inn Hall St.

TO STATION 1/4 MILE

St. Michael's St.

Commarket St.

Broad St.

Ship St.

21

35

Catte St.

New College Lane

Holywell St.

Queen's Lane

Longwall St.

Path along River Cherwell

18

Market St.

36

2

3

New Road

Turl St.

19

20

1

High

4

River Cherwell

17

16

Queen St.

St. Ebbes St.

Tourist Information

Alfred St.

King Edward St.

10

Magpie La.

9

5

Castle St.

GPO

Blue Boar St.

Oriel St.

Merton St.

6

Church St.

15

Pembroke St.

14

Brewer St.

12

11

8

Rose Lane

Old Grey Friars St.

Littlegate St.

Norfolk St.

Speedwell St.

Merton Fields

Botanic Gardens

7

TO LONDON

TO COWLEY

TO READING

St. Aldates St.

Christ Church Meadow

N

Oxford

0   1/4 mile
0   1/4 kilometer

TO ABINGDON, READING, LONDON M4

18 Jesus College
19 Lincoln College
1   All Souls College   20 Brasenose College
2   Hertford College   21 Exeter College
3   New College   22 Balliol College
4   Queen's College   23 Trinity College
5   St. Catherine's College   24 St. John's College
6   Magdalen College   25 Ashmolean Museum
7   St. Hilda's College   26 Regents Park College
8   Merton College   27 Somerville College
9   University College   28 Keble College
10 Oriel College   29 University Museum
11 Corpus Christi College   30 Rhodes House
12 Christ Church   31 Mansfield College
13 Worcester College   32 Wadham College
14 Pembroke College   33 Manchester College
15 Museum of Modern Art   34 Bodleian Library
16 Carfax Tower   35 Sheldonian Theatre
17 St. Peter's College   36 Radcliffe Camera

New College ("new," founded in 1379), University College (1249) and Merton College (1264).

The university is enough, in our opinion, but if you want more than you can see on foot, or if too many of the colleges are closed when you visit, consider The Oxford Story, a kind of theme-park version of Oxford, at which you can tour the city, the colleges, and history as well, in an audio-visual "ride." Located at 6 Broad Street, it costs £5 for adults, £4 for children.

If you have the time, by all means see some of the other excellent sights that the city has to offer. Among the most famous is the Ashmolean Museum, Britain's oldest public museum, full of fascinating objects. Tuesday to Saturday 10:00 to 4:00, Sunday 2:00 to 4:00.

Look also at the Bodleian Library, the first public library in England (founded in 1598). Like the U.S. Library of Congress, it contains every book published in the country concerned, in this case, the entire United Kingdom. Monday to Friday 9:00 to 5:00, Saturday 9:00 to 12:30.

The Sheldonian Theatre, even if nothing is playing, is worth a trip. Designed by Sir Christopher Wren and built in 1669, it is open Monday to Saturday from 10:00 to 12:45 and 2:00 to 4:45; off-season Saturday until 3:45.

The Oxford Canal, built in 1790, provided transport between London and Birmingham, and is still navigable. From the canal, you can see a few remains of Oxford Castle, which dates from Norman times.

The Covered Market, which dates from the eighteenth century, still offers tantalizing food from its stalls.

See also the University Church of St. Mary the Virgin, built in the fifteenth century, one of the city's oldest churches. From the tower, you can get a fine view of the entire city.

Hotel

Hartwell House, Oxford Road, Buckinghamshire HP17 8NL. Phone 011 44 1296 747 444, fax 011 44 1296 747 450.

Twenty miles northeast of Oxford. Expensive. Facilities include a spa, lap pool, sauna, health club, billiards, beauty parlor, excellent dining room, and beautiful countryside. President Clinton stayed here in 1994 during his visit to Britain to celebrate D-Day. Check for discounts when making your reservations. There are excellent Christmas and New Year packages. Reserve well in advance. It is an easy drive from London and very popular for weekend visits.

PARIS, FRANCE

Paris is an excellent one-day trip from London. It is also one of the best off-season destinations. The weather is never too cold. Just carry your umbrella.

Tourist office

In the U.S.: French Government Tourist Office, 444 Madison Avenue, 16th Floor, New York City, N.Y. 10022. Phone 900-990-0040 for information (calls are 50 cents per minute).

The tourist office publishes an excellent newsletter four times a year called *France Insider's News*, which details all of the latest bargains for hotels, restaurants, and sights. It also includes new information about what is going on in Paris as well as the rest of France. You can get a free subscription by calling or writing the French Tourist Office in New York.

In London: French Government Tourist Office, 178 Piccadilly, London W1VOAL. Phone 171 491 7622.

DOCUMENTS: All that is required of North Americans entering France is a valid passport.

CURRENCY: The French currency is the franc, which can be purchased from banks or the Eurostar Station in either London or Paris, or from the airport bank if you fly for the day.

Getting to Paris from London

We think the Eurostar is the easiest way to go to Paris for the day from London. If you prefer, you can fly from Heathrow or Gatwick airports in London to Charles de Gaulle or Orly Airports in Paris, but the train is so much easier. The flight time is one hour, but the hassle to and from the airports in both cities adds at least an hour, if not more, at each end.

EUROSTAR OR LE SHUTTLE

Depart for Paris or Brussels via the Eurostar from Waterloo Station. Be sure to arrive at least twenty minutes prior to train time. If you already have your ticket, check-in is automatic. Insert the ticket in a machine at the turnstile and you will be in the waiting area. Three and a half hours later you are in Paris. Tickets for the Eurostar can be purchased in Britain from Eurostar or a travel agent, a hotel concierge, or by calling 0345 881 881 or 171 834 2345. From the U.S., call BritRail at 1-800-677-8585 or Rail Europe at 1-800-942-4866. For Eurostar in London, call 1345 300 003, in Paris 44 51 06 02, in the U.S., 1-800-387-6782. You can give a credit card number and the tickets will arrive two days later. Be sure to ask for any packages or discounts. They do exist for the asking, but are not usually advertised. Off-season, the trains are less crowded.

A new Eurostar First Premium Service includes taxi transfer upon arrival in downtown Paris or London, a ten-minute check-in lane, Eurostar lounge, newspaper, drink, and deluxe meal with wine served at your seat.

First Class and Standard Class offer various fares, including full, senior, leisure, youth, and child. If you have a Eurailpass, Europass, France Railpass, Benelux Tourrail Pass, or BritRail Pass, you are entitled to a 40 percent discount on your Eurostar ticket (subject to some restrictions, so be sure to ask).

Le Shuttle: in the U.S. 1-800-388-3876, in the UK 990 353 535. This service transports cars from the UK to and from the continent.

Eurostar Web site http://www.raileurope.com. You can also find them on www.railpass.com.

Or from the U.S. call 1-800-EUROSTAR.

It is best to reserve your ticket ahead of time since the trains are usually fully booked. All seats are reserved. The waiting area has a snack bar, magazine, card and souvenir stand, and seating. While on the train you can buy food in a food car. First class has food service at your seat.

The train and stations are wheelchair accessible. (So is the Paris Metro.) Guide dogs ride all trains for free, but if you do plan to return to the UK, be sure that the dog does not have to go into quarantine.

Departures from London start at 6:19am and continue every hour until 6:53pm. Trains depart from Paris every hour from 8:10am until 8:13pm.

Paris: Overview and Arrondissements

1 Cimetière de Montmartre
2 Sacré Coeur Basilica
3 Parc La Villette
4 Parc des Buttes Chaumont
5 Jardins du Trocadero
6 Palais Chaillot
7 Cimetière de Passy
8 American Embassy
9 British Embassy
10 Petit Palais
11 Grand Palais
12 Arc de Triomphe
13 Madeleine
14 Gare St-Lazare
15 Parc Monceau
16 Palais de la Découverte
17 Opéra Garnier
18 Galeries Lafayette
19 Printemps
20 Gare du Nord
21 Gare de l'Est
22 Opéra Bastille
23 Palais Omnisports de Bercy
24 Ministère des Finances
25 Gare de Lyon
26 Parc de Montsouris
27 Cité Universitaire
28 Cimetière Montparnasse
29 Gare Montparnasse

30 Bureau des Objets Trouvés (Lost and Found)
31 Louvre
32 Palais Royale
33 Forum des Halles
34 Musée de l'Orangerie
35 Central Post Office
36 Bourse
37 Bibliothèque Nationale
38 Ecole des Arts et Métiers
39 Archives Nationales
40 Musée Carnavalet
41 Musée Picasso
42 Centre George Pompidou
43 place des Vosges
44 Musée Victor Hugo
45 Notre Dame
46 Mémorial de la Déportation
47 Université de Paris (Sorbonne)

48 Ecole Normal Supérieure
49 Musée de Cluny
50 Museum Nationale d'Histoire Naturelle
51 Panthéon
52 Eglise St-Etienne du Mont
53 La Mosquée
54 Jardin des Plantes
55 Jardins du Luxembourg
56 Eglise St-Sulpice
57 Théâtre Nationale de l'Odéon
58 Eiffel Tower
59 Champs de Mars

60 Ecole Militaire
61 UNESCO
62 Hôtel des Invalides
63 Assemblée Nationale
64 Musée d'Orsay
65 Cimetière de l'Est du Pere Lachaise

BY AIR: Air France and British Air fly almost hourly between London and Paris. Call ahead for fares since they do change, and vary according to day of the week, available specials, advance purchase, your age, and other variables. You can fly from London's Heathrow or Gatwick airports, to Charles de Gaulle or Orly in Paris, all flights taking about one hour. Toll-free phones in the U.S. are: British Air 1-800-247-9297, Air France 1-800-237-2747.

A Day in Paris!

Our first recommendation for Paris is by all means to go; our second is try to go with someone you love. Paris is that kind of city.

If you are going for the day, wear good walking shoes. You can walk all day in Paris, with perhaps a stop for lunch or a cup of tea so you can rest your feet. One glorious street leads to the next.

When you arrive in Paris at the Gare du Nord station, there are many taxis waiting for the arriving passengers, and the taxis keep coming. You can also take the Metro if you know where you want to go.

The Metro is fast and safe, and you can get all over the city using it. A single ticket costs 7F (about $1.20). One-day passes are also available from any Metro station, at airports, and at the Paris Tourist Office.

It is a good idea to have your day planned ahead of time. Because of the time change, which puts Paris one hour ahead of London, the 7am train arrives in time for lunch.

Try to have an itinerary planned for visiting the highlights (including museums), and include time for walking to sights or shopping. Everything is possible in a day in Paris if you keep going from noon until eight!

If you plan on lunch or dinner at a Michelin-starred restaurant, reserve ahead if possible.

What to Do and See (and how to do it in one day—stay longer if you can!)

Paris is definitely one of the most romantic cities in the world. Stroll the streets, snoop in shops, walk along the Seine and (depending on the weather) sit at an outdoor café or inside a bistro or tea shop.

If you are there for just a day, you might want to start with a guided bus tour. Cityrama, 4 Place des Pyramides (Phone 1 44-55-60-00) is your best choice. They have beautiful double-decker buses that take you on a two-hour trip of the highlights. You cannot get off the bus, so be prepared just to look. Tours depart six times per day at a cost of 150F (about $25) per person. Earphones provide an English-language interpretation. You cannot see everything in any case, but using the bus, you can get an overview of this gorgeous city and then, if time permits, go back to what seemed most exciting.

Start the afternoon at Notre Dame Cathedral. From the outside alone, you'll know that Notre Dame is a masterpiece. View it from all sides and from the left bank as well. Just cross the bridge and look. When you see Notre Dame from a short distance away, you can see all of the exterior sculptures, including such scenes as the *Virgin with Child, Christ and his Apostles* and *Christ after the Resurrection.* Go inside to see what was built in the thirteenth century and still stands in such splendor today. Note especially the Gothic interior, with its columns, carved stone choir screen from the fourteenth century, and beautiful windows. The choir screen shows scenes of the Last Supper. See the altar with the fourteenth-century *Virgin and Child.* Behind glass in the treasury are vestments and gold relics. In season you can climb to the top of one of the towers for a breathtaking view.

Off-season (October to May), lectures are held at the cathedral each Sunday at 4:45pm. After that, there is an organ recital and mass.

Behind Notre Dame is the Memorial des Martyrs Français de la Deportation de 1945. It pays tribute to the French martyrs of the Second World War who were sent to death camps. There is an inscription that reads "Forgive, but don't forget." The memorial is open daily from 10am to noon and from 2pm to 7pm.

After the Notre Dame experience, continue on your walking tour. There is not one correct way to see Paris. What follows is our idea of a wonderful day. Perhaps you will discover your own beautiful walk. You cannot go wrong in Paris.

There are a few options:

You can cross the bridge to the left bank, where your entire day can be spent wandering. The Musée D'Orsay, one of the great modern art museums of the world, has eighty galleries with thousands of paintings and sculptures, furniture, photographs, and a movie theater. As it is a very long walk from Notre Dame, you might want to take a taxi. (Closed on Mondays).

Another option is to cross over to the right bank, and head for the Rue de Rivoli. Walk slowly up the Rue de Rivoli, enjoying the sights and the Tuileries Gardens until you arrive at the Musée du Louvre, the world's largest museum and home to the *Mona Lisa, Venus de Milo,* and the *Winged Victory*—and thousands of other masterpieces. Continue on until you reach the Place de la Concorde with its Egyptian obelisk, take some pictures, and continue across the street to walk the beautiful and famous Champs-Elysees. You will be able to see the Arc de Triomphe as you walk up the Champs-Elysees—if your feet make it all the way there. Don't worry—there are plenty of distractions and cafés along the way.

Now it is time for a taxi to the Eiffel Tower, some pictures and a post card, and then back to the train station for your return trip to London. You will be tired, but happy.

If you can stay in Paris more than a day, do so. If not, you will never regret this wonderful day.

We're not going to recommend restaurants or hotels for Paris, as we don't know where a one-day adventure will take you. Just stop, look at the menu outside the restaurant or look inside. If it looks like what you want, stop in. There aren't very many ways to go wrong in Paris.

STRATFORD-UPON-AVON, WARWICKSHIRE COUNTY

Stratford-Upon-Avon is easily reached by train from Paddington Station, London. The trip takes two hours. Call ahead for train times.

Tourist Information Center: Bridgefoot, Stratford-Upon-Avon. Phone 1789 293127, fax 1789 295262.

Stratford-Upon-Avon is best seen off-season when there are few tourists standing in line to see all the sights. The hotels have rooms available, the restaurants are fairly empty, and the theater is at its best. The summer months bring tourists from around the world, and the streets and sights are packed.

William Shakespeare was born in Stratford in 1564 and died there in 1616.

The best way to see Stratford is to stay for a night or two, but if you cannot do so, a day trip is well worth it. By staying in Stratford you can combine it with day trips to Coventry, Warwick Castle, and other places.

What to See and Do in Stratford

Guide Friday Stratford Bus Tours. Phone 01789 294466.
The first thing to do when you arrive in Stratford, whether you

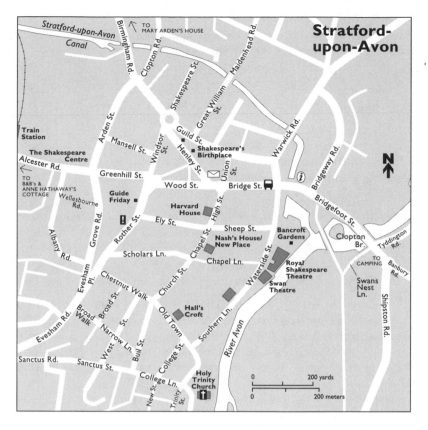

arrive by car or train, is to take the bus tour, which runs all year start-ing from the tourist office. It gives you an excellent overview of what to see before you set out on your own. It's a hop-on hop-off bus, so if you want to spend more time at a sight, get off, do your thing, and with the same ticket wait for the next bus.

Shakespeare Birthplace Trust, Henley Street: The main places of interest are run by the trust; you can buy one ticket to see all five places. If you prefer to see only one or two, you can buy individual tickets. Sights are open daily, off season 10:00 to 6:00, in-season 9:00 to 7:00 except December 24–26, January 1, and Good Friday.

Shakespeare's Birthplace is a half-timbered house. Half the house shows Elizabethan life, the other half has an exhibition about Shake-speare's life and work. There is an attached Shakespeare Centre, which exhibits costumes worn during the playwright's time.

Nash's House, Chapel Street.

Home of Thomas Nash, who was married to Elizabeth Hall, granddaughter of Shakespeare. Open same hours as birthplace.

New Place, Chapel Street.

Shakespeare died here in 1616. It was built in 1483 for the Lord Mayor of London. Open same hours as Hall's Croft House.

Anne Hathaway's Cottage.

Home of Shakespeare's wife in the village of Shottery, just outside of Stratford. He married Anne in 1582. The house is beautiful, with a thatch roof and garden. Open same hours as birthplace.

Hall's Croft, Old Town Street.

The best Tudor town house in Stratford. It has a walled garden. This was the home of Shakespeare's oldest daughter and her husband, Dr. John Hall. His office is on view, as are other rooms and furniture. Open Monday to Saturday, 9:30 to 5:00, off-season to 4:00; Sunday 10:30 to 5:00, off-season 1:30 to 4:00.

Other sights in Stratford: Holy Trinity Church, where are buried William Shakespeare, his wife Anne Hathaway, his daughter Susanna, her husband John Hall and Shakespeare's granddaughter's husband Thomas Nash. In Old Town. Be sure to take a walk along the lovely Avon River. An open market is held in the Market Square on Fridays.

After seeing the sights you can walk the busy streets of Stratford, look in the shop windows, and stop for refreshments in one of the lovely tea shops. The main drag is Henley Street. The other shopping venue is Bridge Street. On these two streets you can find all of the same shops you find in London and every other city and town. Stratford is touristy, but we like it. If you forget a toothbrush or anything else, there is a very large Super Drug. You can even try your luck and buy a lottery ticket.

Theater

The Royal Shakespeare Theatre, Stratford-Upon-Avon CV37 6BB. Phone 01789 295623.

The company that occupies this building divides its time between London and Stratford, and is definitely the best Shakespeare company in the world. Try to see a play in one of the two cities. The season in Stratford is from March to January (off-season), during which five of Shakespeare's plays are performed. There's a lovely restaurant in the theatre—reservations are a must.

The Swan Theatre, behind the Shakespeare Theatre, puts on performances by contemporaries of Shakespeare. The Other Place is a new theatre for experimental productions.

The Stratford-Upon-Avon Shakespeare Birthday Celebration is held annually on the weekend closest to April 23. There are parties and performances. For information, contact Shakespeare Centre, Henley Street, Stratford-Upon-Avon CV37 6QW. Phone 01789 204016.

The Walk

Shakespeare's life in Stratford. For information or tickets stop at the Swan Theatre or call 011 44 1789 412602.

If you like to walk, try this wonderful two-hour walking tour held every Saturday at 10:30am during the off-season. It starts and ends at the Swan Theatre on Waterside. As of this writing, Jonathan Milton is the guide. He is an actor and director of the Traveling Light Shakespeare Company and has coauthored two plays about the life of William Shakespeare. Children under 12 are free if accompanied by an adult (one child per one adult).

Hotels

IF YOU HAVE A CAR

Ettington Park Hotel, Alderminster CV37 8BS. Phone 1789 450123, fax 1789 450472.

This hotel is a restored Gothic country house opened in 1985, and just six miles from Stratford. There are forty-eight rooms and nine suites all individually furnished, all with bath, TV, hair dryer, tea maker, and phone. Hotel facilities and amenities include, room service, indoor pool, sauna, restaurant, bar, two tennis courts, and free parking. It is the only deluxe hotel in the Stratford area. Wheelchair access.

Lygon Arms, Broadway, Worcestershire WR12 7DU. Phone 1386 852 255, fax 1386 858 611.

Built in 1532. Expensive. Included with the price of the room is morning tea, the *Daily Telegraph* newspaper, and Continental breakfast. This hotel offers packages for weekends, Christmas and New Year. Reserve ahead. Available at the hotel are an indoor pool, spa, heath club, and a beauty parlor. The hotel also has an excellent restaurant. The Lygon Arms is accessible to Stratford-Upon-Avon and all of the Cotswold villages. It is also an ideal location for visiting Warwick and Coventry, both described in this chapter.

Welcombe Hotel and Golf Course, Warwick Road, Stratford, Warwickshire. CV37 ONR. Phone 1789 295252, fax 1789 414666.

Two miles from Stratford, the Welcombe is located on 157 beautiful acres. All rooms with bath, robes, phone, TV, some with four-poster beds. Facilities and amenities include room service, restaurant, bar, afternoon tea, eighteen-hole golf course, two lighted tennis courts, and free parking. Superior first class. Wheelchair access.

FIRST CLASS HOTELS WITHIN WALKING DISTANCE OF SIGHTS AND THEATERS

The Arden, Waterside, Stratford-Upon-Avon, CV37 6BA. Phone 1789 415874.

Located opposite the Royal Shakespeare Theatre. All rooms with private bath or shower, TV, phone, tea maker, minibar. Facilities and amenities include room service, laundry service, baby sitting, free parking, restaurant, bar.

The Shakespeare, Chapel Street, Stratford-Upon-Avon, CV37 6ER. Phone 1789 294771, fax 1789 415411.

Located in town. Nicely furnished rooms with bath, TV, tea maker, phone. Facilities and amenities include an elevator, room service, restaurant, bar, free parking. Children under 16 stay free in parents' room. Fireplace in public rooms is lovely in winter.

Stratford Moat House, Bridgefoot, Stratford-Upon-Avon, CV37 6YR. Phone 1789 279988, fax 1789 298589.

Modern 247-room hotel located near the Royal Shakespeare Theatre and Shakespeare Birthplace. All rooms with AC, bath, shower,

TV, tea maker, phone, radio. Facilities and amenities include two restaurants, bar, English pub, indoor pool, sauna, solarium, shops, gardens, free parking. Rooms with river view. Wheelchair access.

The White Swan, Rother Street Stratford-Upon-Avon, CV37 6NH. Phone 1789 297022, fax 1789 268773.

Tudor-style inn dating from 1450, facing Market Square. Five-minute walk from river and town center. All modern rooms with bath, TV, phone, tea maker. Facilities and amenities include room service, restaurant and bar, free parking.

TOURIST-CLASS HOTELS WITHIN WALKING DISTANCE OF SIGHTS

Falcon Hotel, Chapel Street, Stratford-Upon-Avon, CV37 6HA. Phone 1789 279953, fax 1789 414260.

Located near Shakespeare Theatre in fifteenth-century building with modern annex. Beamed ceilings, rooms with bath, TV, phone, tea maker. Facilities and amenities include one four-poster-bed suite, elevator, restaurant, bar, free parking. Children under fourteen stay free in parents' room.

Forte Posthouse, Stratford-Upon-Avon, Bridgefoot CV37 7LT. Phone 1789 266761, fax 1789 414547.

This is a seventeenth-century inn set in private gardens on the Avon, overlooking the Royal Shakespeare Theatre. Nice rooms with bath, radio, TV. The hotel has a dining room, bar, free parking. Wheelchair access.

BED & BREAKFAST

Alveston Cottage, Tiddington Road, Stratford-Upon-Avon CV37 7AE. Phone 01789 292847. Open April to October. No children, no smoking. Rates $113 double, approximately.

This small cottage has only two rooms, one with a bath attached, the other with a private bath down the hall. It is wonderfully located in the heart of Stratford with views of the river from both rooms. Most sights are within walking distance.

Tea

Bensons of Stratford-Upon-Avon, 4 Bard Walk. Phone 01789 261116. Daily except Sunday during the off-season. Wheelchair accessible.

Located near Shakespeare's birthplace, Mary Arden's House, and Ann Hathaway's Cottage, this tea shop is full of English tradition. If you wish to read, newspapers and magazines are available. Tea is served in bone china cups with silver tableware. Fresh flowers are on the tables. Tea consists of sandwiches, scones with jam and cream, and tea. Everything is excellent and homemade.

Richoux, Old Red Lion Court, Bridge Street. Phone 01789 415377. Open daily.

This tea shop is part of a chain of restaurants. They serve a variety of teas, pastries, and scones with jam and cream. Located just off one of the two main shopping streets.

Restaurants

EXPENSIVE: Box Tree Restaurant, Royal Shakespeare Theatre Waterside. Phone 01789 293226. Open only when the theater is open.

Excellent food and views over the river. Try the roast rack of lamb, a house specialty. Also excellent fish dishes. All credit cards accepted.

MODERATE: Liaison, 1 Shakespeare Street. Phone 01789 293400, fax 01789 297863. Lunch Monday to Friday, dinner Monday to Saturday.

Vegetarian meals available, but the regular menu features fish, meats, and some Oriental dishes such as a delicious Thai fish soup. The bread and butter pudding for dessert is excellent. Credit cards accepted.

PUB: Slug and Lettuce, 38 Guild Street. Phone 01789 299700. Open daily.

Very popular pub with good bar food and desserts. Lovely terrace for summer meals and drinks.

WARWICK, WARWICKSHIRE COUNTY

Warwick (pronounced "war-ick") is just nine miles northeast of Stratford-Upon-Avon.

Tourist Office: Located in the court house on Jury Street. Phone 01926 492212.

If you are coming from Stratford by bus, take the X16 bus directly to the main attraction in Warwick—the castle. Warwick is an hour's train ride from London's Paddington Station.

If you arrive by train and want a car and driver, you can call Castle Cars at 01926 494989. They will come to the station and pick you up. The other alternative is a taxi from the station to the castle.

Warwick Castle

April to October daily 10:00 to 6:00, October to March 10:00 to 5:00; closed Christmas day.

Warwick Castle is the most beautiful medieval castle in England. Built on a rise overlooking the Avon River, the castle houses one of England's largest and best collections of medieval weapons and armor. You can visit a torture chamber and dungeon, see a knight in shining armor, and climb the tower. The tower has 250 steps and is one way only, so be sure you want to finish the climb before you start. That's a lot of steps!

Also see the Kingmaker, A Preparation for Battle exhibit, which features the sights and sounds of 1471 as the Earl of Warwick gets ready for battle. The castle has beautiful furniture, paintings by great artists such as Rubens and Van Dyck, and a new addition of life-size Madame Tussaud wax figures, dressed in the appropriate costumes of the time.

The sixty acres the castle is built on are beautifully landscaped and well-kept, even in off-season.

If you have to rest your feet, stop for lunch or tea at the restaurant located on the grounds. There is also a small book shop here.

Before or after visiting the castle, you must walk to the bridge across the Avon, just outside the castle walls, for a beautiful view of the castle and the river below. On a misty off-season day, it can be unforgettable. You will also see rows of houses dating from the middle ages. To get to the bridge, make a right turn as you leave the castle and walk down the hill to the river. You won't regret it.

ALSO IN WARWICK: St Mary's Collegiate Church, where the earls of Warwick are buried; the Beauchamp on Church Street is beautiful and its tower, once climbed, offers a view of the countryside; Lord Leycester Hospital on High Street, a home for old soldiers since 1571, has short tours (Tuesday to Saturday from 10am to 5pm, daily except Good Friday and Christmas Day); St. John's House is a beautiful seventeenth-century mansion, now a museum with exhibits of Victorian costumes, a school room, a kitchen, and musical instruments (daily 10:00 to 5:30). Oken's Doll Museum on Castle

Street (open daily April to October 10am to 5pm) has displays of antique dolls and toys.

Hotel

Tudor House Inn, 90-92 West Street, Warwick CV34 6AW. Phone 1926 495447, fax 1926 492948.

The inn has eleven rooms, six with bath, as well as a restaurant and bar. All credit cards accepted. It was built in 1472, but modernized not too long ago. It remains a simple, small hotel with a lot of atmosphere. The restaurant is not expensive, and the food and service are very good.

Restaurant

Fanshawe's, 22 Market Place. Phone 1926 410590. All credit cards accepted. Monday to Saturday (no lunch Monday).

Very well located on the market square in Warwick, this spot offers a varied menu of either cold sandwiches, lamb, or fish, which is nicely prepared. Game in season.

WINDSOR, BERKSHIRE COUNTY

Windsor is a twenty-five-mile, fifty-minute train ride from London's Waterloo Station to Windsor Riverside Station.

Tourist Office: 24 High Street. Phone 1753 852010. Open summer 9:30am to 6pm, off-season 9:30am to 4pm.

The main sight here is Windsor Castle. Queen Elizabeth II stays at the castle quite often, and when she is there, or on official occasions, the state apartments are closed. If you wish to see them, call the tourist office to check if the Queen is in residence. Other areas are open, but the apartments are so beautiful, it would be a pity to miss them. A beautiful, illustrated guide book of Windsor Castle, which is well worth the price, lays out the route for seeing the place.

Windsor Castle has been the home of British royalty for 900 years. It started as a wooden fortress, built in 1066 by William the Conqueror. Don't miss the changing of the guard, especially if you are with children, who will love this. The new guards leave Victoria Barracks at 10:55am, march along High Street to the castle, where the changing takes place at 11am. The old guards depart the castle at 11:30am along High Street. Stand on High Street or Castle Street for the best views.

After visiting Windsor, you can walk over the river bridge to Eton, home of Eton College, founded in 1440 by Henry IV. It is known by the British as a "public school," but it is actually a private school, England's most famous.

Lunch

The Royal Oak, opposite Riverside Station. Excellent pub food and service. It was opened in 1736, so they know how to run a restaurant!

IF YOU HAVE A CAR

Waterside Inn, Ferry Road, Bray-on-Thames (near Windsor). Phone 0628 20691, fax 0628 784710. Lunch Wednesday to Sunday, dinner Tuesday to Sunday.

The Waterside Inn has seven beautiful rooms and an excellent restaurant. This is a gorgeous and expensive restaurant, but well worth the trip and cost. It is located directly on the river Thames, and you can have your drinks on the terrace in warm weather. The food is French, with a superb menu and wine list. The best buy is the prix fixe lunch or dinner.

Oakley Court Hotel, Windsor Road, Water Oakley (near Windsor). Phone 0628 74141, fax 0628 37011. Daily, breakfast, lunch, and dinner.

This is an attractive hotel with an excellent restaurant, just three miles from Windsor, and built on the banks of the river Thames. The bedrooms are beautiful, some with four-poster beds. There is a nine-hole golf course (pitch and putt), fishing, tennis, and golf nearby. Two restaurants, one formal and one casual. The food is excellent in both. Open all year. No smoking area in restaurant, no dogs (except guide dogs).

Windsor Castle

Index

AARP (American Association of Retired
    People); travel discounts, 14–15
Abbey Tavern (Howth, Ireland), 186–87
Abbey Theatre (Dublin), 175
Access to the Underground (wheelchair
    access), 14
Accession Day, 24
Adelphi Theatre; ghost of William Terriss, 73
Adnams Hotels (Aldeburgh), 152
Adrian's (restaurant) (Howth, Ireland), 187
after-Christmas sales, 23
afternoon tea, 109–11; Brown's Hotel, 110;
    Claridge's Hotel, 110; Fortnum & Mason,
    110, 118, 126; Grosvenor House, 110;
    Harrods, 110; Lanesborough Hotel, 111;
    Richoux, 111; Ritz Hotel, 111
afternoon tea (day trip from London);
    Bensons of Stratford-Upon-Avon, 224;
    Bewley's (Dublin), 185; Canary Restaurant
    (Bath), 157; Mrs. Pickwick's Tea Room
    (Coventry), 169; Richoux (Stratford-Upon-
    Avon), 224; Royal Pavilion tearoom
    (Brighton), 160; Sue Ryder Coffee Room
    (Ipswich), 209
AGA Workshop (cooking school), 129
AIDS and HIV services, 13
Aintree Race Course (Liverpool), 134–35;
    Grand National steeplechase, 134–35
air travel; British Air carry-on restrictions, 4;
    charter flights, 4; consolidators, 4; Europe
    Flight Pass, 3; fly/sail packages, 2; flying
    time, 2–3; major airlines, 3; train service
    (Gatwick and Heathrow to London), 4–5
Alastair Little (restaurant), 96
Alastair Little at Lancaster Road (restaurant),
    96
Aldeburgh (Suffolk County), 150–54;
    Aldeburgh Festival, 30, 151; Britain
    concerts, 31, 151; central bookings, 152;
    Church of St. Peter and St. Paul, 154; hotels
    & accommodations, 152–53; restaurants,
153–54; river trips, 154; shopping, 154;
    sightseeing, 154; traveling to, 151
Aldeburgh Bookshop, 154
Aldeburgh Moot Hall and Museum, 154
Alfred Dunhill (tobacconist), 119
All England Lawn Tennis Championships
    (Wimbledon), 30, 135
All Hallows Church, 68
Alveston Cottage (B & B) (Stratford-Upon-
    Avon), 224
American Airlines, 3
American Museum (Bath), 156
Ancient House (Sparrowe's House) (Ipswich),
    208
animals; attempting to smuggle, 5; quarantine
    of, 5
Ann Hathaway's Cottage (Stratford-Upon-
    Avon), 220
Antenaeum Hotel, The, 81
Antiquarian Book Fair (Olympia), 30, 121
antiques and markets; Antiquarian Book Fair
    (Olympia), 30, 121; Camden Lock
    (Camden High Street), 122; Camden
    Passage at Upper Street (Islington area),
    122; Covent Garden Markets, 121–22;
    Greenwich Markets, 122–23; Grosvenor
    House Antiques Fair, 121; Piccadilly
    Market, 122; Portobello Road, 121
apartments; apartment and home rentals, 11;
    to sublet, 94
Aquascutum (clothing store), 125
Arc de Triomphe (Paris), 218
Arden, The (hotel) (Stratford-Upon-Avon),
    222–23
art exhibits; Royal Academy Summer
    Exhibition, 28, 29, 64
Arundel House (Cambridge), 165
Ascension Day, 29
Ascot Racecourse, 134; Royal Ascot, 29–30, 134
Ashmolean Museum (Oxford), 211
Assaggi (restaurant), 97

Assembly Rooms and Museum of Costume (Bath), 155
At Home Abroad, 11
ATMs and exchange rates, 6
Aubergine (restaurant), 97; wheelchair-accessibility, 109
August Bank Holiday, 31
Austin-Reed (clothing store), 125
Avenue (restaurant), 97

Babbington, Anthony, ghost of, 75
Ballast Quay (Greenwich), 204
ballet. *See* dance
Balmoral Hotel (Edinburgh), 199; restaurant, 201
Bank (restaurant), 97–98
Bank of England Museum, 64
Banqueting House (Whitehall); Rubens ceiling painting, 52
Barclay International (apartments to sublet), 94
Basil Street Hotel, 81–82
Bath (Sumerset County), 154–58; American Museum, 156; Assembly Rooms and Museum of Costume, 155; Bath Abbey, 155; The Circus, 156; Holburne of Menstrie Museum, 156; hotels & accommodations, 156–57; No. 1 Royal Crescent, 156; Pulteney Bridge, 156; restaurants, 157–58; Roman Baths and Pump Room, 155; Roman Baths Museum, 155; Royal Crescent, 155; tourist centre, 155; traveling to, 154
Bath School of Cookery, The, 129–30
Bath Spa Hotel (Bath), 156–57
Battersea Park; bicycling, 135; Easter Parade, 24; London Harness Horse Parade, 24
Battle of Britain Week, 32
Beating Retreat (Horse Guards Parade), 29
Beauchamp (Warwick), 226
Beaufort Hotel, 82
Becket, Thomas, 167
bed and breakfast accommodations; Earl Soham Lodge (Aldeburgh), 152; Grange Farm (Aldeburgh), 152; Ireland, 192; Kiln Farm (Aldeburgh), 152; Old Mill (Coventry), 169
Bed and Breakfast Ireland, 192
Belgo Noord (restaurant), 98
Belvedere, The (restaurant), 98
Bensons of Stratford-Upon-Avon (afternoon tea), 224
Bentham, Jeremy, ghost of, 76
Berk, Burlington Arcade (woolens), 125
Berkeley Court (hotel) (Dublin), 189–90
Berkeley Hotel (London), 82
Bethnal Green Museum of Childhood (Victoria & Albert Museum), 144
Bewley's (restaurant) (Dublin), 185
BHS (British Home Stores), 119
Bibendum Restaurant, 98; wheelchair-accessibility, 109

bicycling, 135–36; London Cyclist's Route Map, 136; rentals, 136; *See also* boating; fitness centers; golf; horse riding; jogging; tennis (as participatory sport)
Big Ben (Houses of Parliament), 47, 139–40
Blacks (sports equipment & clothing), 124
Blair, Tony, 53
Blakes Hotel (restaurant), 98
Blandings Country Homes in England, 11
Blenheim Palace (Woodstock, Oxfordshire), 158–59; restaurants, 159; Tourist Office, 158; traveling to, 158
Blooms (hotel) (Dublin), 191
Blue Badge Guide (Cambridge), 163
Boadicea's Tomb, 77
boat racing; Doggett's Coat & Badge Race, 31; Head of the River Race, 25; Oxford-Cambridge boat race, 25; *See also* cricket; horse racing; horse shows and events; outdoor activities; soccer; Rugby; tennis
boat travel to England; QE2 (Cunard Line), 2
boating, 136; Docklands, 136; rentals, 136; the Serpentine, 136; the Thames, 136; *See also* bicycling; fitness centers; golf; horse riding; jogging; tennis (as participatory sport)
Bodleian Library (Oxford), 211
Body Positive Helpline, 13
Body Shop (soaps & shampoos), 118
Boleyn, Anne, ghost of, 76
Bombay Brasserie (restaurant), 99
book fairs; Antiquarian Book Fair, 30, 121; International Book Fair (Olympia Exhibition Centre), 25
bookstores; Aldeburgh Bookshop (Aldeburgh), 154; Antiquarian Book Fair (Olympia), 30, 121; discount, 119; Hatchards, 118
Boots Drug Stores, 118, 118–19, 125
Bosun's Whistle (restaurant) (Greenwich), 205
Botanic Gardens (Cambridge), 164
Boy Scouts and Girl Guide Memorial Service, 23
Box Tree Restaurant (Stratford-Upon-Avon), 224
boxing day (Christmas season), 37
Bradmore House (restaurant), 111
Brasserie na Mara (restaurant) (Dun Laoghaire, Ireland), 188
Bray (Ireland), 188
Brazen Head Pub (Dublin), 193
Brighton (East Sussex), 160–61; Brighton Marina, 161; Brighton Sea Life Centre, 161; restaurants, 161; Royal Pavilion on the Steine, 160; shopping, 160; sightseeing, 160–61; traveling to, 160; Tourist Office, 160; Veteran Car Run to Brighton, 35; Volk Electric Railway, 161; walking tours, 161
Brighton Arts Festival, 28, 160
Brighton Museum and Art Gallery, 160
British Air Travel Store, 118
British Airways, 3; carry-on restrictions, 4;

Millennium Ferris Wheel, 54
British clothing (shopping for); Aquascutum, 125; Austin-reed, 125; Berk, Burlington Arcade, 125; Gieves & Hawkes, 125; Jaeger's Regent Street, 125; Turnbull & Asser, 119, 125; *See also* haberdashers
British International Motor Show, 35
British Library (St. Pancras Station), 47
British Museum, 46, 47, 61, 144–45; ghost of, 73
British Tourist Authority; American offices, 1; New York City, 195
Britten, Benjamin, 151
Brompton Oratory (RC) Church, 68
Brooklands Grange Hotel (Coventry), 169
Brown's Hotel, 82; afternoon tea, 111
Browns (restaurant) (Brighton), 161
Brudenell Hotel (Aldeburgh), 152
Buckingham Palace, 140; Changing of the Queen's Guard, 22, 48, 140; The Queen's Gallery, 64; Royal Mews, 67, 140; tours, 31, 48–50, 140
Buckstone, John, ghost of, 74
Burger King, 112
Burling Arcade, 118
Burns Night (Robert Burns birthday celebration), 23
bus and underground travel, 9–10, 19; Access to the Underground (wheelchair access), 14; London transport, 9; Travelcards and passes, 9–10
Butley-Orford Oysterage (Aldeburgh), 153

C&A stores (ski clothing), 124
Cabaret Mechanical Theatre, 140
Cabinet War Rooms, 55
Café Nico, 99
Caledonian Hotel (Edinburgh), 199– 220; restaurant, 201
Cambridge (Cambridgeshire County), 161–66; Blue Badge Guide, 163; boat tours & punting (River Cam), 163, 164; Botanic Gardens, 164; Fitzwilliam (museum), 164; Great St. Mary's Church, 163; hotels & accommodations, 165–66; King's College, 163; Magdalene College, 164; map, 162; Oxford-Cambridge boat race, 25; Peterhouse College, 164; Queens College, 164; restaurants, 166; Round Tower, 164; St. John's College, 164; Scott Polar Research Institute, 164; shopping, 163; Shop-mobility Centre, 163; traveling to, 161; Tourist Office, 161; Trinity College, 163; walking tours, 163
Cambridge Folk Festival, 31, 164
Camden Lock (Camden High Street), 122
Camden Passage at Upper Street (Islington area); antique shopping, 122
canal trips, 66
Canary Restaurant (Bath), 157
Canteen (restaurant), 99
Canterbury (Kent County), 166–67;

Canterbury Cathedral, 166–67; Canterbury Heritage Museum, 167; Marlow Theatre, 167; restaurants, 167; Roman Museum, 167; Royal Museum, 167; St. Augustine's Abbey, 167; St. Martin's Church, 167; Tourist Office, 166; traveling to, 166; the Weavers House, 167
Canterbury Festival, 32
Canterbury Heritage Museum, 167
Capital Hotel, 82
Capital Hotel Restaurant, 99; wheelchair-accessibility, 109
Captain's Cabin Restaurant (Aldeburgh), 153
car shows and runs; Classic Car Show (Alexandra Palace), 25; Veteran Car Run to Brighton, 35
Carlyle's House, 64
carry-on luggage restrictions (British Air), 4
Cashmere Clinic, 15
Caswell Hotel, 83
Central Club, 83
Ceremony of the Keys of the Tower of London, 22–23
Champs-Élysées (Paris), 218
Changing of the Guard (St. James's Palace), 22, 52
Changing of the Queen's Guard (Buckingham Palace), 22, 48
Changing of the Queen's Life Guard (Horse Guards Parade), 22
Channing's Brasserie (Edinburgh), 201
charitable trust, 50
charter flights, 4
Chef Imperial (restaurant) (Blenheim Palace), 159
Chelsea Flower Show, 26
Chelsea Football Club (soccer team), 135
Cheltenham (steeplechase races), 134; The National Hunt Festival, 134
Chez Nico (restaurant), 99; wheelchair-accessibility, 109
Chichester, Sir Francis, 202; *Gipsy Moth IV*, 202
children; children's food out, 112–13; London as a vacation destination, 139; traveling with, 5
children (museums of special interest), 143–47; Bethnal Green Museum of Childhood, 144; British Museum, 144–45; London Toy & Model Museum, 66, 145; London Transport Museum, 66, 145; Madame Tussaud's (wax museum), 71, 145; Museum of the Moving Image, 67, 146; National Gallery, 57, 61; National Maritime Museum (Greenwich), 53, 63, 202–3; National Portrait Gallery, 62, 146; Natural History Museum, 62, 146; Pollock's Toy Museum, 67, 142; Royal Air Force (RAF) Museum, 67, 146; Science Museum, 62, 146; Victoria & Albert Museum, 61, 68, 146–47; *See also* museums (special interest)

children (parks), 147–48; Greenwich Park (Greenwich), 147; Hampstead Heath, 148; Hyde Park, 147; Kensington Gardens, 147; Regent's Park, 148; St. James's Park, 148

children (restaurants attractive to); Bradmore House, 111; Deals, 111; Dell Restaurant, 147; Pizza Express, 112; Rainforest Café, 112; Smollensky's Balloon, 112; Sticky Fingers, 112

children (shopping); Davenport's Magic Shop, 141; Disney Store, 118; Hamleys Toy Store, 118, 141; Harrods, 141

children (sightseeing and places of special interest), 139–43; Big Ben, 139–40; Buckingham Palace, 140; Cabaret Mechanical Theatre, 140; Changing of the Guard, 140; Commonwealth Experience, 140; Covent Garden, 140; *Cutty Sark* (clipper ship), 53, 140, 202; *HMS Belfast* (World War II warship), 141; London Aquarium, 59, 141–42; London Bridge, 142; London Dungeon, 70, 142; London Zoo, 59; Russian Submarine, 142; Segaworld (theme park), 142; Tower Bridge, 143; Tower of London, 142–43; Virgin Game Center, 143; Windsor Castle, 227; *See also* parades and marches

chinaware; Chinacraft, 120; Portmeirion Potteries Ltd. (Stoke-On-Trent), 127; Reject China Shops, 120; Royal Doulton Company (Stoke-On-Trent), 127; Royal Worcester (Stoke-On-Trent), 127; Thomas Goode, 120; Wedgewood Visitor Centre (Stoke-On-Trent), 127

Chinese New Year celebrations, 23

Christ Church Cathedral (Dublin), 179, 180

Christ Church College (Oxford), 211

Christ's Hospital March, 32

Christchurch Mansion (Ipswich), 207

Christmas; carol service, 37; Christmas Parade, 37; boxing day, 37; tree lighting (Trafalgar Square), 37

Church of St. Andrew Undershaft; John Stow Memorial Service, 25

Church of St. Bartholomew-the-Great (West Smithfield), 24, 57; Good Friday, 24; Maundy Purses, 24

Church of St. Peter and St. Paul (Aldeburgh), 154

churches and cathedrals; All Hallows, 68; Brompton Oratory (RC), 68; Church of St. Andrew Undershaft, 25; Church of St. Bartholomew-the-Great (West Smithfield), 24, 57; Knights Templar, 57; St. Clements Danes (The Strand), 25, 68; St. Giles Cripplegate, 69; St. Helen Bishopsgate, 69; St. James's (Piccadilly), 69; St. James's Church (Garlick Hill), 75; St. Martin-in-the-Fields (Trafalgar Square), 35, 69; St. Mary-le-Bow Church (Cheapside), 69; St. Olave's Church, 29; St. Paul's Cathedral, 26, 37, 48; Southwark Cathedral, 59; Wesley's Chapel,

House & Museum of Methodism, 69; Westminster Abbey, 23, 24, 32, 34– 35, 45–46, 76; Westminster Cathedral (RC), 59

City of London Festival, 30

Clarence Hotel (Dublin), 190

Claridge's Brook Street (hotel), 83; afternoon tea, 111

Claridge's Restaurant, 99

Clarke's (restaurant), 99–100

Classic Car Show (Alexandra Palace), 25

climate; Dublin, 176; London, 6, 20; Paris, 212; Scotland, 194

Clink Prison Museum, 64

Clock Museum (Guildhall), 64

Coast (restaurant), 100

Cobra (sports clothing & shoes), 123

Cockney children, distribution of oranges and lemons to, 25

Collection, The (restaurant), 100

Commemorative Service for Charles I, 23

Commons, The (restaurant) (Dublin), 192

Commonwealth Experience, 140

Computex (home exchange), 10

Concert Hall Restaurant (Aldeburgh), 153

Connaught Hotel, 83

Connaught Hotel Grill, 100

Conrad Dublin International (hotel) (Dublin), 190

Continental Airlines, 3

cooking schools; AGA Workshop, 129; The Bath School of Cookery, 129–30; Eileen Follows, 130; Hintlesham Hall, 130; Le Cordon Bleu L'Art Culinaire, 130; Le Manoir Aux Quat' Saisons, 131; Leith's School of Food and Wine, 130–31; Roselyne Masselin's Vegetarian Cookery School, 131; Squires Kitchen International (School of Cake Decorations), 131

Cool Britannia, 53

Coolhurst Tennis, Centre, 137

Coral-Eclipse Stakes (Sandown Park), 134

Costermonger's Harvest Festival, 35

Council on International Educational Exchange, 15

Courtauld Institute Picture Gallery, 63

Courtyard by Marriott Ipswich (hotel), 208

Covent Garden, 58, 140; Royal Opera House, 39, 40–41, 58

Covent Garden Markets; antique & general shopping, 119, 121–22

Covent Garden Tube Station; ghost of William Terriss, 73

Coventry (West Midlands County), 168–69; Coventry Cathedral, 168; Guildhall of St. Mary's, 168; Herbert Art Gallery and Museum, 168; Lady Godiva statue, 168–69; Museum of British Road Transport, 168; restaurants, 169; sightseeing, 168–69; Tourist Office, 168; traveling to, 168

Coventry Cathedral, 168; *Christ in Glory* tapestry (Graham Sutherland), 168; engraved-glass screen (John Hutton), 168;

Sir Jacob Epstein's sculptures, 168; stained glass windows (John Piper), 168
Crabbe, George, 151
credit cards; lost, 11; and tennis court reservations, 137
cricket, 133; Cricket Test Matches, 30; Lord's Cricket Ground, 133; MCC Cricket Museum, 66; Oval Cricket Ground, 133; *See also* boat racing; horse racing; horse shows and events; outdoor activities; soccer; Rugby; tennis
Cricketers Hotel (Aldeburgh), 152
Criterion, The (restaurant), 100
Cromwell, Oliver, ghost of, 75
Crown Hotel (Aldeburgh), 152
Crown Passage, 78
Crufts Dog Show, 24
Cuban cigars and U.S. customs, 119
Cunard Line; address/phone number/Web site, 2; fly/sail packages, 2
currency and coins, 6–7; buying pounds sterling before arrival, 7; Euro, 6, 7; in Ireland, 172; in Scotland, 196
Curse of St. Giles Circus, 77
Cutty Sark (clipper ship), 53, 140, 202

D. H. Evans (department store), 119
daily events (year-round), 22–23
dance (events & venues), 41; City of London Festival, 30; Outdoor Theatre Season (Holland Park), 30; Royal Ballet, 39, 41; Sadler's Wells, 41
Daphne's (restaurant), 100
Davenport's Magic Shop, 141
Davidoff (tobacconist), 119
Davy Byrnes Pub (Dublin), 194
day trips from London; Aldeburgh (Suffolk County), 150–54; Bath (Sumerset County), 154–58; Blenheim Palace (Woodstock, Oxfordshire), 158–59; Brighton (East Sussex), 160–61; Cambridge (Cambridgeshire County), 161–66; Canterbury (Kent County), 166–67; Coventry (West Midlands County), 168–69; Dublin (Republic of Ireland), 169– 94; Edinburgh (Scotland), 194–201; Greenwich, 201–5; Hampton Court Palace, 205–7; Ipswich (Suffolk County), 207–9; map, 149; Oxford (Oxfordshire County), 209–12; Paris (France), 212–18; Stratford-Upon-Avon, 218–25; Warwick (Warwickshire County), 225–26; Windsor (Berkshire County), 226–28
De Selby (restaurant) (Dun Laoghaire, Ireland), 188
Deals (restaurants), 101, 111
Debenhams (department store), 119, 126
Dee Gee's Wine and Steak Bar (Howth, Ireland), 187
Dell Restaurant, 147
Delta Airlines, 3

dental emergency care, 13
department stores; BHS (British Home Stores), 119; D. H. Evans, 119; Debenhams, 119, 126; Dickins & Jones, 118; Dr. Martens, 126; Fenwick, 116, 126; Harrods, 52, 111, 119, 121, 126; Harvey Nichols, 119, 126; John Lewis, 119; Liberty, 118, 128; Marks & Spencer, 118, 126; Nicole Farhi, 115–16, 128; Selfridges, 119, 128; Sogo, 118
Derby, the (Epsom Downs), 29, 134
Dhaka (restaurant) (Ipswich), 209
DIAL-A-BED (Edinburgh), 199
Dial-A-Bike (London), 136
Dickens's House, 65
Dickins & Jones (department store), 118
dining; American food, 112–13; children's food out, 112–13; restaurants, 95–108; teas, 109–111; water, 96; wine and beer, 96; smoking/nonsmoking, 95; wheelchair-accessible, 109; *See also* afternoon tea; restaurants
Diplomat Hotel, 83
Docklands (marinas & boat rentals), 136
Doctor Johnson's House, 65
Doggett's Coat & Badge Race, 31
Dorchester, The (hotel), 84
Dorset Square Hotel, 84
Dr. Martens (department store), 126
Drake, Sir Francis, 202
drivers (for hire), 8
driving (in Britain), 8
Drury Lane Theatre; ghost of the Man in Grey, 73–74
duBarry, Madame; and the crown jewels of France, 77– 78
Dublin (Republic of Ireland), 169–94; car rental, 174; currency, 172; electric currents, 173; entrance requirements, 172; golf, 176; horse racing, 184–85; map, 170–71; public holidays, 176; safety reminders, 176, 177; shopping, 173, 179; telephones, 175; theater, 175; Tourist Offices, 172; transportation (bus/rail/taxi), 174–75; travelers with disabilities, 175; traveling to, 177–78; VAT (Value Added Tax) refunds, 173– 74
Dublin (group walks); Historical Walking Tours of Dublin, 184; Literary Pub Crawl, 184; Revolutionary Dublin Tour, 184
Dublin (hotels & accommodations), 189–92; apartment rentals, 178; B & B, 192; Berkeley Court, 189–90; Blooms, 191; Clarence Hotel, 190; Conrad Dublin International, 190; hostels, 178; Jurys, 191–92; Killiney Castle, 190; Merrion Hotel, 190–91; Shelbourne Hotel, 191; Stephen's Hall, 191; Westbury, 191
Dublin (pubs), 179, 193–94; Brazen Head, 193; Davy Byrnes, 194; Kitty O'Shea's Bar, 194; Literary Pub Crawl, 184; O'Dwyer's, 194; The Old Stand, 194

Dublin (restaurants), 192–93; Bewley's, 185; The Commons, 192; Elephant and Castle, 193; Imperial Chinese Restaurant, 193; Les Frères Jacques, 193; Oisin's Irish Restaurant, 193; Roly's Bistro, 192–93
Dublin (sightseeing), 178–79; Christ Church Cathedral, 179, 180; Dublin Castle, 179, 180–81; Dublin City Tour, 179; Dublin's Writers Museum, 183–84; General Post Office, 179, 182; Gray Line Tour Company, 179; Guinness Brewery Centre, 181; Ha'penny Bridge, 182; Irish Jewish Museum, 181–83; Irish Museum of Modern Art, 181; James Joyce Centre, 182; Merrion Square, 183; Molly Malone statue, 183; National Gallery of Ireland, 181; National Library, 181; National Museum of Ireland, 181; O'Connell Street, 182–83; Phoenix Park, 182; St. Patrick's Cathedral, 179, 180; St. Stephen's Green, 182; Temple Bar, 183; Trinity College, 179, 179–80; See also Ireland (Republic of)
Dublin Castle, 179, 180–81
Dublin City Tour, 179
Dublin's Writers Museum, 183–84
Duke's Hotel, 84
Dulwich Picture Gallery (West Dulwich), 68
Dun Laoghaire (Ireland), 187–88; Joyce Tower, 188; National Maritime Museum, 187; restaurants, 188; shopping, 188
Durrants Hotel, 84

Earl Soham Lodge (B & B) (Aldeburgh), 152
Earl's Court; Ideal Home Exhibition, 25; International Boat Show, 23; International Motor Show, 23; The Royal Tournament, 31
Easter Parade (Battersea Park), 24
Easter Sunday Church Parade (Tower of London), 24
Edinburgh (Scotland), 194–201; currency, 196; driving in Scotland, 195; Edinburgh Airport, 195; electric currents, 196; public holidays, 196; senior citizen discounts, 196; shopping, 197; telephones, 196; Tourist Offices, 194; travelers with disabilities, 196; traveling to (air/train/bus), 194, 195; VAT (Value Added Tax) refunds, 197
Edinburgh (hotels & accommodations); Balmoral Hotel, 199; Caledonian Hotel, 199–220; DIAL-A-BED, 199; George Inter-Continental, 200; Howard Hotel, 200; King James Thistle Hotel, 200; Mount Royal, 200; Old Waverley, 200
Edinburgh (restaurants) ; Balmoral Hotel restaurant, 201; Caledonian Hotel restaurant, 201; Channing's Brasserie, 201; Jackson's, 201; L'Auberge, 201; Pierre Victoire, 201; Skippers Bistro, 201
Edinburgh (sightseeing), 197–99; Edinburgh Castle, 197–98; Holyroodhouse Palace, 199; the Royal Mile, 199; walking and bus tours, 197

Edinburgh Castle, 197–98; Regalia Room, 198; St. Margaret's Chapel, 197; Scottish United Service Museum, 198; Scottish War Memorial, 198; Stone of Scone, 78, 198
Edward V, ghost of, 76
Edward Lear Hotel, 84
Edwards and Edwards (ticket broker), 40
Eiffel Tower (Paris), 218
800–FLY-FOR-LESS, 4
Eileen Follows (cooking school), 130
electric currents (necessary converters & plugs); Ireland, 173; London, 9; Scotland, 196
Elephant and Castle (restaurant) (Dublin), 193
Eleven Cadogan Gardens (hotel), 85
Elizabeth I, 202, 207; ghost of, 75
Elizabeth II, 199, 202, 203; and the Scottish regalia, 198
embassies, 9
emergency number, 9
English National Opera, 40
Enniskerry (Ireland), 188; Powerscourt Estate and Gardens, 188–89; restaurants, 189
entry requirements; for American and Canadian citizens, 2
Epsom Racecourse (Epsom Downs), 134; the Derby, 29, 134; Gold Seal Oaks, 134
Eton College (Eton), 227
Ettington Park Hotel (Stratford-Upon-Avon), 222
EurAir. See Europe Flight Pass
Euro, 6, 7
Europe Flight Pass, 3
events (off-season); after-Christmas sales, 23; January, 23; January or February, 23; February, 23–24; February or March, 23–24; February, March, or April, 24; March, 25; March or April, 25; April, 25–26; April or May, 26; May, 26, 28; May or June, 28–29
events (in-season); the traditional season, 27–28; June, 29–30; June or July, 30; July, 30–31; August, 31
events (off-season); September, 32–33; September or October, 33; October, 34, 35; November, 35, 37; December, 37
exchange rates, ATMs and, 6
Expo Garden Tours, 132
eye care, 13

Falcon Hotel (Stratford-Upon-Avon), 223
Fan Museum (Greenwich), 65, 204
Fanshawe's (restaurant) (Warwick), 226
Farlow's (fishing equipment & clothing), 124
Farnborough Air Show, 32
Fawkes, Guy, ghost of, 76
Feathers (restaurant) (Blenheim Palace), 159
Fenwick (department store), 116, 126
ferry sightseeing, 10
festivals (partial listing); Brighton Arts Festival, 28, 160; Canterbury Festival, 32; City of London Festival, 30;

Costermonger's Harvest Festival, 35; Greenwich Festival, 30; Salisbury Festival, 29; Warwick Arts Festival, 31; Windsor Festival, 33; *See also* dance, music festivals and events, opera, theatre
Fexco Tax Free Shopping Limited, 15
Fielding Hotel, 85
Fifth Floor Café, The, 101
fitness centers, 137; *See also* bicycling; boating; horse riding; jogging; tennis (as participatory sport)
Fitzwilliam (museum) (Cambridge), 164
Florence Nightingale Museum, 65
flower shows; Chelsea Flower Show, 26; Hampton Court Flower Show, 30; Royal Horticultural Society Spring Flower Show, 25; Royal Horticultural Society Summer Flower Show, 31; *See also* garden tours; Royal Botanical Gardens
Football Association Cup Final (Wembley Stadium), 26
Footsteps, 19
Forte hotels; off-season bargains, 86
Forte Posthouse (hotel) (Stratford-Upon-Avon), 223
Fortnum & Mason (food shop), 126; afternoon tea, 111; shopping, 118
Fortnum's Fountain (restaurant), 101
47 Part Street (hotel), 85
Four Seasons Hotel, 85–86
Frederick's (restaurant), 101
Freud Museum, 65
Full Tidal Closure of the Thames, 35

Gaiety Theatre (Dublin), 175
Garden House Hotel (Cambridge), 165–66
garden tours; Expo Garden Tours, 132; Gentle Journeys, 132; *See also* flower shows; Royal Botanical Gardens
Gargoyle Club (strip club); ghost of Nell Gwynne, 74
Garter Ceremony (Windsor Castle), 30
Gate Theatre (Dublin), 175
Gatwick Airport; train service to London, 4
General Post Office (Dublin), 179, 182
Gentle Journeys (garden tours), 132
George I, 206
George II, 206; ghost of, 74–75
George IV, 160
George Inter-Continental (hotel) (Edinburgh), 200
ghosts & hauntings; Adelphi Theatre, 73; British Museum, 73; Covent Garden Tube Station, 73; Drury Lane Theatre, 73–74; Gargoyle Club, 74; Green Park, 74; Grenadier Pub (Wilton Row), 74; Hampton Court Palace (Surrey), 74; Haymarket Theatre, 74; Kensington Palace, 74–75; Lincoln's Inn Fields, 75; Old Queen's Head Pub (Isington), 75; Red Lion Square, 75; St. James's Church (Garlick Hill), 75; St. James's Park, 75; Spaniards Inn

(Hampstead Heath), 75–76; Tower of London, 76; University of London, 76; Westminster Abbey, 76
Gieves & Hawkes (men's clothing store), 125
Gipsy Moth IV (Sir Francis Chichester's ketch), 202
Glyndebourne Festival Opera, 28, 40
Godiva, Lady, statue of, 168–69
Gold Seal Oaks (Epsom Downs), 134
golf, 136–37; in Ireland, 176; *Sunday Express Guide to Golf Courses*, 137; *See also* bicycling; boating; fitness centers; horse riding; jogging; tennis (as participatory sport)
Golfing Ireland, 176
Goode's (restaurant), 101
Gore Hotel, 86
Goring Hotel, 86
Grand Hotel (Malahide, Ireland), 186
Grand National steeplechase (Aintree Race Course), 134–35
Grange Farm (B & B) (Aldeburgh), 152
Gray, Lady Jane, ghost of, 76
Gray Line Tour Company (Dublin), 179
Great Eastern Hotel, 87
Great St. Mary's Church (Cambridge), 163
Great White Horse Hotel (Ipswich), 208
Green Olive, The (restaurant), 102
Green Park, ghost of, 74
Greenhouse, The (restaurant), 101
Greenwich, 53–55, 201–5; antique shopping, 122–23, 202; Tourist Office, 201; traveling to (boat/BritRail/bus/ car), 201, 202
Greenwich (restaurants); Bosun's Whistle, 205; Plume of Feathers, 205; Spread Eagle, 205; Trafalgar Tavern, 123, 205; Treasure of China, 205; The Yacht, 123
Greenwich (sightseeing); Ballast Quay, 204; Barge House, 203; *Cutty Sark* (clipper ship), 53, 140, 202; Fan Museum, 65, 204; Flamsteed House, 203; *Gipsy Moth IV*, 202; map, 203; National Maritime Museum, 53, 63, 202–3; Millennium Dome, 53–54, 54–55; Queen's House, 203; Royal Naval College, 204; Royal Observatory, 53, 202–3; Royal Palace of Greenwich, 202; Thames Barrier, 204
Greenwich Festival, 30
Greenwich Mean Time (GMT), 203
Greenwich Park (Greenwich); activities for children, 147
Greenwich Visitor's Guide, 201
Grosvenor House Antiques Fair, 121
Grenadier Pub, ghost of, 74
Grosvenor House Hotel, 86–87; afternoon tea, 111
Guards Museum, 65
Guide Friday Bus Tour; Edinburgh, 197; Stratford-Upon-Avon, 219–20
Guide to British Rail for the Physically Handicapped, A (RADAR), 14
guidebooks; *A Guide to British Rail for the Physically Handicapped* (RADAR), 14;

guidebooks (*continued*)
  London Off-Season and On, 11; *A World of
    Options for the 90's: A Guide to International
    Educational Exchange, Community Service and
    Travel for Persons with Disabilities*, 14
Guildhall (London), 52; Clock Museum, 52,
  64
Guildhall of St. Mary's (Coventry), 168
Guinness Brewery Centre (Dublin), 181
Guinness World of Records, 70
Guy Fawkes' Day, 35

haberdashers; Harvie & Hudson, 119; Hilditch
  & Key, 119; Turnbull & Asser, 119; *See also*
  British clothing
Haigh, John (Kensington Vampire), 77
Halcyon Hotel, 87
Hall's Croft (Stratford-Upon-Avon), 220
Hamleys Toy Store, 118, 141
Hampstead Heath; activities for children, 148;
  bicycling, 135; jogging, 137
Hampton Court Flower Show, 30
Hampton Court Palace (Surrey), 50, 205–7;
  Banqueting House, 206–7; ghosts of, 74,
  206; restaurants, 207; sightseeing, 205,
  206–7; traveling to, 205
Ha'penny Bridge (Dublin), 182
Hard Rock Café, 112
Harrods Department Store, 52, 119, 121, 126;
  afternoon tea, 111
Hartwell House (hotel) (Oxford), 212
Harvey Nichols (department store), 119, 126
Harvie & Hudson (haberdasher), 119
Hatchards (book store), 118
Haymarket Theatre; ghost of John Buckstone,
  74
Head of the River Race (Thames), 25
Heathrow Airport; train service (Heathrow
  Express) to London, 4–5
Hemp, The (hotel), 87
Henry IV, 167   227
Henry VI, 163
Henry VIII, 163, 167, 180, 202, 204, 205
Her Majesty's Theatre (Haymarket), 41
Herbert Art Gallery and Museum (Coventry),
  168
Herzog, Chaim, 181–82
Hess, Rudolph, 144
hidden treasure; the crown jewels of France,
  77–78
"high tea" as a term, 110; *See also* teas
Hilditch & Key (haberdasher), 119
Hilton Park Lane (hotel), 87
Hintlesham Hall (hotel) (Ipswich), 208;
  cooking school, 130
Historical Walking Tours of Dublin, 184
Historical Walks of London, 19
HIV and AIDS services, 13
HMS Belfast (World War II warship), 141
Hogarth's House, 65
Holburne of Menstrie Museum (Bath), 156
Hole in the Wall (restaurant) (Bath), 158

Holland Park; Outdoor Theatre Season, 30;
  tennis courts, 137
Holyroodhouse Palace (Edinburgh), 199
home and apartment rentals, 11
home exchange, 10
Hop-On Hop-Off Thames Ferry, 10
Horse Guards Parade; Beating Retreat, 29;
  Changing of the Queen's Life Guard, 22;
  The Royal Tournament march-past, 31
horse racing; Aintree Race Course, 134–35;
  Ascot Racecourse, 29–30, 134; Brighton,
  160; Epsom Racecourse, 29, 134;
  Cheltenham (steeplechase races), 134;
  Ireland, 184–85; Kempton Park
  Racecourse, 134; Newmarket (Guinness
  Stakes), 26; Royal Windsor Racecourse,
  134; Sandown Park, 134; *See also* boat
  racing; cricket; horse shows and events;
  outdoor activities; soccer; Rugby; tennis
horse riding, 138; Hyde Park, 147; Richard
  Briggs Riding Stables, 138; Roehampton
  Gate Stable, 138; Ross Nye's Riding
  Establishment, 138; *See also* bicycling;
  boating; fitness centers; golf; jogging;
  tennis (as participatory sport)
horse shows and events; Horse of the Year Show,
  33; Horseman's Sunday, 32; International
  Show Jumping Championships, 37; London
  Harness Horse Parade, 24; Royal Windsor
  Horse Show (Home Park), 26; Westminster
  Horse Show (Hyde Park), 31
hostels of Ireland, 178
Hotelink (tickets broker), 135
hotels & accommodations (Aldeburgh), 152–53;
  Brudenell Hotel, 152; Cricketers (Adnams
  Hotel), 152; Crown (Adnams Hotel), 152;
  Earl Soham Lodge (B & B), 152; Grange
  Farm (B & B), 152; Kiln Farm (B & B), 152;
  Ocean House, 152; Seckford Hall, 152;
  Sternfield House, 152; Swan (Adnams
  Hotel), 152; Theberton Grange, 153; White
  Lion Hotel, 153; Wentworth Hotel, 153
hotels & accommodations (Bath), 156– 57;
  Bath Spa Hotel, 156–57; The Priory Hotel,
  157; The Queensberry Hotel, 157; Royal
  Crescent Hotel, 157
hotels (Cambridge), 165–66; Arundel House,
  165; Garden House Hotel, 165–66;
  University Arms Hotel, 165
hotels & accommodations (Coventry), 169;
  Brooklands Grange Hotel, 169; Old Mill (B
  & B), 169
hotels & accommodations (Dublin), 189–92;
  apartment rentals, 178; B & B, 192;
  Berkeley Court, 189–90; Blooms, 191;
  Clarence Hotel, 190; Conrad Dublin
  International, 190; hostels, 178; Jurys,
  191–92; Killiney Castle, 190; Merrion Hotel,
  190–91; Shelbourne Hotel, 191; Stephen's
  Hall, 191; Westbury, 191
hotels & accommodations (Edinburgh,
  Scotland); Balmoral Hotel, 199;

Caledonian Hotel, 199–220; DIAL-A-BED, 199; George Inter-Continental, 200; Howard Hotel, 200; King James Thistle Hotel, 200; Mount Royal, 200; Old Waverley, 200

hotels & accommodations (Ipswich); Courtyard by Marriott Ipswich, 208; Great White Horse Hotel, 208; Hintlesham Hall, 208; The Marlborough Hotel, 208; Station Hotel, 208

hotels & accommodations (London), 80–94; The Antenaeum Hotel, 81; Basil Street Hotel, 81–82; Beaufort Hotel, 82; being built for the Millennium, 54; Berkeley Hotel, 82; Brown's Hotel, 82; Capital Hotel, 82; Caswell Hotel, 83; Central Club, 83; Claridge's Brook Street, 83; Connaught Hotel, 83; Diplomat Hotel, 83; The Dorchester, 84; Dorset Square Hotel, 84; Duke's Hotel, 84; Durrants Hotel, 84; Edward Lear Hotel, 84; Eleven Cadogan Gardens, 85; Fielding Hotel, 85; Forte hotels, off-season bargains, 86; 47 Part Street, 85; Four Seasons Hotel, 85–86; Gore Hotel, 86; Goring Hotel, 86; Great Eastern Hotel, 87; Grosvenor House Hotel, 86–87; Halcyon Hotel, 87; The Hemp, 87; Hilton Park Lane, 87; Howard Hotel, 87–88; Hyde Park Mandarin Oriental, 88; Inter-Continental Hotel, 88; Kensington Close Hotel, 88; The Lanesborough, 88; London Marriott, 89; May Fair Hotel, 89; Le Meridien hotels, off-season bargains, 90; Le Meridien London, 89; The Metropolitan, 89–90; Mornington Hotel, 90; off-season hotel bargains, 86, 89; One Aldwych, 90–91; Park Lane Hotel, 91; Regency Hotel, 91; The Ritz Hotel, 91; Royal Lancaster Hotel, 91; Ruskin Hotel, 91; St. James's Court and Apartments, 92; The Savoy, 92; Sheraton Belgravia Hotel, 92; Sheraton Park Tower Hotel, 92; Sloane Hotel, 92; The Stafford, 93; Twenty Two Jermyn Street, 93; The Westbury Hotel, 93; Whites Hotel, 93; Willbraham Hotel, 93–94

hotels & accommodations (Stratford-Upon-Avon); Alveston Cottage (B & B), 224; The Arden, 222–23; Ettington Park Hotel, 222; Falcon Hotel, 223; Forte Posthouse, 223; Lygon Arms, 222; The Shakespeare, 223; Stratford Moat House, 223; Welcombe Hotel, 222; The White Swan, 223

House of Lords; Law Term opening and procession, 34–35; See also Parliament

Howard, Catherine; ghost of, 74, 76, 206

Howard Hotel (Edinburgh), 200

Howard Hotel (London), 87–88

Howth (Ireland), 186–87; Howth Castle, 186; Howth Transport museum, 186; restaurants, 186–87, 187

Hyde Park, 56; activities for children, 147; bicycling, 135; boat rentals, 136;

Horseman's Sunday, 32; horse riding, 147; jogging, 137; Queen's birthday salute, 26; tennis courts, 137; Westminster Horse Show, 31

Hyde Park Corner, 56

Hyde Park Mandarin Oriental (hotel), 88

Ideal Home Exhibition (Earl's Court), 25

Imperial Chinese Restaurant (Dublin), 193

Imperial War Museum (Duxford), 63, 165

Inaho (restaurant), 102

Independent Holiday Hostels of Ireland, 178

Institute of Contemporary Arts, 62

Inter-Continental Hotel, 88

International Ballroom Dancing championships, 35

International Boat Show (Earl's Court, 23

International Book Fair (Olympia Exhibition Centre), 25

International Home Exchange Network, 10

International Motor Show (Earl's Court), 23

International Show Jumping Championships, 37

Intervac International, 10

Ipswich (Suffolk County), 207–9; Ancient House (Sparrowe's House), 208; Christchurch Mansion, 207; Ipswich Museum, 207–8; St. Stephen's Church, 208; Tolly Cobbold brewery, 208; Tourist Office, 207; traveling to, 207

Ipswich (hotels & accommodations); Courtyard by Marriott Ipswich, 208; Great White Horse Hotel, 208; Hintlesham Hall, 208; The Marlborough Hotel, 208; Station Hotel, 208

Ipswich (restaurants); Dhaka, 209; Kwok's Rendezvous, 209; Marlborough Hotel Restaurant, 208; Mortimer's on the Quay, 209; St. Peter's Restaurant, 209; Sue Ryder Coffee Room (afternoon tea), 209

Ireland (Republic of); car rental, 174; currency, 172; electric currents, 173; entrance requirements, 172; golf, 176; horse racing, 184–85; public holidays, 176; telephones, 175; See also Dublin

Ireland (sightseeing); Bray, 188; Dun Laoghaire, 187–88; Howth & Howth Castle, 186–87; Malahide & Malahide Castle, 185–86; Powerscourt Estate and Gardens (Enniskerry), 188–89; transportation (bus/rail/taxi), 185; transportation (car), 185

Ireland Self-Catering Guide (Cork Kerry Tourism), 178

Irish Horseracing Authority, 185

Irish Jewish Museum (Dublin), 181–83

Irish Museum of Modern Art (Dublin), 181

Irish Racing Calendar, 184

Irish Wheelchair Association, 175

Islington Tennis Centre; indoor tennis, 137; outdoor tennis, 137

Ivy, The (restaurant), 102

Jack the Ripper, 77
Jackson's (restaurant) (Edinburgh), 201
Jaeger's Regent Street (clothing store), 125
Jaffe, Sam, 41
James VI, 198
James Joyce Centre (Dublin), 182
Jason's Trip (canal trips), 66
jazz, 43
Jenny Wren Cruises (canal trips), 66
Jermyn Street, shopping on, 119
Jewish Museum, 65
jogging, 137; See also bicycling; boating; fitness
     centers; golf; horse riding; tennis (as
     participatory sport)
John, King, 181
John Lewis (department store), 119
John Stow Memorial Service, 25
Julie's (restaurant), 102
Jurys (hotel) (Dublin), 191–92

Kay & Co., 11
Keats's House, 65
Keith Prowse (ticket broker), 40
Kempton Park Racecourse, 134; Racal
     Meeting, 134
Kensington Close Hotel, 88
Kensington Gardens, 56, 59; activities for
     children, 147
Kensington Palace, 59; ghost of George II,
     74–75
Kensington Place (restaurant), 102
Kensington Vampire (John Haigh), 77
Kenwood Lakeside Concerts, 30
Kew Gardens (Royal Botanical Gardens), 55
Killiney Castle (hotel) (Dublin), 190
Kiln Farm (B & B) (Aldeburgh), 152
King, Alan, 36
King James Thistle Hotel (Edinburgh), 200
King Sitric (restaurant) (Howth, Ireland), 187
King's College (Cambridge), 163; Adoration of
     the Magi (Rubens painting), 163
Kite Festival (Blackheath Common), 24
Kitty O'Shea's Bar (Dublin), 194
Knights Templar Church, 57
Knightsbridge, shopping, 121
Kwok's Rendezvous (restaurant) (Ipswich), 209

La Tante Claire (restaurant), 102; wheelchair-
     accessibility, 196
Lanesborough Hotel, 88; afternoon tea, 111
L'Auberge restaurant (Edinburgh), 201
Launceston Place (restaurant), 102
L'Aventure (restaurant), 103
Lawn Tennis Association, 138
Le Caprice (restaurant), 103
Le Cordon Bleu L'Art Culinaire (cooking
     school), 130
Le Gavroche Restaurant; wheelchair-
     accessibility, 196
Le Manoir Aux Quat' Saisons (cooking
     school), 131
Le Meridien hotels; off-season bargains, 90

Le Meridien London, 89
Le Palais du Jardin (restaurant), 103
Le Paradis Restaurant (Cambridge), 166
Le Petit Max (restaurant) (Hampton Court
     Palace), 207
Le Pont de la Tour (restaurant), 103–4
legends; Boadicea's Tomb, 77; Curse of St.
     Giles Circus, 77
Lego Land, 141
Leicester Square Half Price Ticket Booth, 41
Leigh's (restaurant), 103
Leith's School of Food and Wine, 130–31
Lemonia (restaurant), 103
Leopardstown (Irish racetrack), 184
Les Frères Jacques (restaurant) (Dublin), 193
Liaison (restaurant) (Stratford-Upon-Avon),
     224
Liberty (department store), 118, 128
Lighthouse Restaurant (Aldeburgh), 153
Lillywhites (sports equipment), 123
Lincoln's Inn, 57
Lincoln's Inn Fields; ghost of Anthony
     Babbington, 75; tennis courts, 137
Literary Pub Crawl (Dublin), 184
Lloyd's of London, 60
L'Odeon (restaurant), 104
London Aquarium (Regent's Park), 59, 141–42
London Bridge, 142
London Butterfly House (Syon House), 67
London Canal Museum, 65
London Cyclist's Route Map, 136
London Dungeon, 70, 142
London Film Festival, 37
London Harness Horse Parade (Battersea
     Park), 24
London Made Easy and wheelchair access, 14
London Marathon, 24
London Marriott (hotel), 89
London Open House, 33
London Planetarium, 71
London Tourist Office; telephone guide to
     London, 12
London Toy & Model Museum, 66, 142, 145
London Transport Museum, 66, 145
London Waterbus Company (canal trips), 66
London Zoo (Regent's Park), 59, 148
Londoner Pub Walks, The, 19
Lord Leycester Hospital (Warwick), 226
Lord Mayor; Michaelmas Day election of, 33;
     procession & show, 37
Lord's Cricket Ground, 133
lost credit cards, 11
Lothian Regional Transport (Edinburgh), 197
Lygon Arms (hotel) (Stratford-Upon-Avon),
     222

McDonald's, 112–13
Madame Tussaud's (wax museum), 71, 145
Madeline Quinn, 19
Magdalen College (Oxford), 211
Magdalene College (Cambridge), 164
major airlines, 3

Malahide (Ireland); hotels & accommodations, 186; Malahide Castle, 185–86; Old Abbey, 187; restaurants, 185–86
Man in Grey (ghost of), 73–74
Manzi's (restaurant), 104
maps; Britain and Ireland, x-xi; Cambridge, 162; Dublin, 170–71; Greenwich, 203; Oxford, 210; Paris, 214–15; Stratford-Upon-Avon, 219
maps (London), 11; Buckingham Palace and Mayfair, 254; Central London street finder, 250; The City, 259; cyclist's route map, 136; day trips from, 149, 257; Bloomsbury, Hilborn, and Fleet Street, 257; Hyde Park, Belgravia and Chelsea, 253; Kensington, Brompton, and Chelsea, 252; Lambeth, South Bank and Southwark, 260; neighborhoods and postal districts, 248; Soho and Covent Garden, 258; theatre district, 38; Westminster and Whitehall, 255
marches. See parades and marches
Marks & Spencer (department store), 118, 126
Marlborough Hotel, The (Ipswich), 208
Marlborough Hotel Restaurant, 208
Marlow Theatre (Canterbury), 167
Mary, Queen of Scots, 197, 198
Maundy Thursday/Maundy Purses, 24
May Bank Holiday, 26
May Fair Hotel, 89
MCC Cricket Museum, 66
medical assistance, 12–14; dental emergency care, 13; eye care, 13; HIV and AIDS services, 13; rape crisis center, 13; travelers with disabilities, 13–14; Worldwide Assistance Services, 12
medication; taking prescriptions with you, 8
Memorial des Martyrs Français (Paris), 217
Merrion Hotel (Dublin), 190–91
Merrion Square (Dublin), 183
Merton College (Oxford), 211
Metropolitan, The (hotel), 89–90
Mezzo (restaurant), 104
Michaelmas Day (election of the Lord Mayor), 33
Midsummer House Restaurant (Cambridge), 166
Millennium Bridge, 54
Millennium Dome, 53–54, 54–55
Millennium Ferris Wheel (British Airways), 54
Millennium preparations, 53–55
Millennium Stadium (Cardiff), 54
Mind-Body-Spirit Festival, 28
Ministry of Sound nightclub, 43
Mobility International, 14
Molly Malone statue (Dublin), 183
Moment's Notice Discount Travel Club, 4
Monument, The, 60
Moon and Sixpence (restaurant) (Bath), 158
Mornington Hotel, 90
Mortimer's on the Quay (restaurant) (Ipswich), 209
Mount Royal (hotel) (Edinburgh), 200

Mrs. Pickwick's Tea Room (Coventry), 169
murders; Jack the Ripper, 77; Kensington Vampire (John Haigh), 77
Musée D'Orsay (Paris), 218
Musée du Louvre (Paris), 218
Museum of British Road Transport (Coventry), 168
Museum of Garden History, 66
Museum of London, 63
Museum of Mankind, 66–67
Museum of the Moving Image, 67, 146
museums (art and design); British Museum, 46, 47, 61, 144–45; Courtauld Institute Picture Gallery, 63; Dulwich Picture Gallery (West Dulwich), 68; Institute of Contemporary Arts, 62; National Gallery, 57, 61; National Portrait Gallery, 62, 146; Percival David Foundation of Chinese Art, 62; The Queen's Gallery (Buckingham Palace), 64; Sir John Soane Museum, 67; Tate Gallery of British Art, 54, 62; Tate Gallery of Modern Art, 54, 62; Victoria & Albert Museum, 61, 146; Wallace Collection, 63; William Morris Gallery, 68; See also art exhibits
museums (day trip from London); Aldeburgh Moot Hall and Museum, 154; American Museum (Bath), 156; Ashmolean Museum (Oxford), 211; Assembly Rooms and Museum of Costume (Bath), 155; Brighton Museum and Art Gallery, 160; Canterbury Heritage Museum, 167; Fitzwilliam (museum) (Cambridge), 164; Herbert Art Gallery and Museum (Coventry), 168; Holburne of Menstrie Museum (Bath), 156; Ipswich Museum, 207–8; Irish Jewish Museum (Dublin), 181– 83; Irish Museum of Modern Art (Dublin), 181; Musée D'Orsay (Paris), 218; Musée du Louvre (Paris), 218; Museum of British Road Transport (Coventry), 168; National Gallery of Ireland (Dublin), 181; National Museum of Ireland (Dublin), 181; Roman Baths Museum (Bath), 155; Roman Museum (Canterbury), 167
museums (science & history); Imperial War Museum (Duxford), 63, 165; Museum of London, 63; National Maritime Museum (Greenwich), 53, 63, 202–3; Natural History Museum, 62, 146; Science Museum, 62, 146; Wellington Museum (Apsley House), 64
museums (special interest); Bank of England Museum, 64; Carlyle's House, 64; Clink Prison Museum, 64; Clock Museum (Guildhall), 64; Dickens's House, 65; Doctor Johnson's House, 65; Fan Museum (Greenwich), 65, 204; Florence Nightingale Museum, 65; Freud Museum, 65; Guards Museum, 65; Hogarth's House, 65; Jewish Museum, 65; Keats's House, 65; London

museums (special interest) (*continued*)
Canal Museum, 65; London Toy & Model
Museum, 66, 145; London Transport
Museum, 66, 145; MCC Cricket Museum,
66; Museum of Garden History, 66;
Museum of Mankind, 66–67; Museum of
the Moving Image, 67, 146; Musical
Museum, 67; National Army Museum, 67;
National Postal Museum, 67; Pollock's Toy
Museum, 67; Royal Air Force Museum, 67;
Royal Mews, 67; Sir John Soane Museum,
67; Syon House (Brentford, Middlesex), 67;
Theatre Museum, 68; Wesley's Chapel,
House & Museum of Methodism, 69;
William Morris Gallery, 68
museums (special interest to children),
143–47; Bethnal Green Museum of
Childhood, 144; British Museum, 144–45;
London Toy & Model Museum, 66, 145;
London Transport Museum, 66, 145;
Madame Tussaud's (wax museum), 71, 145;
Museum of the Moving Image, 67, 146;
National Gallery, 57, 61; National Maritime
Museum (Greenwich), 53, 63, 202–3;
National Portrait Gallery, 62, 146; Natural
History Museum, 62, 146; Pollock's Toy
Museum, 67, 142; Royal Air Force (RAF)
Museum, 67, 146; Science Museum, 62,
146; Victoria & Albert Museum, 61, 68,
146–47
music festivals and events (classical), 39–40, 42;
Annual Music Festival (Spitalfields), 30;
Aldeburgh Festival, 30, 32, 151; City of
London Festival, 30; Kenwood Lakeside
Concerts, 30; orchestras, 42; Prom concerts
(Royal Albert Hall), 31, 42; ticket brokers,
40; Wigmore Hall, 42; *See also* opera
music festivals and events (popular);
Cambridge Folk Festival, 31; nightclubs, 43;
jazz, 43
Musical Museum, 67

Nash's House (Stratford-Upon-Avon), 220
National AIDS Helpline, 13
National Army Museum, 67
National Concert Hall (Dublin), 175
National Film Theatre, 39–40
National Exhibition Center; British
International Motor Show, 35; Crufts Dog
Show, 24
National Gallery (London), 57, 61
National Gallery of Ireland (Dublin), 181
National Hunt Festival, The (Cheltenham),
134
National Library (Dublin), 181
National Maritime Museum (Dun Laoghaire,
Ireland), 187
National Maritime Museum (Greenwich), 53,
63, 202–3
National Museum of Ireland (Dublin), 181
National Portrait Gallery, 62, 146
National Postal Museum, 67

National Rehabilitation Board of Ireland, 175
Natural History Museum, 62, 146
Nelson's Column (Trafalgar Square), 57, 58
New Bond Street. *See* Old and New Bond Street
New College (Oxford), 211
New Place (Stratford-Upon-Avon), 220
New Year's Eve; New Year's Day Parade, 23;
Trafalgar Square celebration, 37
Newmarket; horse racing (Guinness Stakes),
26
Nico Central (restaurant), 104
Nicole Farhi (department store), 115–16, 128;
Nicole's Restaurant, 104–5, 115–16
nightclubs, 43
Nobu (restaurant), 105
Noor Jahan (restaurant), 105
Northwest Airlines, 3
Notre Dame Cathedral (Paris), 217

Oak-Apple Day Parade, 28
Oakley Court Hotel (Water Oakley), 227–28
Ocean House (Aldeburgh), 152
O'Connell Street (Dublin), 182–83
Odette's (restaurant), 105
O'Dwyer's Pub (Dublin), 194
off-season hotel bargains, 86, 89
Oisin's Irish Restaurant (Dublin), 193
Oken's Doll Museum (Warwick), 226
Old and New Bond Street, 57; shopping on,
115–17; Stock Exchange, 60
Old Bailey, 58
Old Mill (B & B) (Coventry), 169
Old Queen's Head Pub (Isington); ghost of
Elizabeth I, 75
Old Stand Pub, The (Dublin), 194
Old Waverley (hotel) (Edinburgh), 200
Oldcastle, Sir John; and the Curse of St. Giles
Circus, 77
Olympia (Dublin), 175
Olympus Sports (equipment & clothing), 123
One Aldwych (hotel), 90–91
152 High Street Restaurant (Aldeburgh), 153
192 (one-nine-two) (restaurant), 105
One O'clock Club (for preschool children),
147
One O'clock Club (for preschool children),
147
One Paston Place (restaurant) (Brighton), 161
Open Air Theatre Season (Regent's Park), 29
opera, 40–41; dress requirements, 40–41;
English National Opera, 40; Glyndebourne
Festival Opera, 28, 40; Outdoor Theatre
Season (Holland Park), 30; Royal Opera
House (Covent Garden), 39, 40–41, 58;
Wexford Opera Festival (Ireland), 40; *See
also* music
Original London Walks, The, 19
Orsino (restaurant), 105
Other Place, The (experimental theatre)
(Stratford-Upon-Avon), 221
outdoor activities; bicycling, 135–36; boating,
136; fitness centers, 137; golf, 136–37; horse
riding, 138; jogging, 137; tennis, 137–38;
waterskiing, 136

Oval Cricket Ground, 133
Oxford (Oxfordshire County), 209–12; hotels & accommodations, 212; map, 210; Tourist Office, 209; traveling to, 209
Oxford (sightseeing); Ashmolean Museum, 211; Bodleian Library, 211; Christ Church College, 211; Magdalen College, 211; Merton College, 211; New College, 211; Oxford Canal, 211; The Oxford Story (audio-visual ride), 211; Sheldonian Theatre, 211; University Church of St. Mary the Virgin, 211; University College, 211
Oxford-Cambridge boat race (Thames river), 25
Oxford Street & Oxford Circus; shopping on, 118–19
Oxo Tower (restaurant), 105–6

Paddington Sports Club, 138
pancake races, 24
parades and marches; Christmas Parade, 37; Easter Parade (Battersea Park), 24; Easter Sunday Church Parade (Tower of London), 24; London Harness Horse Parade (Battersea Park), 24
New Year's Day Parade, 23; Oak-Apple Day Parade, 28; The Royal Tournament march-past, 31; Trafalgar Day Parade, 35; See also Tower of London Church Parades
Parks Paris (France), 212–18; currency, 212; entrance requirements, 212; map, 214–15; restaurants, 218; Tourist Office, 212
Paris (sightseeing); Arc de Triomphe, 218; Champs-Élysées, 218; Eiffel Tower, 218; guided bus tour (Cityrama), 217; Memorial des Martyrs Français, 217; Musée D'Orsay, 218; Musée du Louvre, 218; Notre Dame Cathedral, 217; Place de la Concorde, 218; planning ahead, 216–17; transportation (taxis/Metro), 216
Paris (traveling to), 212; by air, 216; Eurostar, 213; Le Shuttle, 213–14
parks, Park Lane Hotel, 91
parks; activities for children, 147–48; Battersea Park, 24; bicycling, 135; boat rentals, 136; Hampstead Heath, 135; Holland Park, 30; Home Park (Windsor), 26; Hyde Park, 26, 31, 32, 56, 147; jogging, 137; Kensington Gardens, 56, 59; One O'clock Club (for preschool children), 147; Regent's Park, 29, 59, 148; Richmond Park, 135; St. James's Park, 51, 75
Parliament (Houses of), 47–48; Big Ben, 47; State Opening, 35; See also House of Lords
participatory sports. See sports (participatory sports)
Penn, Sybel, ghost of, 74
Percival David Foundation of Chinese Art, 62
Peterhouse College (Cambridge), 164
Phoenix Park (Dublin), 182
Piccadilly, shopping, 118
Piccadilly Market; antique shopping, 122

Pierre Victoire restaurant (Edinburgh), 201
Pizza Express, 112
Place de la Concorde (Paris), 218
Planet Hollywood, 113
Plough and Sail Restaurant (Aldeburgh), 153
Plume of Feathers (restaurant) (Greenwich), 205
Point Theatre (Dublin), 175
Pollock's Toy Museum, 67, 142
Poppies Country Cooking (Enniskerry, Ireland), 189
Portmeirion Potteries Ltd. (Stoke-On-Trent), 127
Portobello Road; antique shopping, 121
Powerscourt Estate and Gardens (Enniskerry, Ireland), 188–89
Priory Hotel (Bath), 157
Prom concerts (Royal Albert Hall), 31, 42
pubs (Dublin), 179, 193–94; Brazen Head, 193; Davy Byrnes, 194; Kitty O'Shea's Bar, 194; Literary Pub Crawl, 184; O'Dwyer's, 194; The Old Stand, 194
pubs (London); Cheshire Cheese, 95; Dirty Dick's, 95; Grenadier Pub (Wilton Row), 74; Mayflower Pub, 95; Old Queen's Head Pub (Isington), 75
pubs (outside of London); Slug and Lettuce Pub (Stratford-Upon-Avon), 225
Pulteney Bridge (Bath), 156

QE2 (Cunard Line), 2
Quaglino's (restaurant), 106
Quasar (virtual reality), 71
Queen's Chapel (St. James's Palace); morning church services, 69
Queen's Gallery (Buckingham Palace), 64
Queen's House (Greenwich), 203
Queen's Official Birthday, 29; real birthday salute, 26
Queens College (Cambridge), 164
Queensberry Hotel (Bath), 157
Quo Vadis (restaurant), 106

Racal Meeting (Kempton Park Racecourse), 134
RADAR (Royal Association for Disabilities and Rehabilitation), 14
Rainforest Café, 112
Raleigh, Sir Walter, ghost of, 76
rape crisis center, 13
Red Lion Square; ghost of Oliver Cromwell, 75
Red Pepper (restaurant), 106
Regatta Restaurant (Aldeburgh), 153
Regency Hotel, 91
Regent Street, shopping on, 118
Regent's Park, 59; activities for children, 148; bicycling, prohibiting, 135; boat rentals, 136; jogging, 137; London Aquarium, 59, 141–42; London Zoo, 59; Open Air Theatre Season, 29; tennis courts, 137
Remembrance Sunday, 35
Rental Directories International, 11

Republic of Texas Embassy (Pickering Place), 79

Restaurant, The; wheelchair-accessibility, 109

restaurants; Quaglino's, 106; *See also* afternoon tea; dining

restaurants (Aldeburgh), 153–54; Adnams Hotels, 152; Butley-Orford Oysterage, 153; Captain's Cabin Restaurant, 153; Concert Hall Restaurant, 153; The Lighthouse, 153; 152 High Street, 153; Plough and Sail, 153; Regatta, 153; Wentworth Hotel Restaurant, 154

restaurants (American in London); Burger King, 112; Hard Rock Café, 112; McDonald's, 112–13; Planet Hollywood, 113; Smollensky's Balloon, 112

restaurants (Bath), 157–58; Canary Restaurant, 157; Hole in the Wall, 158; Moon and Sixpence, 158; Vellore, 158

restaurants (Blenheim Palace); Feathers, 159; The Chef Imperial, 159

restaurants (Brighton); Browns, 161; One Paston Place, 161

restaurants (Cambridge), 166; Le Paradis Restaurant, 166; Midsummer House Restaurant, 166

restaurants (Canterbury), 167; Ristorante Tuo e Mio, 167; Sullys, 167

restaurants (Coventry), 169; Brooklands Grange Hotel, 169; Mrs. Pickwick's Tea Room, 169

restaurants (Dublin), 192–93; Bewley's, 185; The Commons, 192; Elephant and Castle, 193; Imperial Chinese Restaurant, 193; Les Frères Jacques, 193; Oisin's Irish Restaurant, 193; Roly's Bistro, 192–93

restaurants (Edinburgh); Balmoral Hotel restaurant, 201; Caledonian Hotel restaurant, 201; Channing's Brasserie, 201; Jackson's, 201; L'Auberge, 201; Pierre Victoire, 201; Skippers Bistro, 201

restaurants (Greenwich); Bosun's Whistle, 205; Plume of Feathers, 205; Spread Eagle, 205; Trafalgar Tavern, 123, 205; Treasure of China, 205; The Yacht, 123

restaurants (Ipswich); Dhaka, 209; Kwok's Rendezvous, 209; Marlborough Hotel Restaurant, 208; Mortimer's on the Quay, 209; St. Peter's Restaurant, 209; Sue Ryder Coffee Room (afternoon tea), 209

restaurants (London: attractive to children); Bradmore House, 111; Deals, 111; Dell Restaurant, 147; Pizza Express, 112; Rainforest Café, 112; Smollensky's Balloon, 112; Sticky Fingers, 112

restaurants (London by price: moderate); Belgo Noord, 98; Deals, 101, 111; Fortnum's Fountain, 101; The Green Olive, 102; Inaho, 102; Lemonia, 103; Manzi's, 104; Nicole's, 104–5, 115–16; Noor Jahan, 105; 192 (One-Nine-Two), 105; Red Pepper, 106; Richoux, 106; Soho

Soho, 107; Sticky Fingers, 108, 112; Wodka, 108

restaurants (London by price: moderate to expensive); Assaggi, 97

restaurants (London by price: expensive); Alastair Little, 96; Alastair Little at Lancaster Road, 96; Avenue, 97; Bank, 97–98; The Belvedere, 98; Bombay Brasserie, 99; Café Nico, 99; Coast, 100; The Collection, 100; The Criterion, 100; The Fifth Floor Café, 101; Frederick's, 101; Julie's, 102; Kensington Place, 102; Launceston Place, 102; L'Aventure, 103; Le Palais du Jardin, 103; L'Odeon, 104; Mezzo, 104; Nico Central, 104; Odette's, 105; Orsino, 105; Oxo Tower, 105–6; Rules, 106–7; San Frediano, 107; Scalini, 107; Star of India, 108; Sugar Club, 108; Zafferano, 108; Zilli Fish, 108

restaurants (London by price: very expensive); Aubergine, 97; Bibendum Restaurant, 98; Blakes Hotel, 98; Canteen, 99; Capital Restaurant, 99; Chez Nico, 99; Claridge's Restaurant, 99; Clarke's, 99–100; Connaught Hotel Grill, 100; Daphne's, 100; Goode's, 101; The Greenhouse, 101; The Ivy, 102; Le Caprice, 103; Le Pont de la Tour, 103–4; Leigh's, 103; Nobu, 105; Quo Vadis, 106; River Café, 106; San Lorenzo, 107; Santini, 107; Scotts, 107; The Square, 107; Vong, 108

restaurants (London by price: very, very expensive); La Tante Claire, 102

restaurants (London: wheelchair-accessible), 109; Aubergine, 97, 109; Bibendum Restaurant, 98, 109; The Capital Hotel Restaurant, 99, 109; Chez Nico, 99, 109; Le Gavroche Restaurant, 109, 196; The Restaurant, 109; La Tante Claire, 102, 109

restaurants (Stratford-Upon-Avon); Bensons of Stratford-Upon-Avon (afternoon tea), 224; Box Tree Restaurant, 224; Liaison, 224; Richoux (afternoon tea), 224; Slug and Lettuce Pub, 225

Revolutionary Dublin Tour, 184

Richard, Duke of York, ghost of, 76

Richard Briggs Riding Stables, 138

Richmond Park; bicycling, 135

Richoux (restaurant) London), 106; afternoon tea, 111

Richoux (Stratford-Upon-Avon); afternoon tea, 224

Rippers Corner (Mitre Square), 77

Ristorante Tuo e Mio (Canterbury), 167

Ritz Hotel, The, 91; afternoon tea, 111

River Café (restaurant), 106

River Cam (Cambridge); boat tours & punting, 163, 164

Roehampton Gate Stable, 138

Roly's Bistro (Dublin), 192–93

Roman Baths and Pump Room (Bath), 155

Roman Baths Museum (Bath), 155

Roman Museum (Canterbury), 167
Ronnie Scott jazz club, 42
Roselyne Masselin's Vegetarian Cookery
    School, 131
Ross Nye's Riding Establishment, 138
Round Tower (Cambridge), 164
Royal Academy of Arts (Burlington House);
    Summer Exhibition, 28, 29, 64
Royal Air Force (RAF) Museum, 67, 146
Royal Albert Hall Prom concerts, 31, 42
Royal Ascot, 29–30, 135
Royal Ballet, 39, 41
Royal Botanical Gardens (Kew), 55
Royal Court Theatre (St. Martin's Lane), 41
Royal Courts of Justice, 52; Law Term opening
    and procession, 34–35
Royal Crescent Hotel (Bath), 157
Royal Docks Water-ski Club, 136
Royal Doulton Company (Stoke-On-Trent),
    127
Royal Festival Hall, 39
Royal Henley Regatta, 30
Royal Horticultural Society; Spring Flower
    Show, 25; Summer Flower Show, 31
Royal Lancaster Hotel, 91
Royal Mews, 67
Royal Mile (Edinburgh), 199
Royal Museum (Canterbury), 167
Royal National Theatre, 41
Royal Naval College (Greenwich), 204
Royal Oak, The (restaurant) (Windsor), 227
Royal Observatory (Greenwich), 53, 202–3;
    Prime Meridian, 203
Royal Opera House (Covent Garden), 39,
    40–41, 58
Royal Palace of Greenwich, 202
Royal Pavilion on the Steine (Brighton), 160
Royal Shakespeare Theatre (Stratford-Upon-
    Avon), 221; The Other Place, 221; season,
    25, 221; Stratford-Upon-Avon Shakespeare
    Birthday Celebration, 221; Swan Theatre,
    221
Royal Tournament, 31
royal warrants (shopping), 116; Alfred Dunhill
    (tobacconist), 119; Fortnum and Mason
    (food shop), 118, 126; Hamleys Toy Store,
    118, 141; Harrods Department Store, 52,
    111, 119, 121, 126; Harvey Nichols, 119,
    126; Liberty (department store), 118, 128;
    Smythson Stationery, 116; Swaine Adeney
    (leather goods/ equestrian supplies),
    116–17; Thomas Goode (chinaware), 120;
    Turnbull & Asser (haberdasher), 119
Royal Windsor Horse Show (Home Park,
    Windsor), 26
Royal Worcester (Stoke-On-Trent), 127
Royals; protocol concerning, 36; Royals
    watching, 34
Rugby; championships, 23; Millennium Stadium
    (Cardiff), 54; Rugby League Challenge Cup
    Final (Wembley Stadium), 26
Rugby Union Cup Final, 26; Twickenham

stadium, 135; See also boat racing; cricket;
    horse racing; horse shows and events;
    outdoor activities; soccer; tennis
Rules (restaurant), 106–7
Ruskin Hotel, 91

Sadler's Wells ballet, 41
safety, 14
St. Augustine, 166
St. Augustine's Abbey (Canterbury), 167
St. Clements Danes (The Strand), 68; hand
    bell ring and distribution of oranges and
    lemons to, 25
St. David's Day ceremony (Windsor Castle), 25
St. Giles Cripplegate Church, 69
St. Helen Bishopsgate Church, 69
St. James's Church (Garlick Hill); ghost of, 75
St. James's Church (Piccadilly), 69
St. James's Court and Apartments (hotel), 92
St. James's Park, 51; activities for children, 148;
    ghost of, 75; jogging, 137
St. James's Palace, 51–52; Changing of the
    Guard, 22, 52; Queen's Chapel morning
    church services, 69
St. James Terrace (restaurant) (Malahide,
    Ireland), 185–86
St. John's College (Cambridge), 164
St. John's House (Warwick), 226
St. Martin-in-the-Fields, 69;
    Costermonger's Harvest Festival, 35
St. Martin's Church (Canterbury), 167
St. Mary-le-Bow Church (Cheapside), 69
St. Mary's Collegiate Church (Warwick), 226
St. Olave's Church; Samuel Pepys
    Commemoration, 29
St. Patrick's Cathedral (Dublin), 179, 180
St. Patrick's Day, 25
St. Paul's Cathedral; St. George's Day Service,
    26; tours, 48; Watch Night, 37
St. Peter's Restaurant (Ipswich), 209
St. Stephen's Church (Ipswich), 208
St. Stephen's Green (Dublin), 182
San Frediano (restaurant), 107
San Lorenzo (restaurant), 107
Sandown Park (racecourse), 134; Coral-Eclipse
    Stakes, 134; Whitbread Gold Cup, 134
Santini (restaurant), 107
Savoy, The (hotel), 92
Scalini (restaurant), 107
Science Museum, 62, 146
Scotch House, The (woolens), 118
Scotline Tours (Edinburgh), 197
Scott Polar Research Institute (Cambridge),
    164
Scottish Tourist Board (London), 195
Scotts (restaurant), 107
"Season, The," 27–28, 29
Seckford Hall (Aldeburgh), 152
Segaworld (theme park), 142
Selfridges (department store), 119, 128
senior citizens; senior citizen discounts, 196;
    and travel in London, 14–15

Serpentine, the; boating on, 136
Seymour, Jane, ghost of, 74
Shakespeare, William, 219; birthday
    celebration, 26; Globe Theatre (London),
    41; New Place (death place) (Stratford-
    Upon-Avon), 220; Royal Shakespeare
    Company (London), 41; Shakespeare
    Birthplace Trust (Stratford-Upon-Avon),
    220; William Shakespeare Memorial
    (Southwark Cathedral), 59; See also
    Stratford-Upon-Avon
Shakespeare, The (hotel) (Stratford-Upon-
    Avon), 223
Shelbourne Hotel (Dublin), 191
Sheldonian Theatre (Oxford), 211
Shepherd Market, 55
Sheraton Belgravia Hotel, 92
Sheraton Park Tower Hotel, 92
Sherlock Holmes Museum, 71
Shop-mobility Centre (Cambridge), 163
shopping, 15; after-Christmas sales, 23; royal
    warrants, 116; size conversions, 117; street
    markets, 57; VAT (Value Added Tax), 114,
    115
shopping (antiques and markets); Antiquarian
    Book Fair (Olympia), 30, 121; Camden
    Lock (Camden High Street), 122; Camden
    Passage at Upper Street (Islington area),
    122; Covent Garden Markets, 121–22;
    Greenwich Markets, 122–23; Grosvenor
    House Antiques Fair, 121; Piccadilly
    Market, 122; Portobello Road, 121
shopping (bookstores); Antiquarian Book Fair
    (Olympia), 30, 121; discount, 119;
    Hatchards, 118
shopping (British clothing); Aquascutum, 125;
    Austin-reed, 125; Berk, Burlington Arcade,
    125; Gieves & Hawkes, 125; Jaeger's Regent
    Street, 125; Turnbull & Asser, 119, 125; See
    also shopping (haberdashers)
shopping (for children); Davenport's Magic
    Shop, 141; Disney Store, 118; Hamleys Toy
    Store, 118, 141; Harrods, 141
shopping (chinaware); Chinacraft, 120;
    Portmeirion Potteries Ltd. (Stoke-On-
    Trent), 127; Reject China Shops, 120; Royal
    Doulton Company (Stoke-On-Trent), 127;
    Royal Worcester (Stoke-On-Trent), 127;
    Thomas Goode, 120; Wedgewood Visitor
    Centre (Stoke-On-Trent), 127
shopping (department stores); BHS (British
    Home Stores), 119; D. H. Evans, 119;
    Debenhams, 119, 126; Dickins & Jones,
    118; Dr. Martens, 126; Fenwick, 116, 126;
    Harrods, 52, 111, 119, 121, 126; Harvey
    Nichols, 119, 126; John Lewis, 119; Liberty,
    118, 128; Marks & Spencer, 118, 126; Nicole
    Farhi, 115–16, 128; Selfridges, 119, 128;
    Sogo, 118
shopping (haberdashers); Harvie & Hudson,
    119; Hilditch & Key, 119; Turnbull & Asser,
    119; See also shopping (British clothing)

shopping (miscellaneous); Body Shop (soaps
    & shampoos), 118; Boots Drug Stores, 118,
    118–19, 125; British Air Travel Store, 118;
    The Scotch House (woolens), 118;
    Smythson Stationery, 116; Swaine Adeney
    (leather goods/ equestrian supplies),
    116–17; Virgin Megastore, 118
shopping (royal warrants); Alfred Dunhill
    (tobacconist), 119; Fortnum and Mason
    (food shop), 118, 126; Hamleys Toy Store,
    118, 141; Harrods Department Store, 52,
    111, 119, 121, 126; Harvey Nichols
    (department store), 119, 126; Liberty
    (department store), 118, 128; Smythson
    Stationery, 116; Swaine Adeney (leather
    goods/ equestrian supplies), 116–17;
    Thomas Goode (chinaware), 120; Turnbull
    & Asser (haberdasher), 119
shopping (sporting goods & clothing); Blacks
    (equipment & clothing), 124; C&A stores
    (ski clothing), 124; Cobra (clothing &
    shoes), 123; Farlow's (fishing equipment &
    clothing), 124; Lillywhites (equipment),
    123; Olympus Sports (equipment &
    clothing), 123; YHA (Youth Hostel
    Association) Shop, 124
shopping (tobacconists); Alfred Dunhill, 119;
    Davidoff, 119
shopping (woolens); Berk, Burlington Arcade,
    125; The Scotch House, 118; See also
    shopping (British clothing)
shopping streets; Covent Garden, 119; Jermyn
    Street, 119; Knightsbridge, 119, 121; Old
    and New Bond Street, 57, 115–17; Oxford
    Street and Oxford Circus, 118–19;
    Piccadilly, 118; Regent Street, 118
sightseeing; one day, 44–47; two days, 47–48;
    three days, 48–50; four days, 51–55; five
    days, 55–59; six days, 59–60
Sir John Soane Museum, 67
size conversions (clothing), 117
Skippers Bistro (Edinburgh), 201
Sloane Hotel, 92
Slug and Lettuce Pub (Stratford-Upon-Avon),
    225
smoking/nonsmoking sections in restaurants,
    95
Smollensky's Balloon, 112
Smythson Stationery, 116
Snape Malting Riverside Centre (Aldeburgh),
    154
soccer ("football"), 135; Chelsea Football Club,
    135; tickets, 135; See also boat racing;
    cricket; horse racing; horse shows and
    events; outdoor activities; Rugby; tennis
social season, 27–28
Sogo (department store), 118
Soho Soho (restaurant), 107
South Bank (restaurant) (Dun Laoghaire,
    Ireland), 188
Southcut, Joanna; the bishops and her box,
    56

Southwark Cathedral; Shakespeare's birthday celebration, 26; William Shakespeare Memorial, 59

Spaniards Inn (Hampstead Heath); ghost of Dick Turpin, 75–76

Sparrowe's House (Ancient House) (Ipswich), 208

Spencer House, 60

sporting events (spectator); boat racing, 25, 31; cricket, 30, 66, 133; horse racing, 26, 29–30, 133–35; horse shows and events, 24, 26, 31, 32, 33, 37; information and tickets, 133; soccer ("football"), 135; Rugby, 23, 26, 54, 135; tennis, 30, 135; See also boat racing; cricket; horse racing; horse shows and events; outdoor activities; soccer; Rugby; tennis

sporting goods & clothing; Blacks (equipment & clothing), 124; C&A stores (ski clothing), 124; Cobra (clothing & shoes), 123; Farlow's (fishing equipment & clothing), 124; Lillywhites (equipment), 123; Olympus Sports (equipment & clothing), 123; YHA (Youth Hostel Association) Shop, 124

sports (participatory sports); bicycling, 135–36; boating, 136; fitness centers, 137; golf, 136–37; horse riding, 138; jogging, 137; tennis, 137–38; waterskiing, 136

Spread Eagle (restaurant) (Greenwich), 205

Spring Antiques Fair (Chelsea Old Town Hall), 25

Square, The (restaurant), 107

Squires Kitchen International (School of Cake Decorations), 131

Stafford, The (hotel), 93

Star of India (restaurant), 108

Station Hotel (Ipswich), 208

Stephen's Hall (hotel) (Dublin), 191

Sternfield House (Aldeburgh), 152

Sticky Fingers (restaurant), 108, 112

Stock Exchange (Old Bond Street), 60

Stone of Scone, 78, 198

Stratford Moat House (hotel), 223

Stratford-Upon-Avon, 218–25; map, 219; Tourist Information Center, 218; traveling to, 218; See also Shakespeare, William

Stratford-Upon-Avon (hotels & accommodations); Alveston Cottage (B & B), 224; The Arden, 222–23; Ettington Park Hotel, 222; Falcon Hotel, 223; Forte Posthouse, 223; Lygon Arms, 222; The Shakespeare, 223; Stratford Moat House, 223; Welcombe Hotel, 222; The White Swan, 223

Stratford-Upon-Avon (restaurants); Bensons of Stratford-Upon-Avon (afternoon tea), 224; Box Tree Restaurant, 224; Liaison, 224; Richoux (afternoon tea), 224; Slug and Lettuce Pub, 225

Stratford-Upon-Avon (sightseeing); Ann Hathaway's Cottage, 220; Guide Friday Stratford Bus Tour, 219–20; Hall's Croft, 220; Nash's House, 220; New Place, 220;

Shakespeare Birthplace Trust, 220; The Walk, 221–22

Stratford-Upon-Avon (theatre); The Other Place, 221; Royal Shakespeare Theatre, 221; Stratford-Upon-Avon Shakespeare Birthday Celebration, 221; Swan Theatre, 221

Stratford-Upon-Avon Shakespeare Birthday Celebration, 221

street markets, 57

student travel, 15

Sue Ryder Coffee Room (afternoon tea) (Ipswich), 209

Sugar Club (restaurant), 108

Sullys (restaurant) (Canterbury), 167

Sunday Express Guide to Golf Courses (AA Publishing), 137

Swaine Adeney (leather goods/equestrian supplies), 116–17

Swan Hotel (Aldeburgh), 152

Swan Theatre (Stratford-Upon-Avon), 221

Swan Upping, 31

sweater repair, 15

Syon House (Brentford, Middlesex), 67

Take-A-Guide Ltd., 9

Tate Gallery of British Art, 54, 62

Tate Gallery of Modern Art, 54, 62

telephone guide to London, 12

telephone use, 16

Temple, The (London), 57

Temple Bar (Dublin), 183

tennis (as participatory sport), 137–38; credit cards and reservations, 137; indoor tennis, 137; Lawn Tennis Association, 138; outdoor tennis, 137–38; See also bicycling; boating; fitness centers; golf; horse riding; jogging

tennis (as spectator sport); Wimbledon (All England Lawn Tennis Championships), 30, 135; See also boat racing; cricket; horse racing; horse shows and events; outdoor activities; soccer; Rugby

Terriss, William (ghost of); Adelphi Theatre, 73; Covent Garden Tube Station, 73

Thames Barrier (Greenwich), 204; Full Tidal Closure of the Thames, 35

Thames River; bicycling routes, 135; boating on, 136; Doggett's Coat & Badge Race, 31; Head of the River Race, 25; Hop-On Hop-Off Thames Ferry, 10; Oxford-Cambridge boat race, 25; pancake races, 24; Royal Henley Regatta, 30; Swan Upping, 31; waterskiing, 136

theatre, 39–40, 41; City of London Festival, 30; in Dublin, 175; Globe Theatre, 41; Her Majesty's Theatre (Haymarket), 41; Leicester Square Half Price Ticket Booth, 41; Open Air Theatre Season (Regent's Park), 29; Royal Court Theatre (St. Martin's Lane), 41; Royal National Theatre, 41; Royal Shakespeare Company, 41; Royal Shakespeare Theatre season, 25; theatre district map, 38; ticket brokers, 40

Theatre Museum, 68
Theberton Grange (Aldeburgh), 153
time (24-hour system), 17
ticket brokers, 40
tipping, 17
tobacconists; Alfred Dunhill, 119; Cuban cigars and U.S. customs, 119; Davidoff, 119
Tolly Cobbold brewery (Ipswich), 208
Tower Bridge, 143
Tower of London, 44–45, 142–43; Ascension Day, 29; Ceremony of the Keys, 22–23; Crown Jewels, 143; ghosts of, 76; prisoners at, 144; Queen's birthday salute, 26
Tower of London Church Parades; Christmas, 37; Easter Sunday, 24; Whitsunday (Pentecost), 26
Tower Hill Pageant, 72
Turnbull & Asser (haberdasher), 119, 125
Turpin, Dick, ghost of, 75–76
Trafalgar Day Parade, 35
Trafalgar Square, 57–58; Christmas tree lighting, 37, 58; the crown jewels of France and, 77– 78; Nelson's Column, 57, 58; New Year's Eve celebration, 37; police station in a lamppost, 78–79
Trafalgar Tavern (restaurant) (Greenwich), 123, 205
train service (Gatwick and Heathrow to London), 4–5
train travel, 18–19; Tickets to, 18; types of passes, 18; underground or tube, 19
Travelcards and passes, 9–10
travelers with disabilities; in Dublin, 175; in London, 13–14; in Scotland, 196; Shop-mobility Centre (Cambridge), 163; See also wheelchair access
Travelin' Talk Directory ; and travelers with disabilities, 14
Treasure of China (restaurant) (Greenwich), 205
Trinity College (Cambridge), 163
Trinity College (Dublin), 179, 179–80; Book of Kells, 179, 180
Tudor House Gallery (Aldeburgh), 154
Tudor House Inn (Warwick), 226
TWA, 3
Twenty Two Jermyn Street (hotel), 93
Twickenham (Rugby stadium), 135

underground and bus travel, 9–10, 19; Access to the Underground (wheelchair access), 14; London transport, 9; Travelcards and passes, 9–10
United Airlines, 3
University Arms Hotel (Cambridge), 165
University Church of St. Mary the Virgin (Oxford), 211
University College (Oxford), 211
University of London; ghost of Jeremy Bentham, 76
US Airways, 3
U.S. customs, Cuban cigars and, 119

VAT (Value Added Tax), 114, 115; refunds, 173–74, 197
Vellore (restaurant) (Bath), 158
Veteran Car Run to Brighton, 35
Victoria, 51, 160, 205
Victoria & Albert Museum, 61, 146–47; Bethnal Green Museum of Childhood, 144; Theatre Museum, 68
Villas and Apartments Abroad, 11
Virgin Megastore, 118
visa requirements (American and Canadian citizens), 2
Volk Electric Railway (Brighton), 161
Vong (restaurant), 108

Walk, The (Stratford-Upon-Avon), 221–22
walking tours of London, 19
Wallace Collection, 63
Warwick (Warwickshire County), 225–26; hotels & accommodations, 226; restaurants, 226; Tourist Office, 225; traveling to, 225
Warwick (sightseeing), 225–26; Beauchamp, 226; Lord Leycester Hospital, 226; Oken's Doll Museum, 226; St. John's House, 226; St. Mary's Collegiate Church, 226; Warwick Castle, 225–26
Warwick Arts Festival, 31
Warwick Castle, 225–26
Watch Night (St. Paul's Cathedral), 37
Waterside Inn (Bray-on-Thames), 227
waterskiing, 136; Royal Docks Water-ski Club, 136; See also bicycling; boating; fitness centers; golf; horse riding; tennis (as participatory sport)
weather; Dublin, 176; London, 6, 20; Paris, 212; Scotland, 194
Weavers House, The (Canterbury), 167
Wedgewood Visitor Centre (Stoke-On-Trent), 127
Welcombe Hotel (Stratford-Upon-Avon), 222
Wellington Museum (Apsley House), 64
Wembley Arena; Horse of the Year Show, 33
Wembley Stadium; Football Association Cup Final, 26; Rugby League Challenge Cup Final, 26
Wentworth Hotel (Aldeburgh), 153
Wentworth Hotel Restaurant (Aldeburgh), 154
Westbury (hotel) (Dublin), 191
Westbury Hotel, The (London), 93
Westminster Abbey, 45–46; Battle of Britain Week, 32; Boy Scouts and Girl Guide Memorial Service, 23; Chamber of Pyx and the flayed skin of a thief, 78; ghosts of, 76; Law Term opening and procession, 34–35; Maundy Thursday, 24; Stone of Scone, 78, 198
Westminster Cathedral (RC), 59
Westminster Horse Show (Hyde Park), 31
Wexford Opera Festival (Ireland), 40
wheelchair access, 14; Irish Wheelchair Association, 175; restaurants, 109, 111; See also travelers with disabilities

Whitbread Gold Cup (Sandown Park), 134
White Lion Hotel (Aldeburgh), 153
White Swan, The (hotel) (Stratford-Upon-Avon), 223
Whitehall, 52
Whites Hotel, 93
Whitsunday (Pentecost) Church Parade; Tower of London, 26
Wigmore Hall, 42
Willbraham Hotel, 93–94
William the Conqueror, 227
William III, 206
William Morris Gallery, 68
William Shakespeare Memorial (Southwark Cathedral), 59
Wimbledon; All England Lawn Tennis Championships, 30, 135
Windsor (Berkshire County), 226–28; hotels & accommodations, 227–28; restaurants, 227–28; Tourist Office, 227; traveling to, 226

Windsor Castle, 227; Garter Ceremony, 30; Royal Windsor Horse Show (Home Park), 26; St. David's Day ceremony, 25
Windsor Festival, 33
Wodka (restaurant), 108
woolens (shopping for); Berk, Burlington Arcade, 125; The Scotch House, 118; *See also* British clothing
World of Options for the 90's: A Guide to International Educational Exchange, Community Service and Travel for Persons with Disabilities, A, 14
Worldwide Assistance Services, 12
Worldwide Discount Travel Club, 4

Yacht, The (restaurant) (Greenwich), 123
YHA (Youth Hostel Association) Shop; sports equipment & clothing, 124

Zafferano (restaurant), 108
Zilli Fish (restaurant), 108

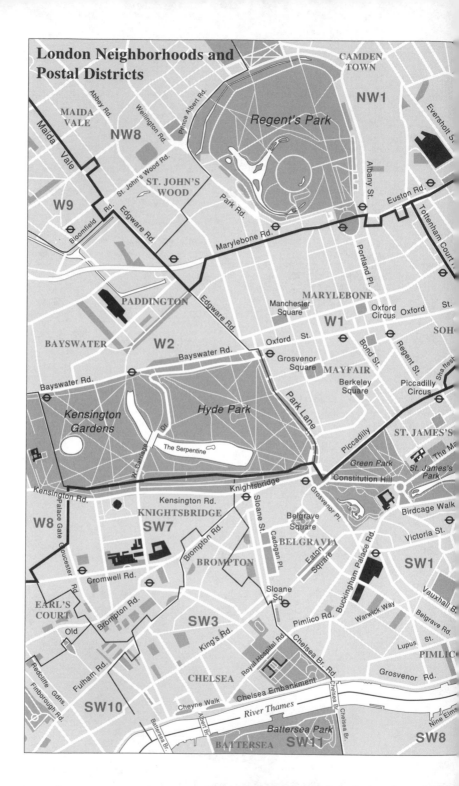

London Neighborhoods and Postal Districts

CAMDEN TOWN

NW1

Regent's Park

MAIDA VALE

Abbey Rd.

Wellington Rd.

Prince Albert Rd.

Eversholt St.

NW8

St. John's Wood Rd.

ST. JOHN'S WOOD

Park Rd.

Albany St.

Euston Rd.

W9

Bloomfield Rd.

Edgware Rd.

Tottenham Court

Marylebone Rd.

Portland Pl.

MARYLEBONE

Manchester Square

PADDINGTON

Edgware Rd.

W1

Oxford Circus

Oxford St.

SOH

BAYSWATER

W2

Bayswater Rd.

Oxford St.

Bond St.

Regent St.

Grosvenor Square

MAYFAIR

Berkeley Square

Piccadilly Circus

Shaftes

Bayswater Rd.

Hyde Park

Park Lane

Kensington Gardens

The Serpentine

Piccadilly

ST. JAMES'S

W. Carriage Dr.

Green Park

The Ma

St. James's Park

Kensington Rd.

Knightsbridge

Constitution Hill

Palace Gate

Kensington Rd.

Grosvenor Pl.

Birdcage Walk

W8

Gloucester Rd.

KNIGHTSBRIDGE

SW7

Brompton Rd.

Sloane St.

Belgrave Square

Victoria St.

Cadogan Pl.

BELGRAVIA

SW1

Cromwell Rd.

BROMPTON

Eaton Square

Buckingham Palace Rd.

EARL'S COURT

Brompton Rd.

Pimlico Rd.

Warwick Way

Vauxhall B.

Old

Sloane Sq.

Belgrave Rd.

SW3

King's Rd.

Lupus St.

Fulham Rd.

Royal Hospital Rd.

Chelsea Br. Rd.

PIMLIC

Redcliffe Gdns.

Finborough Rd.

CHELSEA

Chelsea Embankment

Grosvenor Rd.

Cheyne Walk

Chelsea Br.

SW10

Albert Br.

River Thames

Nine Elms

Battersea Br.

Battersea Park

SW8

BATTERSEA

SW11

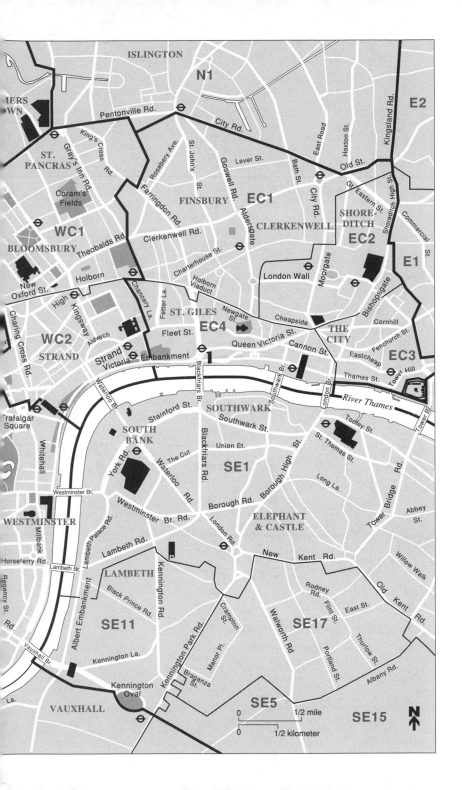

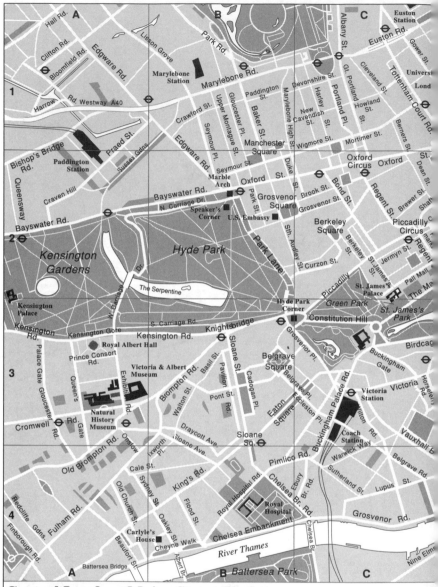

Central London: Major Street Finder

Albert Embankment **D4**	Berkeley St **C2**	Buckingham Palace Rd **C3**	Clerkenwell Rd **E1**
Aldersgate **E1**	Birdcage Walk **C3**	Cannon St **F2**	Constitution Hill **C3**
Aldwych **D2**	Bishops Br. Rd **A1**	Chancery Ln **D1**	Cornhill/Leadenhall St **F2**
Audley(N&S) **B2**	Bishopsgate **F1**	Charing Cross Rd **D2**	Coventry/Cranbourne **D2**
Baker St **B1**	Blackfriars Rd **E2**	Charterhouse St **E1**	Craven Hill Rd/Praed St **A2**
Bayswater Rd **A2**	Bloomsbury Way **D1**	Cheapside **E2**	Cromwell Rd **A3**
Beech St/Chiswell St **E1**	Bond St (New&Old) **C2**	Chelsea Br. Rd **B4**	Curzon St **C2**
Belgrave Pl **B3**	Bow St/Lancaster Pl **D2**	Chelsea Embankment **B4**	Drury Ln **D2**
Beaufort **A4**	Brompton Rd **B3**	Cheyne Walk **B4**	Eastcheap/Great Tower **F2**
Belgrave Rd **C4**	Buckingham Gate **C3**	City Rd **F1**	Eccleston Pl **C3**

Gower St **C1**	Oxford St/New Oxford **C2**	Waterloo Rd **E1**
Grace Church St **F2**	Paddington St **B1**	Westway A40 **A1**
Gray's Inn Rd **D1**	Pall Mall **C2**	Whitehall **D2**
Gt Portland St **C1**	Park Ln **B2**	Wigmore/Mortimer **C1**
Gt Russell St **D1**	Park Rd **B1**	Woburn Pl **D1**
Grosvenor Pl **C3**	Park St **B2**	York Rd **D3**
Grosvenor Rd **C4**	Piccadilly **C2**	
Grosvenor St (Upr) **C2**	Pont St **B3**	RAILWAY STATIONS
Haymarket **C2**	Portland Pl **C1**	Blackfriars **E2**
Holborn/High/Viaduct **D1**	Queen St **E2**	Cannon St **F2**
Horseferry Rd **C3**	Queen Victoria St **E1**	Charing Cross **D2**
Jermyn St **C2**	Queen's Gate **A3**	Euston **C1**
Kensington High St/Rd **A3**	Queensway **A2**	Holborn Viaduct **E1**
King's Cross Rd **D1**	Redcliffe Gdns **A4**	King's Cross **D1**
King's Rd **B4**	Regent St **C2**	Liverpool St **F1**
Kingsway **D2**	Royal Hospital Rd **B4**	London Bridge **F2**
Knightsbridge **B3**	St. James's St **C2**	Marylebone **B1**
Lambeth Palace Rd **D3**	Seymour Pl **A1**	Paddington **A2**
Lisson Grove **A1**	Seymour St **A2**	St Pancras **D1**
Lombard St **F2**	Shaftesbury Ave **C2**	Victoria **C3**
London Wall **E1**	Sloane/Lwr Sloane **B3**	Waterloo East **E3**
Long Acre/Grt Queen **D2**	Southampton Row **D1**	Waterloo **D3**
Long Ln **E1**	Southwark Bridge Rd **E2**	
Ludgate Hill **E2**	Southwark Rd **E2**	BRIDGES
Marylebone High St **B1**	St. Margarets/Abingdon **D3**	Albert **B4**
Marylebone Rd **B1**	Stamford St **E2**	Battersea **A4**
Millbank **D4**	Strand **D2**	Blackfriars **E2**
Montague Pl **D1**	Sydney St **A4**	Chelsea **C4**
Moorgate **F1**	Thames St(Upr&Lwr) **F2**	Hungerford Footbridge **D2**
New Bridge St **E2**	The Mall **C2**	Lambeth **D3**
New Cavendish **C1**	Theobald's Rd **D1**	London Bridge **F2**
Newgate St **E1**	Threadneedle St **F2**	Southwark **E2**
Nine Elms Ln **C4**	Tottenham Ct Rd **C1**	Tower Bridge **F2**
Oakley St **B4**	Vauxhall Br. Rd **C4**	Waterloo **D2**
Old St **F1**	Victoria Embankment **D2**	Westminster **D3**
Old Brompton Rd **A4**	Victoria St **C3**	
Onslow Sq/St **A3**	Warwick Way **C4**	

Edgware Rd **A1**
Euston Rd **C1**
Exhibition Rd **A3**
Farringdon Rd **E1**
Fenchurch/Aldgate **F2**
Fleet St **E2**
Fulham Rd **A4**
Gloucester Pl **B1**
Gloucester Rd **A3**
Goswell Rd **E1**

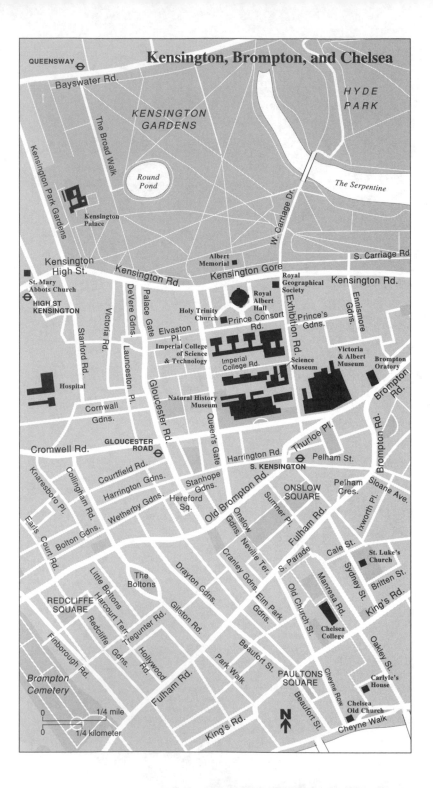

Kensington, Brompton, and Chelsea

QUEENSWAY

Bayswater Rd.

HYDE PARK

KENSINGTON GARDENS

The Broad Walk

Kensington Park Gardens

Round Pond

The Serpentine

Kensington Palace

W. Carriage Dr.

S. Carriage Rd.

Albert Memorial

Kensington High St.

Kensington Rd.

Kensington Gore

Kensington Rd.

St. Mary Abbots Church

HIGH ST KENSINGTON

Royal Geographical Society

DeVere Gdns.

Palace Gate

Holy Trinity Church

Royal Albert Hall

Kensington Rd.

Victoria Rd.

Elvaston Pl.

Prince Consort Rd.

Prince's Gdns.

Ennismore Gdns.

Stanford Rd.

Launceston Pl.

Imperial College of Science & Technology

Imperial College Rd.

Exhibition Rd.

Science Museum

Victoria & Albert Museum

Brompton Oratory

Hospital

Cornwall Gdns.

Gloucester Rd.

Natural History Museum

Queen's Gate

Brompton Rd.

Cromwell Rd.

GLOUCESTER ROAD

Harrington Rd.

Thurloe Pl.

Pelham St.

Brompton Rd.

Knaresboro Pl.

Collingham Rd.

Courtfield Rd.

Stanhope Gdns.

S. KENSINGTON

ONSLOW SQUARE

Pelham Cres.

Sloane Ave.

Harrington Gdns.

Hereford Sq.

Old Brompton Rd.

Sumner Pl.

Ixworth Pl.

Earls Court Rd.

Wetherby Gdns.

Onslow Gdns.

Fulham Rd.

Bolton Gdns.

Neville Ter.

S. Parade

Cale St.

Sydney St.

St. Luke's Church

Little Boltons

The Boltons

Drayton Gdns.

Cranley Gdns.

Elm Park Gdns.

Old Church St.

Manresa Rd.

Britten St.

King's Rd.

REDCLIFFE SQUARE

Harcourt Terr.

Redcliffe Gdns.

Tregunter Rd.

Gilston Rd.

Chelsea College

Oakley St.

Finborough Rd.

Hollywood Rd.

Fulham Rd.

Park Walk

Beaufort St.

PAULTONS SQUARE

Cheyne Row

Carlyle's House

Brompton Cemetery

King's Rd.

Beaufort St.

Chelsea Old Church

Cheyne Walk

0   1/4 mile
0   1/4 kilometer

N

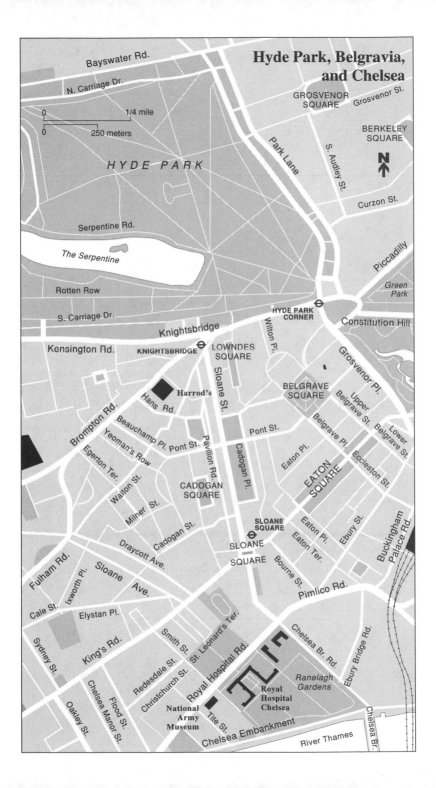

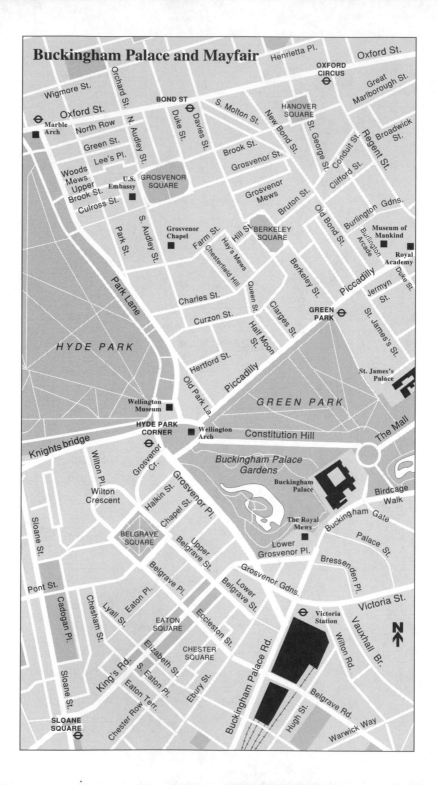

Buckingham Palace and Mayfair

Henrietta Pl.
Oxford St.

OXFORD CIRCUS

Wigmore St.
Oxford St.
Great Marlborough St.

Marble Arch
North Row
BOND ST
S. Molton St.
HANOVER SQUARE

Orchard St.
Duke St.
Davies St.
New Bond St.
St. George St.
Conduit St.
Regent St.
Broadwick St.

Green St.
Lee's Pl.
N. Audley St.
Brook St.
Grosvenor St.
Clifford St.

Woods Mews
Upper Brook St.
U.S. Embassy
GROSVENOR SQUARE
Grosvenor Mews
Bruton St.
Burlington Gdns.

Culross St.
Museum of Mankind
Burlington Arcade
Royal Academy

Park St.
S. Audley St.
Grosvenor Chapel
Farm St.
Hill St.
BERKELEY SQUARE
Old Bond St.
Piccadilly
Jermyn St.
Duke St.

Chesterfield Hill
Hays Mews
Berkeley St.

Park Lane
Charles St.
Queen St.
Clarges St.
GREEN PARK
St. James's St.

HYDE PARK
Curzon St.
Half Moon St.

Hertford St.
Old Park La.
Piccadilly
St. James's Palace

Wellington Museum
GREEN PARK

HYDE PARK CORNER
Wellington Arch
Constitution Hill
The Mall

Knightsbridge
Grosvenor Cr.
Buckingham Palace Gardens
Birdcage Walk

Wilton Pl.
Halkin St.
Grosvenor Pl.
Chapel St.
Buckingham Palace
Buckingham Gate

Wilton Crescent
BELGRAVE SQUARE
Upper Belgrave St.
The Royal Mews
Palace St.

Sloane St.
Belgrave Pl.
Lower Belgrave St.
Lower Grosvenor Pl.
Bressenden Pl.

Pont St.
Cadogan Pl.
Chesham St.
Lyall St.
Eaton Pl.
Eccleston St.
Grosvenor Gdns.
Victoria St.

King's Rd.
EATON SQUARE
Elizabeth St.
Ebury St.
CHESTER SQUARE
Victoria Station
Wilton Rd.
Vauxhall Br.

Sloane St.
SLOANE SQUARE
Chester Row
Eaton Terr.
S. Eaton Pl.
Buckingham Palace Rd.
Hugh St.
Belgrave Rd.
Warwick Way

N

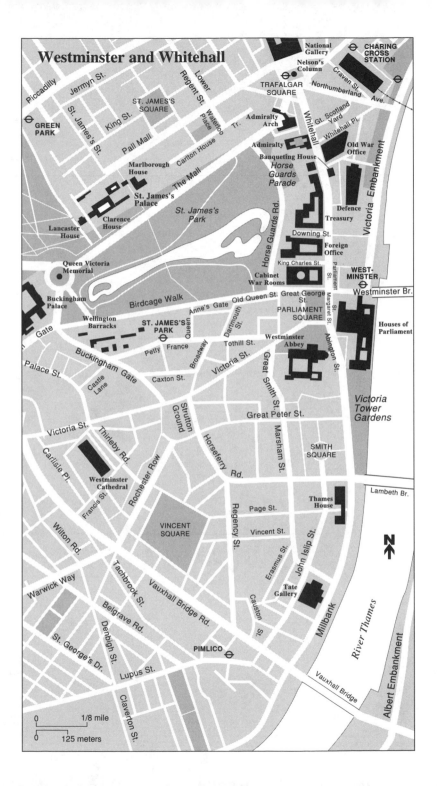

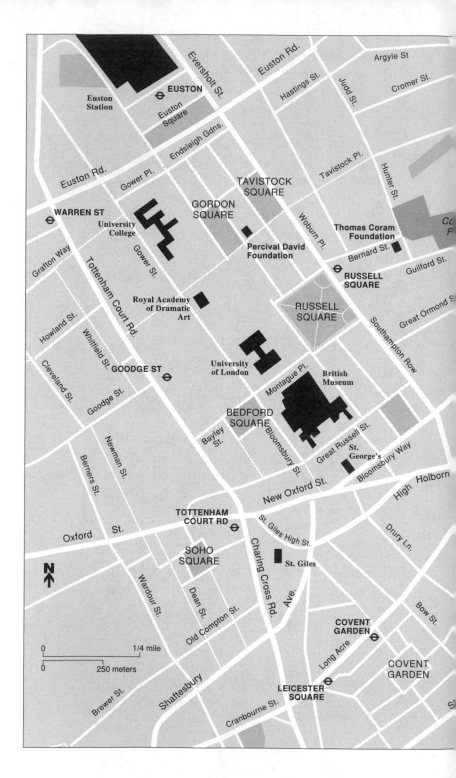

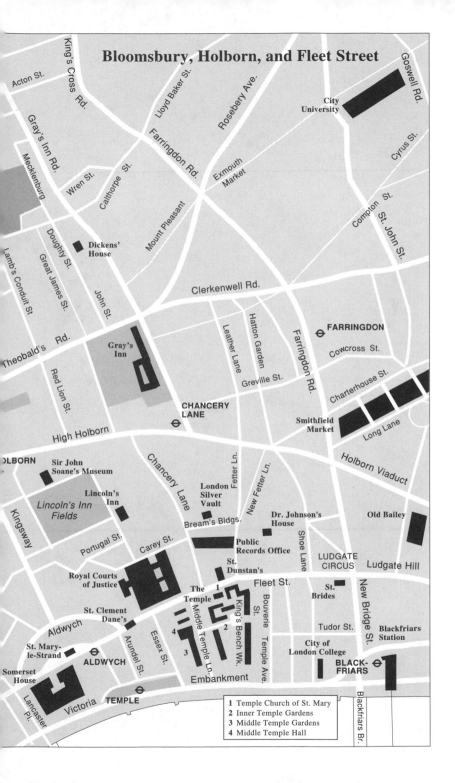

Bloomsbury, Holborn, and Fleet Street

King's Cross Rd.
Acton St.
Lloyd Baker St.
Rosebery Ave.
Goswell Rd.
City University
Gray's Inn Rd.
Farringdon Rd.
Mecklenburg
Wren St.
Calthorpe St.
Exmouth Market
Cyrus St.
Mount Pleasant
Compton St.
St. John St.
Doughty St.
Dickens' House
Lamb's Conduit St.
Great James St.
John St.
Clerkenwell Rd.
FARRINGDON
Theobald's Rd.
Gray's Inn
Leather Lane
Hatton Garden
Farringdon Rd.
Cowcross St.
Red Lion St.
Greville St.
Charterhouse St.
CHANCERY LANE
High Holborn
Smithfield Market
Long Lane
OLBORN
Sir John Soane's Museum
Chancery Lane
Fetter Ln.
New Fetter Ln.
Holborn Viaduct
Lincoln's Inn Fields
Lincoln's Inn
London Silver Vault
Dr. Johnson's House
Old Bailey
Kingsway
Bream's Bldgs.
Shoe Lane
Portugal St.
Carey St.
Public Records Office
St. Dunstan's
LUDGATE CIRCUS
Ludgate Hill
Royal Courts of Justice
The Temple
1
Fleet St.
St. Brides
New Bridge St.
St. Clement Dane's
Middle Temple Ln.
King's Bench Wk.
Bouverie St.
Temple Ave.
Tudor St.
Blackfriars Station
Aldwych
4
2
City of London College
St. Mary-le-Strand
Arundel St.
Essex St.
3
BLACK-FRIARS
Somerset House
ALDWYCH
Embankment
Blackfriars Br.
Lancaster Pl.
Victoria
TEMPLE

1 Temple Church of St. Mary
2 Inner Temple Gardens
3 Middle Temple Gardens
4 Middle Temple Hall

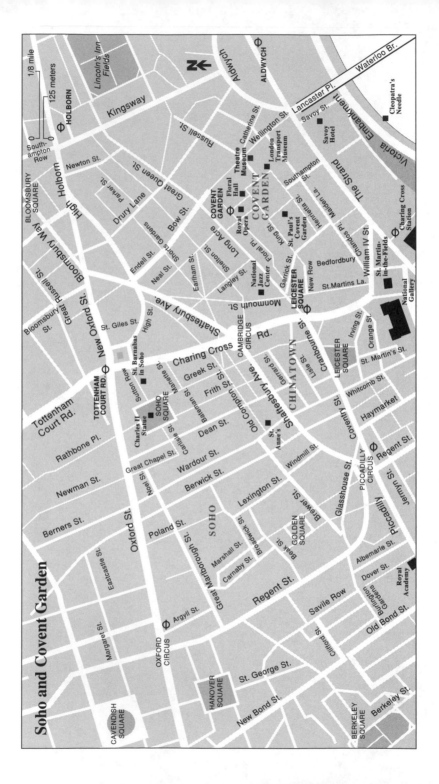

Soho and Covent Garden